Second Edition

Paying Teachers
for What They
Know and Do

Second Edition

Paying Teachers
for What They Know and Do

New and Smarter Compensation Strategies
to Improve Schools

ALLEN ODDEN CAROLYN KELLEY

CORWIN PRESS, INC.
A Sage Publications Company
Thousand Oaks, California

For information:

Corwin Press, Inc.
A Sage Publications Company
2455 Teller Road
Thousand Oaks, California 91320
E-mail: order@corwinpress.com

Sage Publications Ltd.
6 Bonhill Street
London EC2A 4PU
United Kingdom

Sage Publications India Pvt. Ltd.
M-32 Market
Greater Kailash I
New Delhi 110 048 India

Printed in the United States of America

Library of Congress Cataloging-in-Publication Data

Odden, Allan.
    Paying teachers for what they know and do: New and smarter compensation strategies to improve schools / by Allan Odden and Carolyn Kelley.—2nd ed.
       p. cm.
       Includes bibliographical references and indexes.
       ISBN 0-7619-7887-9 (c: acid-free paper)—ISBN 0-7619-7888-7 (p: acid-free paper)
       1. Teachers—Salaries, etc.—United States. 2. Merit pay—United States. 3. Teacher effectiveness—United States. I. Kelley, Carolyn.
    II. Title.
       LB2842.22 .O33 2001
       331.2′813711′00973—dc21   2001002191

01   02   03   04   05   10   9   8   7   6   5   4   3   2   1

Acquiring Editor:	Robb Clouse
Associate Editor:	Kylee Liegl
Corwin Editorial Assistant:	Erin Buchanan
Production Editor:	Olivia Weber
Editorial Assistant:	Cindy Bear
Typesetter/Designer:	Rebecca Evans
Cover Designer:	Tracy Miller

Contents

Preface

The country seems to be launching another round of efforts to change how teachers are paid. Except for changes made at the beginning of the century when the single-salary schedule was created, and some of the 1990s changes, nearly all change efforts have failed to produce lasting effects. Most previous efforts at changing how teachers are paid have focused on individual merit or incentive pay, pay strategies that work in only a few private-sector organizations and do not work in education or other organizations in which the most productive work is characterized by collegial and collaborative interaction.

But despite this record of flawed proposals, it is possible to make the current round of teacher compensation innovation a success and a contribution to education rather than another set of failed efforts. A major purpose of this book is to steer state and local efforts toward teacher compensation change into strategies that are appropriate for education, that contribute to the national goal of teaching all students to high standards, that strengthen teaching as a profession, and that contribute to higher pay for teachers. The path to teacher compensation change is not easy, but there are new ideas about how to pay educated workers, such as teachers, on bases other than years of experience, education units, and degrees. The book describes these strategies, discusses how they fit within several broader elements of change in the education system, gives examples of changes that are being implemented across the country, and suggests ways that states and districts can proceed to make progress on this important agenda.

Although teacher compensation technically includes both teacher salary and benefits, the book uses the phrases *teacher pay, teacher salary,* and *teacher compensation* interchangeably. Odden and Conley (1992) addressed the broader issue of teacher compensation, with suggestions with which we generally agree for changes in teacher benefit packages. But the major difficulty over this century has been designing workable and helpful changes in the teacher salary structure, which is the subject of this book.

We also take the position that teaching should be viewed as a full-time job and that teacher salaries can appropriately be compared to the salaries of other jobs that more formally cover a 12-month period. Although teachers are in the classroom for less than 8 hours a day and teach only 180 working days a year, fully engaged professional teachers put in many more hours than that formal schedule suggests, easily working a full 8-hour day if not more and working during considerable periods of the summer as well. The job of a teacher consists not only of teaching students (and correcting their work) but also of continually developing new knowledge and skills, improving the curriculum, and increasingly helping to manage their schools. Both anecdotal and research evidence imply that high-quality teaching, as envisioned by standards-based school reform, cannot be accomplished within a 6-hour day and a 9-month school year, and that the best teachers—those whom the system needs to retain and who should be paid more—work substantially beyond these minimums.

We believe that the driving public concerns about schools are safety, academic standards, and student achievement. The public wants schools to improve—to produce higher levels of student learning. Thus our proposals for changing teacher compensation are best understood within a broader set of strategies that will improve the quality and results of America's public schools. We have the conviction that if schools get better, they will also gain stronger public support, which will be accompanied by increased funding as well. Thus we address teacher compensation within the broader context of improving schools. From experience in other organizations and, lately, from experiences within education, the teacher compensation changes suggested in this book can serve as interlinking strategies to improve America's schools. They can also serve as a means to improve the salaries of the teacher leaders who need to take the primary local leadership roles for accomplishing current education reform goals.

The first few chapters in the book reflect this education reform orientation. Chapter 1 has two sections. The first section provides an overview of changes in the levels of teacher pay over several decades. It concludes, somewhat in contradiction to public perception, that average teacher salaries have not increased that much over the past several decades and that the salary potential for an individual entering teaching is very limited. The second section shows how teacher compensation change fits into two major initiatives within education—the standards-based reform movement and efforts to strengthen teaching as a profession. This section also summarizes the new compensation strategies that have been created in private-sector and nonprofit organizations—knowledge- and skills-based pay, contingency-based pay, and group-based performance awards—and suggests that they have potential for application in education as well.

Chapter 2 makes several major points. First, it shows that teacher compensation has changed over the years, although most of the change occurred in the 19th and early 20th centuries, before nearly all who are now in education entered teaching or some other position in the education system. Second, it argues that teacher compensation changed when the broader economy changed and the structure of worker compensation in general changed. Third, it argues that the economy today is again changing—from an industrial to an information, high-performance economy—and that many organizations outside of education have already designed and implemented different pay structures that might work in education as well. Fourth, this chapter shows how the structure of compensation should be linked to the nature of the school organization—its goals, human resources policies, management, and so forth—and shows how the changing nature of schools and the unchanging nature of teacher compensation suggest that teacher compensation change should be high on the education agenda.

Chapter 3 reviews the major elements of pay that should be considered for any system—beginning pay, membership (seniority) pay, performance pay (either for individuals, teams, or groups), and contingency pay. It describes different versions of each of these pay elements, giving possible education examples for each.

Chapter 4 reviews the linkages between pay and motivation. The chapter reviews this important topic for workers in all types of organizations as well as specifically for education. The chapter argues that individuals, including teachers, are motivated by a variety of intrinsic and extrinsic factors including pay. A rich research literature in noneducation organizations and beginning research in education show, moreover, that adding an extrinsic element, such as a performance bonus, to an intrinsic motivator, such as accomplishing goals, does not undermine the intrinsic motivator but rather enhances overall motivation. The combined set of findings on what motivates workers generally and what motivates teachers suggests that several new structures for compensation, including knowledge- and skills-based pay and group-based performance awards, have high potential for contributing to stronger motivation of teachers.

Chapters 5 and 6 discuss the two major promising new elements that could be included in a revised teacher compensation structure—knowledge- and skills-based pay as well as collective, generally school-based, performance awards. Knowledge- and skills-based pay would provide salary increments for teachers who developed new knowledge, skills, and professional expertise that are needed by schools. These would include increasingly sophisticated curriculum and instructional skills, professional and curriculum development expertise, or competencies to engage wisely in school-based management. In a full-fledged, knowledge- and skills-based pay plan, expertise would replace experience and education units as the basis for salary increases above beginning pay. Chapter 5 discusses the cutting-edge, new pay plans in Douglas County, Colorado; Menomonee Falls, Wisconsin; Cincinnati, Ohio; and the Vaughn Next Century Learning Center. Interestingly, each of the plans provides a permanent salary increase for certification from the National Board for Professional Teaching Standards (which is discussed in Chapter 1). The latter two make substantial use of new teaching standards and a performance assessment system. Chapter 5 also discusses various strategies for developing the infrastructure for administering a knowledge- and skills-based pay plan—particularly, descriptions of teaching practice to professional standards and of assessment systems that can gauge each individual teacher's practice to those standards.

We have used the term *knowledge- and skills-based pay* in the second edition of the book rather than the *competency label,* which was used in the first edition. Although the terms mean the same thing, the private sector uses competency pay for professional workers and managers and uses skills-based pay for manufacturing workers. In education, however, competency pay connotes merit pay to many, so we have decided to use the more generic and descriptive term *knowledge- and skills-based pay.*

Chapter 6 provides a lengthy, analytic discussion of group- or school-based performance awards. The chapter distinguishes the idea of a collective award from the individual incentive and merit pay programs of the past, which have not worked in education. In contrast, a group performance award would provide a bonus to all workers in a school—all professional staff and all classified staff as well. This chapter discusses all the major elements that need to be addressed in designing a school-based performance award, including financing. The chapter recommends that such awards should have student achievement as the primary factor in the performance measure; that performance awards should be provided only for value-added, that is, for improving performance; and that the awards should be provided to everyone in the school, including dollars for the student body fund if possible. The chapter includes descriptions of several promising but not perfect performance awards that were implemented already during the 1990s. Interlaced throughout this chapter are research findings about the operation and effects of several of the programs.

Chapter 7 discusses a series of design and implementation issues that are key to effective teacher compensation change. This chapter makes several key points. First, involving all major parties in the development and change process should create teacher compensation change; involvement generates trust, and trust is the key ingredient in making new approaches to pay work. Second, the chapter suggests three major activities to help prepare districts and schools for designing and implementing pay changes: setting the foundation for the need for change and gathering information from the local context that will help in designing certain portions of any specific new compensation element, learning from other organizations and schools about why and how they changed pay structures, and piloting new ideas when possible. The tone of this chapter is that process is as important as technical issues for an activity as complicated as changing how individuals—teachers—are paid.

Chapter 8 is a new chapter and describes the wide-ranging teacher compensation initiatives and proposals that are emerging around the country. The fact is that teacher quality is a top issue on many state and district policy agendas, and new and better ways of paying teachers—and paying teachers more—are critical elements of those agendas. Numerous states and districts are seeking to pay teachers more; to provide recruiting incentives, including signing bonuses; to pay more for teachers in shortage areas and for teachers willing to work in struggling, high-poverty schools; and to pay the top salaries to teachers with the most expertise. The topic of teacher pensions and how to make them more attractive is also creeping onto the teacher compensation agenda. The chapter suggests that efforts to change the structure of teacher salaries could be even more comprehensive than the topics outlined in more depth in the book.

Finally, we must make a few comments on the financing of teacher compensation change. Many would argue that teacher compensation can only change if more money is added to the education system. Until the education system follows private-sector practice and uses technology to replace workers and uses funds saved to raise teacher salaries, higher salaries will probably only happen if more money is put into the education system. Although that seemed a far reach in the middle of the 1990s, it seems more possible today. Nearly half the states have either teacher quality or teacher compensation task forces; nearly all recommendations suggest more money is needed. Furthermore, we find that the new salary structures proposed in this book meet most policymakers' demands for a new system for paying teachers. Although many policymakers are reluctant to increase salaries through the current teacher salary structure, most are less reluctant and even enthusiastic about doing so for the proposed new structures. Only time will tell if funding follows rhetoric, but in the short to medium term, teacher salary levels can rise only if more money is budgeted to the education system.

We do make a specific set of suggestions for how to finance school-based, value-added performance awards. These programs need separate and protected funding sources because they work in the medium to long run only if they remain an enduring feature of the education system. These programs should not be started if policy leaders are not prepared to maintain their funding.

We are optimistic about the ideas we put forth in this book. We know compensation change is never easy. We know the history of change in education compensation is dismal and is basically a history of failed efforts—until recently. We also know that poorly designed and implemented compensation change can have a detrimental impact on system productivity and employee morale. But done appropriately, compensation change potentially can create a positive, motivating, and rewarding work environment; contribute to enhanced education system productivity; and produce higher salaries for teachers. This book is written, in part, to encourage state, district, and union policymakers to adopt approaches to change in compensation that can enhance rather than deplete educational productivity.

We also believe that the imperative of education improvement today is as important as it has ever been, and we believe that teacher compensation change can be part of the numerous strategies that, combined, will help make reform work. We hope the ideas put forth in this book will become a feature of the teacher compensation landscape across the country over the next decades.

Acknowledgments

The contributions of the following reviewers are gratefully acknowledged:

Robert F. Chase
President, National Education Association
Washington, DC

Kathleen T. Ware
Associate Superintendent, Cincinnati Public Schools
Cincinnati, OH

Yvonne Chan
Principal, Vaughn Next Century Learning Center
San Fernando, CA

Gene Wilhoit
Commissioner, Kentucky Department of Education
Frankfort, KY

Sandra Feldman
President, American Federation of Teachers
Washington, DC

About the Authors

Allan Odden is Professor of Educational Administration at the University of Wisconsin–Madison. He formerly was Professor of Education Policy and Administration at the University of Southern California (USC) and Director of Policy Analysis for California Education, an educational policy studies consortium composed of USC; Stanford University; and the University of California, Berkeley. At Wisconsin, he is Co-Director of the Consortium for Policy Research in Education (CPRE), which is funded by the U.S. Department of Education.

CPRE is a consortium of the Universities of Wisconsin–Madison, Pennsylvania, and Michigan, in addition to Harvard University and Stanford University. He is the principal investigator for the CPRE Teacher Compensation Project, funded by the Pew Charitable Trusts, the Carnegie Corporation, and private donors. He is an expert on teacher compensation, school finance, educational policy, school-based management, and educational policy implementation.

He helped Cincinnati develop its far-reaching, new, teacher compensation system, and he worked with the Vaughn Next Century Learning Center as it restructured how it paid its teachers. He has also worked in numerous states and districts around the country on teacher compensation reform.

He worked with the Education Commission of the States for a decade (1975 to 1984), serving as Assistant Executive Director, Director of Policy Analysis and Research, and Director of its educational finance center. He was President of the American Educational Finance Association from

1979 to 1980 and served as research director for special state educational-finance projects in numerous states around the country. He has consulted for the U.S. Congress, the U.S. Secretary of Education, governors, state legislators, chief state school officers, national and local unions, superintendents in many local school districts, the National Alliance for Business, the Business Roundtable, and New American Schools. He has written widely, publishing over 200 journal articles, book chapters, and research reports, as well as 25 books and monographs.

His books include *Reallocating Resources: How to Boost Student Achievement Without Spending More,* written with Sarah Archibald (Corwin, 2000); *School Finance: A Policy Perspective* (2nd edition), written with Lawrence Picus (2000); *School-Based Financing,* coedited with Margaret Goertz (Corwin, 1999); *Financing Schools for High Performance,* written with Carolyn Busch (1998); *Paying Teachers for What They Know and Do* (1st edition), written with Carolyn Kelley (1997); and *Educational Leadership for America's Schools,* written with Eleanor Odden (1995).

He was a mathematics teacher and curriculum developer in New York City's East Harlem for 5 years. He received his PhD and MA degrees from Columbia University, a Master of Divinity degree from the Union Theological Seminary, and his BS from Brown University.

 **Carolyn Kelley** (PhD, Stanford University) is Associate Professor of Educational Administration at the University of Wisconsin–Madison and a Senior Research Associate for CPRE. Her expertise is in educational policy; organizational theory; and teacher compensation, incentives, and accountability. She has conducted extensive research on the role of teacher compensation as an element of strategic, human resource management in schools. Her current research examines the structure and scope of human resources management and the role of the principal in schools with successful knowledge- and skills-based teacher pay and evaluation systems.

She has also served as a researcher and policy analyst for SRI International, the University of California at San Francisco, the University of Michigan, the Illinois State Scholarship Commission, the Illinois Board of Higher Education, the U.S. Department of Health and Human Services, and the U.S. Senate. Her publications include over 30 journal articles, book chapters, and research reports. Recent coauthored publications include *Financial Incentives for National Board Certification* with Allan Odden (in press), and *Payment for Results: The Effects of The Kentucky and Maryland Group-Based Performance Award Programs,* written with Sharon Conley and Steve Kimball (2000).

She has consulted for the U.S. Department of Education, the Organization for Economic Cooperation and Development, numerous states, local school districts, national associations of educational policymakers and practitioners, and national and state teachers' unions.

How Are Teachers Compensated?

1

Teacher compensation is a high-interest issue. Some think teachers are paid too little. Others think teachers are paid too much. Today, however, there are many efforts across the country to pay teachers more, in part because higher pay is key to recruiting and retaining the quality of teachers needed to educate students to high-achievement standards. The challenge is to determine how to pay which teachers more.

One problem in accomplishing this goal is that many do not like the way teachers currently are paid; they are reluctant to use the current structure to pay teachers more. Most districts pay teachers according to a single-salary schedule that provides salary increases for objective differences among teachers—education units, university degrees, and years of teaching experience. Over a 50-year period, up to about 1995, state and local policymakers enacted several well-publicized efforts to link teacher pay to performance—either their own performance or the performance of their students. Those efforts were largely ineffective, unsuccessful, and short-lived. As a result, teacher compensation structures today look pretty much as they did decades ago, and relative teacher pay levels are not better, and in many cases are worse, than they were decades ago.

This book is about both changing the way teachers are paid and raising teacher salary levels. We do not propose raising teacher salary levels across the board. But we have concluded that if the country is to accomplish the aspirations of standards-based education reform—educating many more students to much higher levels of performance—then recruiting and retaining quality teachers must be a high-priority issue. And paying teachers differently—as well as paying them more—must be part of this equation.

This book uses *teacher compensation* and *teacher pay* interchangeably. Technically, teacher compensation would include salary as well as fringe benefits, such as health and life insurance, retirement, sick leave, and so forth. Odden and Conley (1992) discuss some of these nonsalary issues, but this book primarily addresses the salary issue, using *salary, pay,* and *compensation* as synonyms.

Because teacher compensation is the largest portion of the education budget, how teachers are paid is key to effective use of educational resources. If teachers are paid below market, salaries need to be increased or the quality, and thus the effectiveness, of individuals entering and remaining in teaching is likely to fall (Manski, 1987; Murnane, Singer, Willett, Kemple, & Olsen, 1991; National Commission on Teaching and America's Future, 1996; Rosen & Flyer, 1994). If better methods exist for paying teachers, they should be considered and adopted, especially if they will contribute to improved schools and more effectively paid, higher-paid teachers. But finding and implementing more effective ways to pay teachers is a stiff challenge, and, as Chapter 2 discusses, the history of this search in our country is quite dismal.

As the book argues, however, the more recent history of paying teachers differently holds more promise. For several reasons, the education system has begun to meet more successfully the challenge of designing better ways to pay teachers. In this book, we identify a variety of new compensation structures that can be used in conjunction with other organizational strategies to enhance teacher capacity and effectiveness, improve school performance, increase student achievement, raise teacher salaries, and, perhaps, even bolster teacher morale. We discuss these strategies in an attempt to provide guidance to policymakers and practitioners in how to design and successfully undertake teacher compensation reform.

In this chapter, we describe how the level of teacher pay has changed since 1960, provide an overview of current teacher compensation structures, and discuss how the context surrounding teaching today is conducive to revisiting the issue of teacher compensation.

Current Status of Teacher Compensation: Pay Levels and Salary Structures

In general, today's teachers are paid according to a single-salary schedule that provides salary increments according to a teacher's years of experience and number of college or university units and degrees. This teacher salary schedule, first implemented in several big-city districts in the late 1920s and early 1930s, has not changed much over the course of the 20th century. For the 45 years from 1950 to 1995, moreover, teacher salaries did not change dramatically relative to other occupations, but toward the end of the 1990s, they began to take a turn for the worse. This began just when the nation needed more and better teachers, more because of enrollment rises and teacher retirements and better because of the demands of standards-based education reforms.

Teacher Salary Levels

Most teachers are public employees. Local school boards set teacher salaries, sometimes with state-guaranteed minimums. This is an unlikely context for producing very high salaries. Although some districts pay teachers an annual salary that can exceed $80,000, the national average in 1999 was $40,574, a relatively low level given the average education and experience of the teaching force.

Teacher salaries have changed significantly over time. In some periods, teacher salaries have risen or fallen with the salaries of other workers, and in other periods—particularly in the 1980s—the policy goal was to boost teacher salaries ahead of other occupations to make teaching more attractive. As the following discussion shows, however, relative teacher salaries in 1995 were about where they were 25 years earlier, but declines began to occur in the late 1990s.

Table 1.1 displays average teacher salaries over the 39-year period from 1960 to 1999. Although nominal teacher salaries rose by more than eightfold over this time period, from $4,950 in 1960 to $40,574 in 1999, the change is much smaller when the numbers are adjusted for inflation using the Consumer Price Index. As Table 1.1 shows, average inflation-adjusted teacher salaries rose from just $28,210 in 1960 to $40,574 in 1999, a 39-year increase of 44%.

But the numbers also show other factors buried in this 39-year change. The largest change in average salaries occurred during the 1960s, the period when the baby-boom generation entered public education, swelling school enrollments. Real salaries increased from $28,210 to $36,514 between 1960 and 1970, a 29% increase in just a decade. During the next 29 years, from 1970 to 1999, however, average inflation-adjusted teacher salaries rose only 11% more to just $40,574.

Table 1.1 Estimated Average Annual Teacher Salaries, 1960 to 1999

Year	Constant 1999 Dollars
1960	$28,210
1970	$36,514
1980	$31,398
1990	$39,430
1991	$40,226
1992	$40,239
1993	$40,406
1994	$40,208
1995	$40,285
1996	$39,861
1997	$40,032
1998	$40,308
1999	$40,574

SOURCE: Based on American Federation of Teachers, 1999 Salary Survey, Table II-2 (American Federation of Teachers, 2000).

NOTE: Consumer price index used as inflation adjustment.

But during the 29 years from 1970 to 1999, teacher salaries went on a roller-coaster ride. First, just as did many salaries during the inflationary period of the 1970s, inflation-adjusted teacher salaries dropped during the 1970s from $36,514 to $31,398, a loss of 14%. Then, during the 1980s, when policymakers decided that teacher salaries needed to increase, real teacher salaries rose 26%, not only gaining back the loss of the 1970s but also gaining an additional 8% over the previous 1970 high. But from 1990 to 1999, average teacher salaries remained essentially flat (paralleling the overall flat level of inflation-adjusted, per-pupil, education funding).

In short, taking 1960 as a base, teacher salaries in 1999 were almost 50% higher, but the bulk of teacher pay increases occurred during the 1960s. Furthermore, since 1970, teacher salaries increased less than an average of 0.4% a year, and after 1990, inflation-adjusted teacher salaries essentially did not increase at all. At least for the last quarter century, this is not a story of fiscal success. Indeed, since the average years of experience of teachers also increased from 1970 to 1999, it could be that when adjusted for years of experience, average teacher salaries today are no higher than they were 29 years ago.

Table 1.2 Beginning Teacher Salaries Compared to Salaries
          of Other College Graduates

	Beginning Salary				
	1972	*1980*	*1990*	*1995*	*1999*
Teaching	$6,970	$10,657	$20,635	$24,463	$26,639
Engineering	10,608	20,136	32,304	36,701	44,362
Accounting	10,356	15,720	27,408	28,398	35,555
Business Administration	8,568	14,100	26,496	28,434	36,886
Liberal Arts	8,328	13,296	26,244	28,715	34,776
Economics/Finance	9,240	14,472	26,712	29,484	38,234
Computer Science	—	17,712	29,100	33,663	42,500
Ratio of Other Occupations' Salaries to Teaching Salaries					
Engineering	1.52	1.89	1.57	1.50	1.67
Accounting	1.49	1.48	1.33	1.16	1.33
Business Administration	1.23	1.32	1.28	1.16	1.38
Liberal Arts	1.19	1.25	1.27	1.17	1.31
Economics/Finance	1.33	1.36	1.29	1.21	1.44
Computer Science	—	1.66	1.41	1.38	1.60

SOURCE: Based on American Federation of Teachers, 1999 Salary Survey, Table III-3 (American Federation of Teachers, 2000).

Of course, these national figures varied dramatically by state and region. The highest average teacher salary in 1999 was $51,692 and was paid in New Jersey, where salaries increased by 57% in nominal terms over the decade from 1989 and 1999. The lowest average teacher salary in 1999 was $28,386 and was paid in South Dakota, where salaries increased by only 38% the previous decade. In three states—Alaska, Wyoming, and Arizona—salaries increased by less than 25% in nominal terms over the previous decade. In Louisiana, moreover, teacher salaries actually remained essentially unchanged (in real terms) during the quarter of a century from 1970 to 1995 but then increased modestly at the end of the 1990s. In short, the national averages played out very differently depending on the region, state, and local district in which a teacher worked.

Average teacher salaries and changes over time, however, are not the only salary parameters of importance. Table 1.2 shows estimated, average, beginning teacher salaries as well as average beginning salaries for several other categories of college graduates, over about the same period—1972 to 1999. These comparisons are important because one key factor in the ability of education to recruit able individuals into teaching is the competitiveness of the beginning salary. Research shows that the higher the beginning salary, the more able the individuals who enter into teaching (Ferris & Winkler, 1986).

Several aspects of the figures in Table 1.2 stand out in comparing *beginning* salaries of teachers to those of college graduates entering different professions. First, beginning teacher salaries in 1999 were significantly below those of all liberal arts graduates, the primary competitive pool for teachers, and the gap had increased to the highest level during this 27-year time period. A modest goal for any state or district would be to have beginning teacher salaries at least at the level for other, beginning liberal arts graduates. The education system was farther from this modest goal in 1999 than at any time during the previous 25 to 30 years.

Second, this might not be a sufficiently high beginning salary. Education must also compete with more technical fields for talent. The data show, however, that competition on these other fronts has become more intense. Although progress was made in matching beginning salaries for individuals entering accounting and business administration up until 1995, nearly all gains were lost between 1995 and 1999, when the gap between beginning salaries for teachers and those for accounting and business majors nearly reached an all-time high.

Third, if teaching is to attract able individuals into mathematics, science, and technology instruction, beginning salaries are even less competitive. Beginning engineers and computer scientists make substantially more—nearly two thirds more—than beginning teachers, as do individuals who enter the economics and finance world.

Finally, although the gap between beginning teacher salaries and those of many other professions narrowed in the early 1990s, the flat level of education funding over the decade reversed this progress, and as the national economy boomed in the 1990s, raising salaries for many occupations, comparative beginning salaries for teachers lost ground. If district and state policymakers continue to keep their eye off the competitive market for teachers and do not make beginning salaries competitive—especially as many teachers retire, enrollment grows, demands rise, and large numbers of quality new teachers are needed—education is likely to remain disadvantaged in recruiting their fair share of bright, able individuals into teaching.

Table 1.3   Ratio of Average Teacher Salary to Average Salary of All
Full-Time Employees in Economy

School Year	Ratio
1961	1.08
1971	1.14
1981	1.01
1991	1.21
1993	1.19
1995	1.20
1997	1.15
1999	1.12

SOURCE: Based on American Federation of Teachers, 1999 Salary Survey, Table II-2 (American Federation of Teachers, 2000).

These admonitions also pertain to *average* salary levels. Teacher salary levels and their changes over time are important in themselves but are also important in relation to other occupations. Even if teacher salaries were stagnant, teaching could still have a relative advantage if the salaries of other workers were falling. But that is not the case. Tables 1.3 and 1.4 provide some comparative data on average teacher salaries, again over the last 30 or so years. Table 1.3 shows the ratio between average teacher salaries and average salaries for all people in the workforce. The numbers pretty much reflect the overall trends in teacher salaries. First, teacher salaries gained relative to the salaries of all workers between 1961 and 1971, growing from just 8% more to 14% more. But nearly all this gain and more were lost during the 1970s. By 1990, however, comparative teacher salaries had risen not only back to their high of 1970 but also a little higher to 21% above the average worker's salary. But 1990 seemed to be the high watermark. The gain dropped from 21% to 12% by 1999 and will probably continue to drop unless more money is added to teacher salary budgets. Although teacher quality was the number-one issue on many state policy agendas at the end of the 1990s, that concern really needs to be bolstered with the dollars to enhance the education system's comparative advantage in both recruiting and retaining quality individuals in teaching.

Moreover, teacher salaries should be substantially higher than the average salary for all other workers, because nearly all teachers are college graduates and a large percentage have master's or even higher-education

Table 1.4 Estimated Average Salaries of Teachers and Selected
            Other College Graduates

	1962	1970	1980	1990	1994	1999
Teachers	$5,512	$8,635	$16,100	$31,347	$35,764	$40,574
Accountant III	7,416	10,686	21,299	35,489	39,815	49,257
Attorney III	11,844	16,884	33,034	59,087	71,328	69,104
Computer Systems Analyst	—	—	—	47,958	55,998	68,782
Engineer	10,248	14,695	28,486	49,365	56,191	68,294
Assistant Professor, Public University	7,700*	10,800	17,800	32,730	37,220	41,940
Ratio of Other Occupations to Teachers						
Accountant III	1.34	1.24	1.32	1.13	1.11	1.21
Attorney III	2.15	1.96	2.05	1.88	1.99	1.70
Computer Systems Analyst	—	—	—	1.53	1.57	1.70
Engineer	1.86	1.70	1.77	1.57	1.57	1.68
Assistant Professor, Public University	1.40*	1.25	1.11	1.04	1.04	1.03

SOURCE: Based on American Federation of Teachers, 1999 Salary Survey, Table II-5 (American Federation of Teachers, 2000).
NOTE: *Data are from 1964.

degrees. Indeed, teachers are among the most highly educated workers in the country's economy, and most teachers engage in ongoing professional training each year to enhance their professional expertise. Given their level of education and training, they should have a significant earning advantage compared to all other workers. Unfortunately, that advantage was only 12% in 1999, which should bring a sense of urgency to most policymakers to raise teacher salaries.

As Table 1.4 reveals, moreover, teachers generally are paid less than people in many other occupations who have similar levels of education and training. Since 1962, average teacher salaries have made some gains with respect to accountants and assistant professors but are still substantially below that of attorneys, engineers, and computer systems analysts. Attorneys made about twice as much as teachers in 1962 and retained a large fiscal advantage in 1999; those who question the litigious nature of U.S. society might smile at the drop in the salary differential of lawyers versus teachers, although the average lawyer still earns 70% more than the average teacher. The alarming aspect of Table 1.4 is that several professions—law, computers, and engineering—offer a salary advantage of 70% over teaching. Unless things change, education will simply not be able to compete effectively for talent. Perhaps the most striking element of Table 1.4 is that the average salary of a teacher is now close to the same as that of an assistant professor at a public university, even though the latter requires a doctorate. But it is probably also true that the average assistant professor is much younger than the average teacher is, as assistant professor is the entry point into the professorate. The fact is that educators—teachers or professors—tend to earn less than people in many other professions, particularly those in mathematics, science, and technological fields.

In sum, it would be fair to say that teacher salaries today are modest. They are just above the median family income in America. They have changed over time but very little since 1970. They are much lower than for many other occupations with similar levels of education and training, although they are modestly higher than the averages of all workers in the economy.

The salary changes that have occurred, however, can be put into a different fiscal context by comparing them to the more than 200% increase in inflation-adjusted, per-pupil funding that occurred between 1960 and 1999 (Odden & Picus, 2000). Clearly, the bulk of new education dollars did not increase the salary of individual teachers; the large bulk, as other research has shown, was used to hire more teachers to provide more services for students in areas such as special and compensatory education (Odden, Kellor, Heneman, & Milanowski, 1999).

The Single-Salary Schedule

Most teachers across the country are paid according to a single-salary schedule. This does not mean that all teachers earn the same salary. Individual teacher salaries vary, and they vary according to the attributes of individual teachers. Teachers with more years of experience have larger salaries. Teachers with more education units have larger salaries. Teachers with master's degrees earn higher salaries. The structure even pays more for additional jobs; coaches earn a salary supplement; advisors of clubs and other cocurricular activities often earn a salary increment. Increasingly, teachers in leadership positions earn salaries above those in the schedule. But the bulk of salaries that teachers earn is determined by the

Table 1.5 Typical Teacher Single-Salary Schedule, 1999-2000

Step	Bachelor's	BA+15	Master's	MA+15	Doctor's
1	$29,885	$30,421	$32,884	$34,662	$37,661
2	31,793	32,326	34,770	36,548	39,547
3	33,141	33,677	36,420	38,195	41,197
4	34,512	35,048	37,768	39,547	42,547
5	36,677	37,213	39,675	41,454	44,452
6	38,304	38,839	41,561	43,337	46,338
7	39,932	40,468	43,466	45,245	48,243
8	41,839	42,375	45,652	47,431	50,429
9	44,023	44.559	48,095	49,872	52,872
10	46,467	47,002	50,815	52,594	55,592
11	49,165	49,700	53,792	55,570	58,571
12*	52,457	52,993	57,084	58,863	61,861
13*	54,606	55,142	59,212	60,990	63,989
14*	56,229	56,755	60,834	62,613	65,611

NOTE: *Steps 12, 13, and 14 are longevity steps payable upon completion of four years service in steps 11, 12, and 13, respectively.

steps-and-lanes schedule, with steps providing salary increases for years of experience and lanes providing increases of education units or degrees.

And critical to the success of the single-salary schedule is that the basis for paying teachers different amounts—for years of experience, education units, and different jobs—be objective, measurable, and not subject to administrative whim.

Table 1.5 displays the major features of a salary schedule for a typical school district from 1999 to 2000. The data show that the beginning salary in this district was $29,885. Nationally, that was about 85% of the beginning salary for all college graduates with a liberal arts degree entering the workforce in that year.

The maximum salary was $65,611, about 120% above the beginning salary. Assuming this type of salary structure remains, which it has for nearly three fourths of a century, the most teachers in this district could expect financially over the course of their career would be to slightly more than double their beginning salary in real terms. But this salary doubling would occur only after working 22 years and investing in substantial graduate training, including earning a doctorate!

For the first 11 years, the teacher automatically receives a salary increment of between $1,348 and $3,188 each year without earning any additional credits. These increases typically are called seniority, years of experience, or step increases. But after 11 years, automatic annual salary increments would stop and be replaced by *longevity* increments that take more than a year to earn. Indeed, the longevity increases for each of steps 12 through 14 require an additional 4 years of teaching. In short, to earn the step-14 salary level requires 22 years of teaching experience, a large part of the full career of most teachers.

Not indicated on the schedule is the placement of an experienced teacher who is new to the district. Although the procedure is changing, common practice has been to limit a teacher to a maximum of 4 to 6 years of experience, which would mean teachers who did not stay in one district for their entire career—the most common behavior—might never reach the highest salary step (step 14 for this district) regardless of their professional expertise.

Table 1.5 shows that earning advanced credits and degrees also produces salary increases. For the first 15 units after the bachelor's degree, the increment is $536 at all levels of experience. But both the dollar amount and the percentage increase for the master's degree rises with the years of experience. So, for example, a teacher with a master's degree at step 1 would earn an 8%, or $2,460, salary increase for the master's, and at step 7, that would produce a 7.4%, or $3,000, increase, and at step 14, a 7.2%, or $4,070, increase. These increases would be added to a teacher's base salary and thus would be earned for every year after the master's degree was earned.

For average teachers who earned a master's degree by their 11th year of teaching, their salary would have risen about 80% above their starting salary. If these teachers did not earn any more degrees or take any more education credits, they would then earn just 13% more (the longevity increases) over the next 12 years, which would put their salary at 103% above their beginning salary.

A doctorate pushes these maximum-earning numbers a bit higher. A doctorate within the first 11 years of teaching produces a salary of $58,571, or 96% above the beginning salary; that would rise by just another $7,040 over the next 12 years of experience to a maximum of $65,611. But only a very few teachers earn a doctorate, and thus enjoy such salary levels.

These data do not include extra salary increments for additional jobs such as coaching a sport, advising a team or other extra curricular activity, or assuming a teacher leadership role.

Certainly, salary schedules around the country vary from the one shown in Table 1.5, with both lower and higher salaries at different points in the steps-and-lanes matrix as well as greater or fewer steps and lanes. Nevertheless, the data in Table 1.5 are a good overall indicator of how teachers are paid. Teachers tend to start with a salary below that of other college graduates with liberal arts degrees and below that of all college graduates. They can, at most, double their salary over a long time period, and only with substantial graduate training, and after a large number of years—often their entire teaching career. They pretty much top out on annual increments within the first 15 years of teaching (in their mid-30s if they begin teaching in their early 20s). And their extra pay for more years of experience is limited—unless they work at a different job during the summer. In short, the typical teacher has modest earning power.

Finally, larger salaries are available to teachers but only for those who leave teaching and enter administration—assistant principal, principal, central office supervisor, or numerous other out-of-classroom jobs. Except for recent salary increases for earning certification from the National Board for Professional Teaching Practice (discussed below) and the very beginnings of pay for knowledge and skills, teachers with a greater array of professional expertise do not earn more than those with fewer skills and competencies, and only in rare circumstances are teachers, who provide the most crucial direct service to students—instruction—able to earn more than individuals who do not work in the classroom.

There are better ways to pay teachers and better ways to let teachers—the linchpin in the education system for reaching the goal of teaching students to high standards—increase their maximum pay beyond levels now possible in the typical school district while also allowing them to remain in the classroom teaching children for the bulk of the working day.

Winds of Change

The need to understand how to design and implement effective, workable, and new teacher compensation structures has an additional urgency because the taxpaying public, the business community, and policymakers continue to pressure the education system to produce results and to link pay—even school finance structures more broadly—to performance. This was an explicit call by the 1999 Education Summit of governors and the nation's business leaders. As Chapter 2 shows, however, the problem is that previous innovations in teacher compensation also seemed promising, such as merit pay for individuals, teachers, or administrators, or career ladder programs; but the promises were not fulfilled (Freiberg & Knight, 1991; Hatry, Greiner, & Ashford, 1994; Heneman & Young, 1991; Murnane & Cohen, 1986; Schlechty, 1989).

Although this dismal history has led many educators to believe that changes in teacher compensation of any sort are not possible in education, particularly performance awards (Bacharach, Lipsky, & Shedd, 1984; Cohen, 1996; Darling-Hammond, 1996; Johnson, 1986; Kohn, 1993; Lipsky & Bacharach, 1983), a new round of teacher compensation changes already has begun to spring up around the country. School-based performance awards have been created in nearly two dozen states including Arizona, California, Florida, Kentucky, and North Carolina, and in a similar number of large districts (Charlotte-Mecklenburg, North Carolina; Dallas, Texas; Fairfax County, Virginia; Memphis, Tennessee; and New York, New York). All use the money for teacher salary bonuses; other states and districts have such programs but require that the money be used for school improvement initiatives. California, Colorado, and Minnesota enacted legislation in 1995 that encourages districts to implement teacher compensation innovations, and Florida passed a bill requiring districts to allocate 20% of teacher salaries on the basis of performance.

Several states and districts have begun to add elements of knowledge- and skills-based pay. Currently, 28 states and more than 50 districts provide salary bonuses to teachers who earn a certificate from the National Board for Professional Teaching Standards (Kelley & Kimball, in press). This was the first major knowledge- and skills-based pay element to enter teacher pay systems. But many other districts are developing local aspects of knowledge- and skills-based pay. Douglas County, Colorado, created one of the first systems, but an additional variation was created by Rochester, New York. In 2000, Cincinnati became the first district in the country to adopt a full-fledged, knowledge- and skills-based, teacher salary structure, as did the Vaughn Next Century Learning Center. In January 2001, a bill was introduced in Iowa to create such a system statewide, essentially scaling up the Cincinnati structure to a statewide strategy coupled with a performance-based system for providing the teaching license (Youngs, Odden, & Porter, 2000). These and other recent initiatives will be discussed in more detail in Chapter 5.

Although these are the two basic structural changes that are occurring, many other compensation initiatives are developing across the country. Several states (e.g., Arizona, Iowa, Nebraska, and South Carolina) and numerous districts (e.g., New York City, Philadelphia) want somehow to raise teacher salary levels to compete for teacher talent in the labor market. Other districts are providing higher pay for teachers in shortage areas (mathematics, science, and technology), and still others are providing pay incentives for individuals who take jobs in hard-to-staff, high-poverty, or low-performance schools to increase the level of teacher quality in those difficult schools. District and state teacher compensation task forces are also using or proposing signing bonuses, moving expenses, and housing allowances in high-cost communities (big cities and Silicon Valley). In short, numerous, varied, and rapidly emerging innovations in teacher compensation all suggest that the time is ripe for change, and all will provide a rich, natural laboratory for research and analysis.

As we have argued throughout this book, we find appealing the claim that changes in teacher compensation plans that improve their alignment with reform goals can contribute to better education for students. However, we also know that within education and the education policy community, we are still at the beginning of the learning curve on what new teacher compensation structures are viable and with what effects. It is quite possible that some plans developed in the future will not draw on the workable new concepts and will constitute just another round of merit pay and thus will not elicit responses that will motivate teachers or improve the quality of education provided to students. Given the vast resources devoted to compensation, the continued pressures from stakeholders outside of education, and the skepticism about viable compensation change by many within education, getting the word out on compensation innovations that show promise—knowledge- and skills-based pay and group performance awards—is a critical need and a primary purpose of this book.

New Concepts of Compensation

The above new ideas for how to pay teachers differently are paralleled by new strategies for paying other individuals, including professional knowledge workers, which have been developed and used quite successfully in organizations, particularly high-performance organizations, in the private and nonprofit sectors. Many organizations in the broader economy are undergoing a dramatic change in both the structure of their workplace and the way they pay employees, including professionals (Crandall & Wallace, 1998; Heneman, Ledford, & Gresham, 2000; Lawler,

1990, 2000b; Heneman & Ledford, 1998; Schuster & Zingheim, 1992; Zingheim & Schuster, 1995a, 2000). A force driving these broader changes is the need to improve productivity, which is also the challenge for education if the lofty goals of education reform are to be attained (Odden & Busch, 1998; Odden & Clune, 1995, 1998).

Although they vary, there are several commonalties in the pressures to improve productivity in nonschool settings. One is an intense focus on quality and results, with the requirement that quality improve in quantum, not just marginal, amounts. To produce quantum improvements, organizations tend to restructure and reorganize. In this process, they usually decentralize their management systems and flatten their organizational structures. They create multifunctional work teams, give them power and authority to accomplish organizational and team goals, and hold them accountable for results. Considerable ongoing investment in training work team members must accompany this new strategy for it to work. Team members are trained in technical areas, in new functional areas for which teams are responsible, and in the business skills needed to engage in self-management (Hammer & Champy, 1993; Heneman et al., 2000; Katzenbach & Smith, 1993; Lawler, 1986, 1992).

These changes represent the "new logic" for organizing higher-performance systems in the 21st century (Lawler, 1996). Moreover, ample research has shown that this way of organizing work is particularly well suited to education and applies quite well to schools (Crandall & Wallace, 1998; Darling-Hammond, 1996; Galbraith & Lawler, 1993; Mohrman, Lawler, & Mohrman, 1992; Mohrman, Wohlstetter, & Associates, 1994; Odden & Busch, 1998; Odden & Odden, 1995).

Many organizations following this new logic also have designed new forms of compensation to have their pay practices enhance the core knowledge and competencies needed in their new organizations. Such core competencies include team-based leadership and management skills; new technical, analytical skills to support continuous improvement; and skills needed to work across traditional functional lines (Crandall & Wallace, 1998; Heneman et al., 2000; Lawler, 1990, 2000b; Zingheim & Schuster, 1995a, 2000).

As a result, concepts such as knowledge- and skills-based pay, pay for knowledge, pay for professional expertise, collective rewards for adding value to performance, and gain sharing have become the core of new compensation strategies. Under these compensation strategies, individuals are not paid on the basis of seniority or for doing a particular job. They are paid on the basis of the knowledge, skills, and competencies they need to perform their many new job tasks and of their success as a group in producing organizational results.

Many organizations also are beginning to pay individuals in hot areas (e.g., information technology fields) a higher salary, even though their job tasks may be similar to other workers. In this way, internal pay equity for comparable jobs is beginning to erode because of external market pressures. If companies do not pay such employees more, the employees leave the organization for higher wages paid by other companies, and the productivity of their former employers declines.

Furthermore, a portion of each team member's pay can depend on the results of the team's effort measured by team and organizational performance. Group performance awards, team bonuses, and gain-sharing plans reflect these compensation innovations.

In sum, many private and nonprofit organizations are beginning to replace job-based pay, experience-based pay, and individual merit and incentive pay with knowledge- and skills-based pay, contingency pay, and team-based performance awards. In short, compensation is being changed to align organizational incentives and rewards with the strategic needs of the workplace (Crandall & Wallace, 1998; Heneman & Von Hippel, 1995; Heneman et al., 2000; Lawler, 2000b; Ledford, 1995a, 1995b; Ledford, Lawler, & Mohrman, 1995).

Shifting pay increments from years of experience and loosely related education units to more direct measures of professional knowledge and skills, adding a mechanism that undergirds the need for ongoing training and assessment of instructional strategies, and adding group-based performance bonuses are compensation changes that could reconnect how teachers are paid with the evolving strategic needs of new school organizations and with calls for teacher professionalism and the core requirements of standards-based education reform. Providing salary increments for teachers who are certified by the National Board for Professional Teaching Standards as accomplished teachers, a policy increasingly adopted by states and districts, is a direct knowledge- and skills-based pay element and represents specific movement on teacher compensation reform; the Web page of the National Board (www.nbpts.org/state_local/where/index.html) describes these latter state and local compensation incentives (Conley & Odden, 1995; Darling-Hammond, 1996; Kelley & Kimball, in press; Kelley & Odden, 1995; Mohrman, Mohrman, & Odden, 1996; Odden, 1996).

The Changing Context of Teaching

These evolving new notions about how to pay knowledge workers, including teachers, are compatible with, and even reinforce, the broader reform context surrounding teaching and education. First, there are serious efforts to transform teaching into a much stronger profession. These efforts include a new understanding of what constitutes good teaching; actions by teachers to describe and assess what beginning, midcareer, and advanced teachers know and can do; and creation of incentives for teachers to learn these new teaching practices. Second, the standards-based education reform movement, in which teachers are playing leading roles, is identifying curriculum content standards and student performance standards that require a greater level of teacher professional competence to implement. The standards-based reform movement includes notions of school restructuring and site-based management, both of which require that teachers play new and key roles in organizing and managing their work environment; these roles also require additional teacher competencies as well as incentives for teachers to develop them.

Thus the context surrounding teaching could be reinforced by change in teacher compensation. If this round of change draws from the new ideas that have been used successfully in other organizations to pay knowledge workers who work best collegially, it has the potential to be more successful than the failed efforts of the individual merit and incentive pay schemes of the past 50 years (Hatry et al., 1994; Heneman & Young, 1991; Murnane & Cohen, 1986) and career ladders of the more recent past (Bellon, Bellon, Blank, Brian, & Kershaw, 1989; Freiberg & Knight, 1991; Schlechty, 1989; Southern Regional Education Board, 1994).

The Push to Professionalize Teaching

The proper context for understanding the need to change teacher compensation is within the larger issue of how to enhance the profession as a whole. There are several initiatives across the country focused on enhancing the professional condition of teaching. Since 1986, when the Carnegie Forum on Education and the Economy released a report on the need to transform teaching into a full-fledged profession, the country has experienced numerous initiatives to do just that. In 1995, the National Commission on Teaching and America's Future was created. In September 1996, it issued a set of proposals (National Commission on Teaching and

America's Future, 1996) close to the 10-year anniversary of the Carnegie report *A Nation Prepared: Teachers for the 21st Century* (Carnegie Forum on Education and the Economy, 1986). The 1995 report made numerous recommendations to improve instruction and the professional nature of teaching, including new forms of teacher compensation. The report specifically mentioned knowledge- and skills-based pay and some sort of group incentives based on improved student learning. This was the first report with proposals to enhance teaching as a profession that also included proposals to change teacher compensation.

Three components of the efforts to professionalize teaching are particularly relevant to a discussion of teacher compensation: (a) a new view of teaching as an intellectually complex, multifaceted activity critical to having all students achieve to high standards; (b) creation of detailed, written descriptions of teaching practice and development of standards that can be used to describe and assess practice to external criteria; and (c) development of assessments for beginning, midcareer, and advanced teachers that indicate the level of teaching practice relative to external standards.

New Understandings of Good Teaching

Based primarily on advances from cognitive psychology, a realization is rapidly growing that all but the most disabled students can achieve to high academic standards. Producing this higher level of learning, however, requires a different type of pedagogy and, indeed, a new understanding of what constitutes good teaching and learning (Bransford, Goldman, & Vye, 1991; Bruer, 1993; Knapp, Shields, & Turnbull, 1995; Lehrer, 1993; Odden & Odden, 1995, Chapter 3; Resnick & Klopfer, 1989).

Good teaching today requires a deep understanding of content, that is, knowledge of the conceptual underpinnings of a subject area, the principles that tie the concepts together, and the ability to use both the principles and the concepts to engage in analysis both to advance understanding of the subject area and to solve real problems. Good teaching also requires a similarly deep understanding of how students learn the content, including the developmental stages children move through as they construct deeper subject matter understanding and the types of predictable errors they make and incorrect theories they construct. Finally, good teaching requires knowing and learning how to use an ever-increasing array of pedagogical practices that lead students through a set of experiences that, over time, help them know and understand the subject matter (for a summary, see Bransford, Brown, & Cocking, 1999).

Effective teaching occurs when students learn to high standards and consists of applying the knowledge of content, student learning, and pedagogy to the tasks of teaching—planning, instruction, assessment, diagnosis, and classroom management—in the context of a particular subject area and with a particular group of students (Darling-Hammond, Wise, & Klein, 1995; Newmann & Associates, 1996). Although good teaching requires a wealth of knowledge, studies also show that good teaching is quite contextualized; a major strength of expert teachers is the degree to which their classroom strategies are conditioned on their personal, practical knowledge of their students—both their specific cognitive abilities and their various learning styles. Good teachers use this personal, practical knowledge as a lens through which they understand classroom events and thus as a guide for developing classroom instructional experiences that will help each student individually as well as the class as a whole construct long-term and deep understandings of the subject matter they study.

In short, good teaching—teaching to high professional standards—is informed by understanding of content, knowledge about learning, and knowledge about content-specific pedagogy, and is grounded in the actual realities of a particular classroom with a set of real, individual children. Furthermore, good teaching is codependent on the effect of any set of instructional activities on the student; good teachers take in information about how students respond and learn (or do not learn) and modify, adapt, and plan future instructional activities with those responses in mind (Cohen, McLaughlin, & Talbert, 1993). In short, as Shulman (1986, 1987) concludes, good teachers engage continuously in pedagogical reasoning (see also Stronge & Tucker, 2000).

This new understanding of effective teaching is quite different from the teaching that is typically found in most classrooms (Elmore, 1996; Goodlad, 1984; Sizer, 1992) and the type of teaching that is the focus of most teacher training or professional development programs (Cohen et al., 1993; Darling-Hammond et al., 1995). At the same time, this type of teaching is quite effective in educating students to high-achievement standards (Newmann & Wehlage, 1993, 1995). Thus there is a rapidly emerging understanding of the new kind of teaching that is needed in the classrooms of the nation's schools to accomplish the goal of teaching all but the severely disabled student to high-achievement standards.

Development of Written Standards
of Professional Teaching Practice

Not only is a new understanding of more effective teaching practice emerging but so also are efforts to articulate and describe this new form of teaching. Indeed, efforts to write detailed descriptions of good teaching practices as well as to write a set of high and rigorous standards by which good teaching practice can be gauged is a significant and major innovation for both professional and lay understanding of teaching.

There are at least four major efforts to write standards describing high-quality, effective teaching practice. The National Board for Professional Teaching Standards (NBPTS) began this effort. The board was created in the aftermath of the 1986 Carnegie Forum on Education and the Economy report; its purpose was to develop an assessment system that could be used to Board certify experienced teachers whose expertise met or exceeded high and rigorous standards of accomplished practice (Bradley, 1994; National Board for Professional Teaching Standards, 1995; National Board for Professional Teaching Standards, 1999). After a developmental period of several years, the board began to certify teachers in late 1994. The board now provides certification in over 30 areas of teaching. The first Board certificates were awarded to 81 teachers in January 1995. In December 2000, there were a total of 9,524 Board-certified teachers. To date, the number of Board-certified teachers has about doubled each year. The goal is to have 100,000 Board-certified teachers by 2005.

As part of this process, the board has created a series of documents that describe standards for teaching practice that must be met for a teacher to become certified. Each of these documents identifies both the areas in which a teacher must be knowledgeable and the standards that would represent accomplished practice. The areas include, among others, understanding of subject matter and how students learn that content, knowledge of pedagogical practices and new forms of student assessment, engagement in professional activities within the school but outside the teacher's own classroom, and outreach to parents. Each document runs between 30 and 40 printed pages; the goal is to describe the array of professional knowledge and competencies teachers are expected to know and be able to deploy to earn Board certification (National Board for Professional Teaching Standards, 1994a, 1994b, 1994c, 1994d; and the National Board's Web site: www.nbpts.org/standards/standards.html).

In a parallel effort, the Interstate New Teacher Assessment and Support Consortium (INTASC), which is housed at the Council of Chief State

School Officers in Washington, DC, is creating a similar set of standards of practice for beginning teachers. The INTASC project seeks to develop an assessment system that states can use as a basis for providing a professional teaching license. Again, the INTASC project is creating 7 or so documents, each about 30 to 40 pages, that describe the knowledge, skills, competencies, and dispositions that are to be expected of individuals who seek a license to begin work in the teaching profession (Interstate New Teacher Assessment and Support Consortium, 1995a, 1995b).

The PRAXIS project of the Educational Testing Service is the third national effort to develop written standards for teaching practice. Just as with INTASC, the focus of PRAXIS is on beginning teachers, and the goal is to provide a way to license beginning teachers on the basis of what they know and can do, not just on the basis of taking a set of courses in an approved teacher training university program (Dwyer, 1994).

The fourth effort is the development of the Framework for Teaching by Danielson (1996). Danielson, who worked at the Educational Testing Service on the initial development efforts for both PRAXIS III and the first National Board assessments, concluded that a description of teaching practices that covered the full range of a teacher's career and that was aligned with standards for licensure and standards for advanced recognition was needed. Hence she developed her Framework for Teaching, which appeared as the 1996 yearbook of the Association for Supervision and Curriculum Development. The framework includes 22 teaching standards organized into four domains: planning and preparation, the classroom environment, instruction, and professional responsibilities. The framework also includes a performance evaluation structure that assesses teachers to four different levels of practice: unsatisfactory, basic, proficient, and advanced.

All these efforts also fit with the professional teacher initiative of the National Council for the Accreditation of Teacher Education (NCATE). NCATE sets standards used to accredit university-based teacher training programs. The Professional teacher initiative suggests that the licensure process should become performance-based and require teachers to pass tests of content, learning, and instructional knowledge as well as a rigorous assessment of clinical skills. The goal is to align the standards required for accreditation with the standards expected for beginning teaching practice (Wise, 1995; Wise & Liebbrand, 1993). Indeed, licensing teachers in two stages—first, a provisional license granted upon graduation from a preservice training program and second, a professional license after assessment of clinical practice within the first years of teaching—is a growing practice around the country (Youngs et al., 2000).

In short, for the first time in history, there are efforts to describe in detail on paper what good teaching entails, including a series of professional standards that would need to be met both to earn a professional teaching license and to earn recognition for midcareer, proficient, advanced, and accomplished practice. As will be explained in later chapters, such documents are critical to implementing a knowledge- and skills-based pay structure for teacher compensation.

Development of Assessment Instruments and Procedures
to Identify What Teachers Know and Can Do

Not only are the National Board, the INTASC project, the PRAXIS program, and Danielson's Framework for Teaching creating standards that describe teaching practice, but they also are creating assessment procedures and instruments that can be used to determine whether an individual's teaching practice meets the written standards as a condition of licensure for INTASC and PRAXIS, to different levels of practice (basic, proficient, and advanced) for the Framework, and for advanced recognition for Board certification.

In other words, these efforts are developing performance assessment approaches to determine what teachers know and can do. INTASC and PRAXIS have two types of tests. A multiple-choice and essay test will assess teacher knowledge of subject matter and professional knowledge of how students learn and of pedagogy. The more ambitious assessment will actually assess clinical teaching practice in the classroom sometime during the first, second, or third year of teaching. This assessment will consist of a combination of on-demand tasks, simulation tasks, and more authentic assessments using portfolios and observations.

The portfolios for both the INTASC and NBPTS assessments are structured similarly; reflect an ambitious, professional, and performance-based strategy for assessing what teachers know and can do; and include several key tasks. One task requires individuals to outline how they would teach an instructional unit; the task is intended to have the candidates indicate both their understanding of the key content aspects of the unit and how students learn that unit. The task asks for demonstrations of problem solving, reasoning, and communication within the subject area as well as the types of manipulative and other tools that would be used in the classroom. A second task requires a video of how the teacher actually taught a lesson to a class that focused on teaching a procedure or a concept and demonstrated teacher-student discourse. A third task asks for different ways teachers assess student learning and achievement. Another task seeks information on how the teacher would facilitate a small-group lesson for a subgroup of students in the classroom. An additional task asks teachers to discuss student work that shows understanding of the content matter being taught, such as mathematical problem solving, understanding and communication, and how student responses were used by the teacher to modify instructional strategies in order to produce better learning. Finally, there is a task that requires evidence of broader collaborative activities with colleagues, which included analysis of one's own teaching and contributions to the teaching field more generally. The key differences between the NBPTS and INTASC assessments are the number of different elements within each task. The board might require several instructional units for task 1, and work for several students in task 5, whereas INTASC would have fewer such items within each task.

These assessments have broken new ground in assessing the professional practice of teachers because they provide solid, psychometrically defensible results for making summative judgments on the nature of a teacher's professional skills with respect to externally set standards describing teaching practice (Bond, 1998; Dwyer, 1998; Jaeger, 1998; Milanowski, Odden, & Youngs, 1998; Moss, Schutz, & Collins, 1998). They are being used for high-stakes decisions—licensure in the case of INTASC and PRAXIS and certification in the case of the National Board. Several states and districts are paying a salary increment for teachers who earn Board certification and make Board certification a condition for advanced opportunities, such as lead teacher roles, mentor teacher programs, and the like. And as Chapter 5 shows, districts and states are beginning to use the results for new knowledge- and skills-based pay structures as well.

Conclusion

In sum, a new and ambitious view of teaching is emerging; written documents that describe sophisticated teaching skills have been published; standards are being developed to assess practice with respect to the written descriptions; assessments are being created to determine whether an individual's practice meets the standards; and important, high-stakes decisions—including additional pay—are being made on the basis of the assessment results.

It should be noted that although these initiatives describe, assess, and either license or pay teachers for performance, they do so to professional, external standards as opposed to just comparing individual teachers to one another. Past efforts to link high-stakes decisions to teacher performance generally tried a more norm-referenced approach to identify the best or the top teachers in a school or a district. In contrast, the above efforts use a criterion-referenced approach with high and rigorous professional standards and seek to identify teachers whose knowledge, clinical skills, and dispositions meet or do not meet professional standards. The best teachers in many schools today may not meet the standards to earn Board certification; the bulk of teachers in an excellent school could quite possibly meet those standards.

The standards describe an ambitious notion of teaching, indeed, a concept of teaching that would be effective in educating students to high standards. The assessments that have been developed show whether the practice of any individual teacher meets those standards, not whether that teacher is better or worse than some other teacher in the school or district.

Finally, from conversations with several individuals who have been developing these assessments, we have concluded that there are *steps* or *levels* in between the level of practice needed for licensure and the level of practice needed for Board certification. The Danielson Framework is a good example. It is these intervening levels that, as we describe more fully in the book, can be and are being used for significant salary increments—and the focus of professional development—as professional expertise expands from beginning to advanced status over the course of a teacher's career.

The Standards-Based Education Reform Movement

The standards-based education reform movement is integrally connected to these new understandings of teaching. The goal of reform—to teach all students to high standards—is substantively based on cognitive research findings showing that students can learn to much higher levels. And by linking high-quality curriculum standards, teacher training, and professional development to the above notions of good teaching, standards-based reform depends fundamentally on deployment of such teaching to accomplish its goal.

Standards-based education reform has three strategic elements: (a) a focus on school performance and student achievement results; (b) a focus on new curricula and the professional skills that they require for effective implementation; and (c) understanding that schools need to be restructured to provide this type of teaching and thus produce the new level of student achievement. Each of these strategic elements suggests needed compensation elements.

First, focusing on results reminds teachers and educational organizations of what needs to be achieved. Focusing on results can encourage continuing curricular and organizational change in the quest for better outcome performance. Student achievement is the complex result of individual differences and educational experiences. In turn, educational experiences are a function of the overall organization and teacher capabilities within the schools. By having the system focus on results, teachers know they need to work on establishing the professional knowledge and skills that allow them to produce achievement results by linking individual student needs with appropriate educational experiences.

Compensation practices can focus attention on results by tying them to rewards based on schoolwide performance in terms of results and not of individual performance. Appropriate rewards would be based on school results. One purpose of this book is to outline how such a practice might work.

Second, research shows that although there is strong, positive, local teacher response to new, ambitious, curriculum frameworks, teachers generally have not been equipped with the knowledge, skills, and competencies to implement this new curriculum well (see, for example, Ball, Cohen, Peterson, & Wilson, 1994; Cohen, 1990; Cohen & Ball, 1990; Goertz, Floden, & O'Day, 1995). The new curriculum requires deeper and more conceptual understandings of curricula content, an array of new pedagogical strategies that focus on concept development and problem solving and that are tailored to the developmental needs of each individual child, and a set of new assessment strategies that identify both what students know and what they can do. Indeed, many teachers must engage in a paradigm shift from what and how they are now teaching to an entirely different mode of pedagogy. This will require new knowledge and expertise, and the specifics of this new expertise will vary by school context (Cohen et al., 1993; Darling-Hammond et al., 1995).

Creating this new professional expertise will require substantial investment of time and energy on the part of teachers as well as substantial investment of funds by the education system in ongoing professional development. Although enhancement of professional expertise could be reward enough for teachers to engage in this process (McLaughlin & Yee, 1988), a change in the compensation structure to stimulate this engagement and to reward those who develop and use such new knowledge could also be warranted. Such a compensation structure could link funds spent on compensation directly to the expertise teachers need to effectively teach the new curriculum and increase student achievement. Another purpose of this book is to sketch how this element of compensation could be designed.

Third, there is a substantial knowledge base on how to design decentralized management systems, including changes in compensation, despite conventional wisdom to the contrary. Incomplete design and poor implementation have largely caused past problems with decentralized management in education (Murphy & Beck, 1995; Wohlstetter & Odden, 1992). Research has found that effective, school-based management strategies operate by decentralizing power, knowledge, information, and rewards; creating an instructional guidance focus for change; and providing facilitative principal leadership. This more comprehensive decentralization creates conditions that help professionals in schools to reorganize curriculum and instruction toward the above notions, as the primary objective of change in school and classroom organization as well as use of resources (Smylie, 1994). This research also found that school-based management strategies could be strengthened if coupled with new compensation strategies (Darling-Hammond, 1996; David, 1994; Mohrman et al., 1994; Newmann & Wehlage, 1995; Odden & Busch, 1998; Odden & Odden, 1994; Odden & Wohlstetter, 1995; Odden, Wohlstetter & Odden, 1995; Robertson, Wohlstetter, & Mohrman, 1995; Wohlstetter, Smyer, & Mohrman, 1994).

In short, standards-based education reform suggests at least the following new elements for compensation: (a) knowledge- and skills-based pay to develop the wide array of skills needed to teach a high-quality curriculum well and to engage in effective school-based management; and (b) group performance awards for meeting specified improvement in school results.

This book also assesses in detail the degree to which these and other new compensation ideas could apply to education. As background, the next chapter discusses the history of change in teacher compensation and argues that the same macrofactors that led to teacher compensation change years ago are operating today, thus presaging another round of change along the lines just discussed.

What Have We Learned From Attempts at Change?

2

The single-salary schedule represents one of three dominant approaches that have been used to compensate teachers in the United States over the past 200 years. The history of the emergence of the single-salary schedule provides a rich source of information about the context that can lead to successful teacher compensation reform and identifies successes as well as past mistakes that can be avoided in future compensation change efforts. Thus this chapter examines the history of teacher compensation reforms that stuck as well as those that proved to be more fleeting. These experiences suggest that when compensation reforms have been successful, strong relationships existed among teacher compensation and the attributes of teachers, the school organization, and the institutional environment within which schools operated. The importance of these relationships will be explored, with particular attention to what the current characteristics of teachers, schools, and public attitudes suggest about the possibility that we may now be embarking on a fourth major era of teacher compensation reform.

Three Approaches to Compensating Teachers

Since the early 1800s, there have been three major approaches to compensating teachers: boarding 'round, a grade- or position-based salary schedule, and the current single-salary schedule (see also Protsik, 1996).

Boarding 'Round

In the 1800s, a major portion of teacher compensation consisted of free room and board provided in the homes of pupils' parents. Typically, each week, the teacher would move to another student's house and be provided with room and board as part of the pay for teaching (Spring, 1994).

Today, moving from house to house and living with students' families may seem more like punishment than compensation, but at the time, the system met local needs. In the 1800s, most Americans lived in rural areas with limited tax bases, and the schools specifically catered to these agricultural communities. School calendars accommodated agricultural cycles; teachers were hired from among members of the community and were often relatives of school trustees (Tyack & Strober, 1981).

Teachers themselves rarely had more than an elementary education, and most were quite young. For example, 77% of female teachers in southeastern Michigan in 1860 were between 17 and 24 years of age (Spring, 1994). Job requirements focused on basic knowledge of reading, writing, and arithmetic—and possession of a "certified moral character" and a middle-class appearance (Tyack & Strober, 1981, p. 134). The transitory nature of work in teaching and the nature of the curriculum discouraged investments of time or money in professional training.

Classroom lessons focused on recitation and memorization work by students and heavy use of teacher-proof curricular materials such as the *McGuffey Reader* (Fuller, 1982). In the few instances where passage of county examinations were required of teachers, the certificate awarded was little more than "the limit above total ignorance to be reached before a candidate could receive it" (Fuller, 1982, p. 162).

For women, a job in teaching acted as a transition from the parents' home to the husband's home. Teaching was rarely considered a career; in fact, once married, most areas prohibited women from working in the classroom. Likewise, many men frequently taught only as a supplementary source of income to farming. Other men used the public role of a teaching job to gain the community trust necessary to become a preacher or an elected official (Fuller, 1982).

In this context, the boarding 'round method of compensating teachers provided the local community with the ability to monitor the moral character of teachers. By providing room and board to teachers, the community had constant supervision over their comings and goings, which was particularly important if the teacher was new to the area (Tyack, 1974). Teachers in one-room schoolhouses had a large amount of discretion over what went on in the classroom. At the end of each school term, students performed in community shows featuring plays, recitations of poems, and spelling bees. But with the exception of this public display of their work, teachers generally were left to their own devices in the classroom, and families had little access to knowledge about what went on there (Fuller, 1982). Instead, competence was evaluated by the way teachers conducted their personal affairs in the community. Thus the boarding 'round system enabled schools to operate with minimal public expenditures and served to meet the needs of community members interested in monitoring moral characteristics of teachers. The limited training requirements for teachers meant that those in need of subsistence could quickly move in and out of teaching as economy and agricultural opportunity necessitated.

Despite these advantages, eventually, the boarding 'round pay system petered out under the forces of demographic change and education reformers' will.

Grade-Based Salary Schedule

Beginning in the late 1800s and continuing through the early 1900s, the boarding 'round system was gradually replaced by a grade- or position-based salary schedule. The grade-based salary schedule reflected changes in the training of teachers and in the organization of schools and society. Under the grade-based system, teacher pay was based on years of experience, gender, race, and grade level taught. School administrators could also factor a subjective measure of merit into teachers' salaries, a measure that teachers came to view as overly arbitrary (Tyack & Strober, 1981).

The grade-based salary schedule provided higher wages for teachers, as many states adopted minimum salary requirements in attempts to address the problem of high teacher turnover (English, 1992). At about the same time, however, individual cities adopted differentiated or position-based salary schedules for men and women and for whites and blacks. For example, in Boston in 1876, salaries ranged from $1,700 to $3,200 for male grammar school teachers and $600 to $1,200 for female grammar school teachers. High school teachers were paid more: Men earned $1,700 to $4,000; women earned $1,000 to $2,000 (Katz, 1987). The ranges were set based on the grade level a teacher taught, and where the teachers fell within the range reflected years of experience and the administrators' assessment of their merit. Under this system, accountability for the teacher's work shifted from the rural community members to county-level administrators.

These changes in teacher compensation were precipitated by three major changes relating to teachers, schools, and society. First, concerns about the quality of schools and a new belief in scientific management led to increased training requirements for teachers. Second, quality and efficiency concerns led to the consolidation of rural schools and the creation of larger, graded schools run under bureaucratic administrative structures. And third, the United States was shifting from an agrarian to a more urban, industrial society, increasing the demand for urban education.

In 1896, the National Education Association Committee of Twelve on Rural Schools reported that rural schoolteachers were inefficient, incompetent, and in dire need of training (Fuller, 1982). A new and widespread belief in scientific management led professional educators to believe that there were scientific principles underlying teaching and that proper training could "cure" bad teaching (Fuller, 1982, p. 164).

The resulting training for most teachers took place at county teacher institutes led by county superintendents. The institutes were inexpensive and lasted for only a few days to a month. The institutes focused primarily on subject matter knowledge, although, over time, teaching-method courses were expanded. The emphasis on subject matter was particularly important, given widespread implementation of the "new education" curriculum, a response to the overly "bookish" curriculum of the rural schools (Fuller, 1982, p. 204). Rather than lead students through distinct lessons on spelling and math, teachers were supposed to integrate lessons on grammar, literature, arithmetic, geography, and history. Over time, the fields of agriculture and natural science were added to the curriculum in an attempt to enthrall students with the rural way of life.

With the reformers' new focus on training, states adopted teacher licensing procedures, which required passage of difficult county examinations. These exams were typically administered at the end of attendance at a teacher institute, often taking 2 full days to complete. County superintendents graded the exams and, over time, failed more candidates than they passed, despite teacher shortages. And although evidence on the efficacy of the exams for improving teaching was not strong, the exams did offer some assurance of teacher quality.

A second effort to improve the quality and efficiency of rural schools was the consolidation of schools into larger districts, to be run by the expert supervision of the county superintendents. Consolidation, reformers claimed, would produce larger and thus more efficient schools and save money (Fuller, 1982; Tyack, 1974). Education professionals could more successfully standardize equipment and textbooks across a broader geographic area and more easily supervise teachers. Additionally, consolidated schools brought city-like education conditions to rural areas, which educators hoped would raise rural students' performance. Consolidated schools became common by 1903 in the Midwest, once state legislatures passed laws allowing public education funds to be spent on transportation of students by wagon to the central schools. The consolidation movement enabled rural schools to become somewhat more like their larger, urban counterparts.

Third, the gradual shift in the United States from an agrarian to a more urban, industrial economy necessitated major changes in the nation's schools. The number of children attending schools rose as fewer worked on the farms (Tyack, 1974). As a result of consolidation and urbanization, the number of one-room schoolhouses gradually declined, and the number of graded, consolidated schools grew rapidly. For the first time, students were placed by age and ability into classrooms with a more rigid curriculum. The highly bureaucratic, graded schools were typically supervised by male principals and superintendents. Local communities forfeited control over the hiring of teachers in exchange for what they hoped would be improved, consolidated schools run by professionals. At the same time, new laws lengthened the school year by an average of 40 days during the period from 1890 to 1940 (Hanushek, 1994). Given the increasing requirements to earn a teaching certificate and the longer school year, few white men were attracted to seasonal teaching positions as a secondary occupation. In contrast, with limited occupational alternatives, many women still found the level of teacher pay attractive despite these added costs. The result was a hierarchical, graded school system with an almost exclusively female teaching force and a male-dominated administration.

The larger tax base of consolidated school districts, management oversight by professionals, increased training requirements for teacher candidates, and a longer school year all made the boarding 'round system impractical and obsolete. Under the new position-based compensation system, teachers across a city received a fairly uniform level of pay, contributing in one sense to a higher level of equity within the profession (English, 1992). This salary schedule also recognized the fact that secondary school teachers typically had more years of formal educational training and could command higher pay rates in other fields. Furthermore, the growing number of professional school administrators increased the costs of public education. The ability to pay the mostly female teaching force less was one effective way a district could keep costs under control (Richardson & Hatcher, 1983). Finally, the state-set minimum salary level may have impacted the high teacher turnover rates; the average city schoolteacher now remained for almost a decade (Rothman, 1978).

Despite these advantages, the graded pay schedule was overtly racist and sexist. Black teachers at both the elementary and secondary school levels were paid less than white teachers, and the mostly female, elementary school teaching force was paid less than the largely male (though more educated) high school teaching force. In 1893, the Massachusetts Board of Education admitted that women's wages, when compared to men's, "are so low as to make it humiliating to report the two in connection" (Rothman, 1978, p. 59). This led to resentment and a sense of inequality among teachers. Many felt that teaching was teaching, regardless of the grade level taught, and they should be paid for the job. It was this exploitation of female and black teachers that led to the slow demise of the differentiated salary schedule. An increasingly assertive female workforce collectively demanded higher salaries under the principle of equal pay for equal work, eventually leading schools toward today's single-salary schedule.

The Single-Salary Schedule

In 1921, Denver and Des Moines became the first cities to introduce the single-salary schedule to teachers (Sharpes, 1987). This compensation system was so named because all classroom teachers in the city were paid on the same scale regardless of gender, race, grade level taught, or family status of the teacher (Educational Research Service, 1978). Pay level was determined solely by a teacher's years of experience and level of academic preparation. By 1950, 97% of all schools had adopted the single-salary schedule (Sharpes, 1987).

The creation and rapid growth of the single-salary schedule was due largely to changes in schools and society. The growth of the women's movement and the organization of labor led to several efforts to develop a salary schedule that would provide equal pay for equal work. For example, the Interborough Association of Women Teachers (IAWT) in New York, originally called the Women Teachers' Organization, fought a long battle for equal pay for equal work in teaching. In 1900, the New York State Davis Law brought the school districts of the five boroughs of New York City under one Board of Education, creating one position-based salary schedule for teachers. Whereas previously, women teachers in Brooklyn received equal pay for equal work, now their pay was cut to a level below men's salaries. Each year from 1907 to 1910, the IAWT successfully lobbied the state legislature for passage of a law requiring equal pay for equal work in teaching. However, each time the bill made it through the legislature, either the governor or the New York City mayor vetoed the bill, as the mayor was permitted to do on issues affecting the city. Male teachers, organized as the Association of Men Teachers and Principals of the City of New York, fought these equal pay bills by claiming that

> women did not require the same standard of living as men, that women did not deserve equal pay, because they were intellectually inferior to men, and that equal pay would result in more women avoiding marriage in favor of work. (Carter, 1992, p. 48)

Many men were simply afraid that equalization would mean a necessary cut in their own pay to stay within budget. Only after the election of a new governor and mayor in 1910, Democrats John Alden Dix and George B. Gaynor, respectively, was the bill establishing equal pay for equal work for teachers signed into law—in 1911 (Carter, 1992). This victory supported women's groups lobbying across the country. By 1925, 80% of women in the nation's largest cities had won equity in pay (Tyack, 1974).

Thus when first implemented, the single-salary schedule addressed two important teacher needs: equity and objectivity. Teachers were paid for teaching, not for the grade level they taught. The salary schedule was accessible, giving all teachers an equal chance to earn a pay raise under the same rules. The education component of the single-salary schedule successfully encouraged greater numbers of teachers to attend a 4-year college and earn a bachelor's degree. Additionally, salary increases were no longer partially based on what teachers viewed as arbitrary administrative assessments of their merit. This profoundly changed the nature of the working relationship between teachers and their supervisors. In effect, the single-salary schedule helped to eliminate administrative control over teachers' work, giving teachers greater autonomy in the classroom (English, 1992; Lipsky & Bacharach, 1983; Spring, 1994).

The single-salary schedule has more advantages than just providing pay equity across grade levels, gender, race, and ethnicity. As stated above, it removed the essentially arbitrary and often capricious administrator assessments of teacher "merit," a notion that was very seldom defined explicitly. Furthermore, the single-salary schedule made teacher pay predictable; it showed any individuals entering teaching what their salary would be over a long time period and what they needed to do, other than continue in teaching, to earn salary increases. In addition, by paying each teacher with similar education units and experience the same salary, it eliminated competition among teachers for more pay, a desired characteristic for a system that depends on cooperation and collegiality for best results. Finally, the single-salary schedule was easy to administer; the bases for changing an individual's pay were neutral, objective, and understandable. In short, the single-salary schedule has several inherent strengths that made it appropriate for schools when it was initially implemented and that account in large part for why it remained, through the rest of the 20th century, as the primary way teachers are paid (Lipsky & Bacharach, 1983).

Some Recent Short-Lived Efforts
to Reform Teacher Compensation

Nevertheless, because of the implementation of the single-salary schedule, concerns have been raised about its appropriateness. But even in the face of significant changes in the role of teachers, schools, and society, the single-salary schedule has remained much the same as it was when it was first implemented in the 1920s. Its significant advantages—familiarity, predictability, and ease of administration—have made the single-salary schedule resilient and hard to change. And as collective bargaining strengthened in the last half of the 20th century, the single-salary schedule was typically viewed by teacher organizations as the only salary structure that provided fair and equitable representation for all teachers (Kerchner, Koppich, & Weeres, 1997).

But the single-salary schedule has not been without its critics. Some have expressed concern that the single-salary schedule is unfair because it rewards equally teachers with the same education and experience despite different levels of effort, skills, professional competencies, or student results. Thus in 1983, *A Nation at Risk* recommended that teacher salaries be "professionally competitive, market-sensitive, and performance-based" (National Commission on Excellence in Education, 1983, p. 30). Districts and states across the nation responded with a flurry of activity by establishing merit pay, career ladders, and other incentive pay programs for teachers, most of which were short-lived.

The 1980s were not the first time these types of programs had been tried. The first-known merit pay plan was attempted in 1908 in Newton, Massachusetts (English, 1992). Even the differentiated salary schedules of the early 1900s, which provided salary differentials for teaching roles that differed in terms of levels of responsibility, contained a merit component. Yet the 1980s were the first period where there was a national call for improving teacher performance through monetary incentives. President Reagan led the way, making merit pay one of his "bully pulpit" issues (English, 1992).

Merit Pay Plans

A wide variety of merit pay programs have been tried in districts across the nation, meeting with great publicity and limited success. Merit pay plans ostensibly award teachers bonuses for excellent performance, usually determined by a supervisor although sometimes by peer review. The success of merit pay depends greatly on the ability of principals and peer teachers to identify and define good performance, a very difficult task. Hanushek (1994) states that "no single set of teacher characteristics, teacher behaviors, curricular approaches, or organizational devices guarantees a high probability of success in the classroom" (p. 86). Essentially, different groups of students respond in different ways to different teaching practices.

Several studies have sought to understand why merit pay programs have never stuck. Nearly all the studies have reached the same conclusions about merit pay (Educational Research Service, 1978; Hatry, Greiner, & Ashford, 1994; Jacobson, 1987; Johnson, 1986; Murnane & Cohen, 1986). First, most merit plans create competition among teachers by trying to identify a small percentage of the "best" or "excellent" teachers. Such a program is at odds with the collegiality and cooperative culture that is created in the most effective schools (Rosenholtz, 1989) and thus is a pay element that undermines rather than reinforces good school performance.

Second, *excellent* (or *best*) is rarely defined well. Sometimes it pertains to teaching practice. Sometimes it pertains to activities outside the classroom, even activities that have little if anything to do with teaching. But without a clear definition of best, the incentive goal of merit pay is undermined, and it becomes, essentially, a useless organizational element.

Third and related, the procedures for defining best and then selecting teachers who fit the definition and allegedly meet the standards of best are usually flawed, often embarrassingly flawed. For such a system to work and to be viewed as fair, it must respond accurately and specifically to a teacher who asks, "Why wasn't I selected, and what do I need to do to be selected?" (Murnane & Cohen, 1986). Very few merit programs have been able to answer that simple question. As such, the programs are viewed with caution if not skepticism, thus further undermining their intent.

Fourth, districts and states rarely provide stable funding for such programs. The programs are initially enacted with great expectation. They are usually funded at below required levels, and then funding is eliminated in a few years at the first signs of district fiscal stress. Again, this undermines any potential incentive effect of the program; teachers know that *merit*, however defined or administered, is unlikely to be rewarded. This miserable funding record also suggests that merit programs are rarely conceived as critical elements of a state's or district's education program. Core elements are always funded; noncore elements are funded in good times but then dropped as soon as budgets become squeezed.

Pay strategies that vary from the single-salary schedule must overcome these fatal flaws of past merit pay programs. And unless funded over the long haul, even well-conceived, new pay approaches will not provide the incentives for a skeptical teaching force to adopt new behaviors (Smylie & Smart, 1990).

Murnane and Cohen (1986) found that the merit programs that remained over time were generally found in very wealthy school districts that had ongoing funds for the program. They also found that the long-term programs tended to reward a large percentage of teachers, if not all teachers, and rewards were most often provided for performing additional tasks rather than for excellent teaching. As a result, the programs may have been termed "merit programs," but they actually accorded additional pay for additional tasks in which all teachers engaged.

One district that exemplifies the typical ups and downs associated with merit pay is Fairfax County Public School District, Virginia. Adopted in 1987, the Fairfax County Merit Pay plan was fully implemented in the district's 165 schools by the 1989 to 1990 school year. Bonuses equaled 9% of salaries and were awarded each year for 4 years to teachers rated "skillful" or "exemplary" (Hatry et al., 1994). Although the procedures for identifying skillful and exemplary teachers were given some considerable attention in the plan's design and implementation, the plan did not, in those first 4 years, gain the support of the bulk of teachers or the teacher union. The plan was suspended in 1992 because of overall district budget cuts. The program was restored 2 years later but in a scaled-down version.

Although public support existed for the plan, the two major local teacher organizations believed that the plan was too costly and that it undermined teacher collegiality by creating a competitive work environment (Richardson, 1994).

The Fairfax plan, then, experienced a fate similar to the merit pay plans discussed above. The Fairfax plan suffered from problems of administration and implementation (even granting that it represented an ambitious and even professional effort to identify teaching expertise), creation of a competitive rather than a collegial environment, and funding suspension at the first signs of fiscal stress. Unless a new teacher compensation approach can overcome such hurdles, it is unlikely to remain over time.

Career Ladders

Another type of teacher compensation innovation attempted in the 1980s was the teacher career ladder. A career ladder program sought to identify teachers whose performance met or exceeded standards for practice and then to provide them with leadership positions, such as curriculum or professional development. Career ladders were an attempt to address the flat career structure of teaching and to reward "good" teachers with both recognition and additional leadership responsibilities in the school. Some career ladder plans made a strong effort to maintain the presence of teacher leaders in the classroom rather than maintaining the current career structure, in which career advancement tends to move teachers out of the classroom and into administrative positions. But most career ladder programs also removed such teachers from the classroom for some time to engage in other tasks, which spanned the range from curriculum development to teacher training. In addition, most teacher career ladder programs had quotas on the number of teacher leader positions.

An April 1994 survey of state career ladders conducted by the Southern Regional Education Board's Career Ladder Clearinghouse found only four states that still funded career ladder programs: Arizona, Missouri, Tennessee, and Utah. Evaluation of these showed mixed results. In Arizona, students taught by teachers in the career ladder program showed increased achievement, lower dropout rates, and increased graduation rates (Cornett, 1994). These improvements were especially great in districts where the career ladder program focused on developing and improving teachers' classroom skills (Conley & Odden, 1995). Despite these positive results, the state failed to provide consistent funding for the program (Cornett, 1994).

The career ladder plan in Utah has also met with state funding problems along with some teacher opposition. The highly decentralized Utah program allowed districts to design their own plans. According to Timar (1992), some districts responded by making genuine organizational changes focused on teacher improvement, whereas other districts did not comply with the program's general intent and gave teachers across-the-board raises without including a performance-, skill-, or job-based requirement.

Summary

Overall, in a study of 18 school district programs since 1983, Hatry and colleagues (1994) found that most school districts that implemented merit pay and career ladder plans for teachers were unsuccessful in creating lasting and effective programs. Some districts reported positive effects, such as reduced teacher turnover and absenteeism. Most, however, cited significant teacher morale problems stemming from competition, unfair evaluation practices, and the use of quotas in determining the number of teachers to receive awards. Programs were also viewed as costly (when funding was stable) and difficult to administer. And most programs were dropped within a few years.

The 1980s efforts at teacher compensation change thus fell to the same foibles as previous efforts at merit pay: funding curtailment, poor assessment and administrative procedures, quotas, and other features that created competition within a desired cooperative culture as well as opposition by teacher unions.

A Time for Change?

But some recent efforts at compensation reform, described in Chapters 5 and 6, have avoided many of these problems. Significant advances in the development of state standards, in student assessment and teacher evaluation technology, in group-based performance and individual knowledge and skills pay designs, and a willingness on the part of both local and national union leadership to explore new ideas and at least consider alternatives to the single-salary schedule have created a new environment. For the first time in over 50 years, there is a window of opportunity for meaningful and lasting compensation reform.

All compensation schemes implicitly send messages to teachers about desired professional behaviors. The single-salary schedule encourages teachers to further their graduate education even (in most districts) if the courses are not directly related to teaching assignments, in order to move to the right on the salary schedule, that is, to the higher-priced salary lanes (Clardy, 1988). However, there is only modest evidence that graduate coursework is a reliable indicator of teacher quality or classroom performance (Hanushek, 1994). Murnane (1983) reported that teachers who hold bachelor's degrees are typically just as effective as those who hold master's degrees. Furthermore, there is only modest evidence that experience is related to teaching effectiveness; the relationship is strong only for the first few years of teaching (Ferris & Winkler, 1986; Hanushek, 1997; Murnane, 1983).

Although there is some debate on the efficacy of either typical pre-service, undergraduate—or typical graduate—teacher training courses to improve teaching effectiveness, there is evidence that well-designed and well-taught courses can have a major impact (Darling-Hammond, Wise, & Klein, 1995). Because, as we shall argue, graduate courses and degrees could in some circumstances serve as indicators of knowledge-and-skill attainment in a knowledge- and skills-based pay system, it is important to note that research on the efficacy of course taking concerns typical teacher training courses and may not be relevant to recent programs and courses that were rigorously designed to develop competencies that reflect new teaching standards.

Perhaps the most common criticism of the single-salary schedule is that it treats as equals teachers with the same education level and experience, despite potentially unequal performance and skills (Lipsky & Bacharach, 1983). As far back as 1867, the superintendent of the Adams County, Pennsylvania, schools, Aaron Sheeley, claimed that paying all teachers the same wages "offers a premium to mediocrity, if not to positive ignorance and incompetence. Inducements should always be held out to teachers to duly qualify themselves for their work" (English, 1992, p. 6).

These problems are not new, but changes in the organization of schools, the roles of teachers, and an increasingly internationally competitive environment have heightened the importance of developing clearly aligned and directed incentive structures in schools. The loose coupling between the compensation incentives embedded in the single-salary schedule and the goals of schools is becoming increasingly costly to schools with limited resources and increasing demands for improved performance. Thus new and expanding roles for teachers, changes in the school organization, and societal demands may once again be pushing the teacher compensation system toward obsolescence and renewal (see Kelley, 1997, for an expanded version of this argument).

Table 2.1 summarizes characteristics of teachers, schools, and society for each of the three eras of teacher compensation reform; however, the table divides the third era, the single-salary schedule (1950 to the present), into three specific school models: the scientific-management model of the 1950s; the effective-schools model that was advocated in the 1970s; and the high-standards, high-involvement model, which reflects current notions of a modern, effective school and the type of school envisioned by standards-based education form.

Scientific Management

The scientific-management model represents the typical school at the beginning of the single-salary schedule era, that is, in the first half of the 20th century. In this model, as under the position-based salary schedule, the role of the teacher was essentially to implement a teacher-proof curriculum. Skill levels for teachers were basically taught in preservice training but were still low relative to other occupations or to current, skill-level demands for teachers. Rewards for additional educational units and certification requirements for promotion to administrative positions meant that many teachers continued their education beyond initial licensure; the primary incentive for the units element of the schedule was to encourage elementary teachers to earn a full bachelor's degree and to pay more to teachers, usually high school teachers, who had earned such a degree. Educational-administration and graduate teacher education programs emerged over time to provide postbachelor's-degree training that also was rewarded. The single-salary schedule was designed in part to encourage teachers to take advantage of more education by guaranteeing them a return on their investment (Conley & Odden, 1995).

The scientifically managed school maintained similar goals, structures, and leadership responsibilities as in the previous era; the primary goal was to teach basic skills for employment. The school structure remained hierarchical and bureaucratic, with a predominantly female teaching force and a predominantly male administrative structure. The superintendent maintained authority as the educational leader in the district. He, very seldom she, was responsible for the results of the system.

Table 2.1 Changes in U.S. Teachers, Public Schools, and Society as They Relate to Teacher Compensation, 1800-2000

| | *Boarding 'Round* (Early to Mid-1800s) | *Position-Based* (Late 1800s to Mid-1900s) | *Scientific Management* (1950s) | *Single-Salary Schedule* | |
				Effective Schools (1970s)	*High Standards/High Involvement* (1990s)
Teachers					
Teacher's role	Moral leadership	Implement teacher-proof curriculum	Implement teacher-proof curriculum	– Provide services – Teach basic skills – Develop schools as communities	– Produce high-level student achievement – Leadership/Shared decision making
Preservice training	Elementary school	High school/Teacher training institutes	College/Normal school	College/Graduate school	College/Graduate school
Licensing	None	State license/Passage of rigorous country examination	State license/Minimal skills	State license/Minimal skills	State license/Wide variation in skill requirements among states
Inservice Training					
Goals	N/A	N/A	Teacher education and administrative credentialing	Teacher education and administrative credentialing; training in pedagogy	Advanced disciplinary content; pedagogy; leadership, management, and decision making

(continued)

Table 2.1 Continued

| | Boarding 'Round (Early to Mid-1800s) | Position-Based (Late 1800s to Mid-1900s) | Scientific Management (1950s) | Single-Salary Schedule | |
				Effective Schools (1970s)	High Standards/High Involvement (1990s)
Source	N/A	N/A	Higher-education administrator and teacher education programs	Higher-education administrator and teacher education programs; district staff development	Higher-education disciplines and teacher education/leadership programs; school staff development; professional development
Needs served	N/A	N/A	Promotion	– Promotion – Development	Development
Schools					
Goals	– Teach basic literacy – Moral character	Teach basic skills for employment and citizenship	Teach basic skills for employment	– Provide basic skills for employment – Focus on low-income and urban populations	– Provide high outcomes for all students – High competency and problem-solving skills

				– Address human growth needs – Schools as communities	– Flexibility and diversity in the workforce – Teacher professionalism – Decentralized/Participative work organization
Structure	One-room schoolhouse	Bureaucratic	Bureaucratic	Bureaucratic	Decentralized/Flat
Leadership	Teacher/Community	Superintendent	Superintendent	Principal	Teacher teams
Society					
Frame of reference	Local community	City/County	State	State/Nation	State/Nation/Global economy
Expectations	– High moral character – Basic literacy	– Good citizens – Basic employment skills	Basic skills for employment and democratic participation	Equity concerns; basic skills for all despite adverse environmental conditions	Internationally competitive workforce

Principals and teachers implemented, in a fairly uniform manner, the school directives that emanated from the superintendent and central office.

Societal demands on schools focused on interest in an educated citizenry with basic and stable skills for employment and the ability to participate fully in the democratic process. Teacher knowledge and pedagogy learned in preservice teacher training generally were sufficient to teach the standardized school curriculum.

The single-salary schedule, designed in this era, treated teachers equally, with a uniform, base pay amount and rewards for additional years of experience. In addition, the single-salary schedule acknowledged a belief in the utility of scientific training by rewarding continuing education. Although compensation for education units loosely reflected skills, it represented a small portion of overall compensation and initially was taken advantage of by few teachers. Indeed, the extra units were most often tapped as a way to earn extra compensation while taking the courses needed to leave teaching and enter the administrative ranks. There was no reward for producing results.

Effective Schools

In the 1970s, a new model of good schooling began to emerge, reflecting renewed national interest in equity concerns, new roles for teachers and administrators, instructional skills beyond those learned in most teacher training programs, and a more conscious, school-based focus on student achievement results. Research published in the 1960s suggested that educational outcomes were the result of differences in environment related to family socioeconomic status rather than to differences in the quality of education or student aptitude. The notion that schools were unable to overcome inequities in family circumstance was abhorrent to many educators. The effective-schools movement arose in response in an attempt to identify effective means of overcoming environmental barriers to education (Cohen, 1983; Purkey & Smith, 1983).

Thus the goal of the effective school was to provide basic skills for employment, with a particular focus on low-income, urban, and minority populations. The focal point for education effectiveness moved from the district to the school site. Schools were responsible for producing results. Schools also emphasized the importance of attending to human growth needs and to developing schools as communities within which all children—particularly low-income and minority children—could learn basic skills. The principal rather than the superintendent was identified as the instructional leader in an otherwise bureaucratic and hierarchical organizational structure.

Teachers in effective schools were thrust into new roles and were expected to engage in schoolwide, education improvement activities. Because effective schools also recognized the importance of attending to the human side of students, teachers were expected to work to develop schools as communities that could meet the needs of each individual student.

Preservice training for the effective school focused on developing a large tool bag of pedagogical approaches. However, the range and depth of skills required in some cases, including specialized skills related to the specific needs of the local student population, meant that inservice training began to expand significantly beyond that rewarded in the single-salary schedule. District pedagogical experts provided staff development opportunities to enable teachers to continue to develop an array of effective teaching skills after they were hired by the district (Brophy & Good, 1986; Cohen, 1983; Rosenshine & Stevens, 1986).

Furthermore, training in effective-school characteristics also emerged, in many places, adding an understanding of school organization, structure, and culture to the knowledge base expected of teachers (Cohen, 1983; Purkey & Smith, 1983). Inservice training for principals in new instructional-leadership skills also expanded quite dramatically. Moreover, the focus on the school and the results it produced grew in intensity.

But the single-salary schedule remained virtually untouched. It was not expanded for either teachers or principals to provide incentives or rewards for learning and using their new teaching and administration expertise. Moreover, teachers received no rewards for developing the expertise to engage productively in schoolwide improvement activities. Finally, no rewards were provided for improving schoolwide student achievement results—even though the goal of eliminating disparities in basic skill achievement across race and income lines was ambitious and desired. In short, although the roles, competencies, activities, and responsibility for results changed dramatically in the effective-schools movement, the salary schedule remained the same, providing incentives for the old bureaucratic structure, levels of expertise, and roles—thus not undergirding the development of effective schools and, in some ways, undercutting those efforts.

The High-Standards and High-Involvement Model

The high-standards, high-involvement model combines elements of standards-based reform (Fuhrman, 1993) and site-based, high-involvement management (Mohrman et al., 1994; Odden, Wohlstetter, & Odden, 1995). This model arose in the 1990s in an era of increasing global competition. Changes in the structure of the workplace have created demands for public school graduates who have learned considerably richer problem-solving skills, as well as greater content knowledge, particularly in mathematics, science, writing, communication, and social studies.

The high-standards, high-involvement model is a school with very ambitious goals—all but the severely disabled learning to high-achievement standards for complex subject matter—and different management structures designed to better achieve those goals. High standards means that schools are to produce a high level of student achievement with a strong focus on high outcomes for all students, extending concerns of the effective-schools model but with much higher performance expectations for students. Student outcomes are to include a high capacity for problem solving, the ability to adapt to a changing work environment, and the ability to access and maintain a high level of understanding of difficult subject matter.

High involvement alludes to the importance of teachers centrally involved in not only school improvement but also school management for the purpose of achieving the ambitious, new-school goals. The high-involvement model means that schools are led by teacher teams who are responsible for instructional leadership and school management (see Mohrman et al., 1994; Newmann & Wehlage, 1995; Odden & Wohlstetter, 1995; Robertson, Wohlstetter, & Mohrman, 1995).

As a result of this high-standards, high-involvement model, extremely high-skill and performance demands are placed on teachers. Teachers need to develop and improve advanced-content knowledge and advanced-pedagogical knowledge (to produce high performance from all students) as well as leadership, management, and decision-making skills that traditionally have been the purview of principals or district-level administrators.

The high-standards, high-involvement model places high demands on teacher training programs. It suggests not only the need for rigorous skill requirements for licensure but also the need to continue learning an array of skills once initial licensure has been earned (Darling-Hammond, Wise, & Klein, 1995). Because the skill requirements to successfully operate within this type of environment are so high, it is also likely that few teachers will have mastered the variety of skills needed in preservice. Thus the high-standards, high-involvement model also places high demands on *inservice* training and professional development, which could be obtained from a variety of sources: higher educational institutions (disciplines as well as teacher education and leadership programs); school-led staff development; and professional development opportunities offered through professional associations, unions, networks of teachers, or independent consultants.

Currently, preservice, licensure, and inservice training tend to be woefully inadequate to address the needs of the professional teacher in this model of schooling. However, a variety of efforts, described in Chapter 1, are currently underway that have the potential to radically alter the current structure of teacher training and ongoing professional development.

The inadequacies of the single-salary schedule become patently apparent when considered in light of this third model of schooling: no rewards for teachers to develop ongoing skills needed by the school, improve outcomes for students, or achieve school goals.

As both the effective-schools and the high-standards, high-involvement school models reveal, the single-salary schedule, despite its considerable strengths, does not provide the type of incentives that would strengthen either of these newer models of schooling. What both these models suggest is that as changes occur in the expected results from schools and in the roles and expertise needed by the faculty within schools, changes in compensation could also be created that reward teachers and administrators for implementing these changes. This is not to say that the single-salary schedule created in the first half of the 20th century is deficient; indeed, it accommodated the school system for which it was created. It may simply be less than adequate for the school system teachers and administrators are trying to create for the 21st century. In short, the current single-salary schedule needs to be rethought in relation to the needs of the education system of today.

Other Factors Supporting Compensation Reform

The standards movement described in the previous chapter is creating a new mindset in education. Increasingly, educators and policymakers are interested in understanding, evaluating, and rewarding results. The increased emphasis on state standards and assessments has led to significant experimentation and advancement in the technology of student assessment. The experiences of states like Kentucky, Maryland, and Vermont with performance-based assessment have helped researchers and policymakers work through some of the pitfalls of student assessments that are designed to inform and support the development of effective teaching practices.

Similarly, the work of the National Board for Professional Teaching Standards, the Interstate New Teacher Assessment and Support Consortium, and the Educational Testing Service—to develop meaningful evaluation and assessments for teachers at various stages of career preparation and professional practice—provides an opportunity for the first time to meaningfully evaluate and reward teacher knowledge-and-skill development. These assessments differ from previous efforts because those in the profession have developed them, and teachers' associations and professional networks have received them well.

And increasingly, the policymaker community is making better-informed decisions about designing licensure and compensation systems that build professional practice (Youngs, Odden, & Porter, 2000). These systems are also informed by an understanding of incentive structures and are better aligned with state-, district-, and school-level goals for focusing and enhancing teaching practice to enable all students to achieve high standards of performance.

Perhaps as a result of these important changes in context and in the role of teachers, national and local teacher union leadership has shown increased willingness to explore compensation structures that better reflect the needs of teachers (for professional growth) and schools (to provide clear, identifiable, and measurable performance objectives) (see Urbanski & Erskine, 2000). Local union leaders were at the table with administrators directing the efforts of nearly all the districts currently at the forefront of compensation reform. And in 2001, the American Federation of Teachers adopted a resolution that supports experimentation to "enhance the traditional compensation schedule using approaches that contribute to more effective teaching and learning." The resolution identified a number of new approaches to compensation worth considering, including schoolwide performance bonuses, knowledge- and skills-based pay, and incentives to recruit teachers to hard-to-staff schools and shortage areas such as math and science (Archer, 2001).

In the next chapter, we explore elements of pay that could be used to better align the compensation system with current expectations for teacher roles, organizational goals, and societal expectations of schools.

The Elements of Pay and Compensation

3

Traditional compensation systems have been designed to promote tenure, predictability, and internal equity for employees (Zingheim & Schuster, 1995a). New compensation systems are being designed to promote the ongoing acquisition of skills and competencies; labor market realities in terms of pay levels; commitment to the key goals of the organization; accomplishment of results; and, in many organizations that in some places include schools, reduction of costs as well (Crandall & Wallace, 1998; Heneman, Ledford, & Gresham, 2000; Lawler, 2000a; Zingheim & Schuster, 2000).

As argued in Chapters 1 and 2, the single-salary schedule designed at the turn of the 20th century was adequate for the issues of tenure, predictability, and internal equity then but is not adequate for the issues of knowledge and skills, labor market realities, involvement in school management, and high levels of performance that schools require today. The single-salary schedule replaced grade-based pay specifically as a result of concerns about internal equity issues. Unlike previous pay systems, the single-salary schedule paid teachers on the basis of the same criteria, regardless of race, gender, or grade level taught (Education Research Service, 1978).

Although possessing some unique features, such as payment for additional educational credits and degrees, this pay system typified the dominant approach to compensation used in business at the time. In fact, for nearly the past 100 years, businesses and education systems have paid people on the basis of the jobs they occupied. A key administrative task

49

was to manage jobs. Activities were divided into numerous categories, jobs for different tasks were identified, the skills for each of the many jobs were identified, and people were selected for jobs when they had the requisite skills. The salary for each job was then set within a fixed range, with a beginning salary and annual increases up to a maximum level.

Most organizations tried to provide salary equity across many different jobs by equating the tasks of various jobs, often assigning them "Hays" points, using the methodology of the Hays national compensation consulting firm.

To earn a salary beyond the maximum for a job, individuals needed to develop skills required for a different and higher-paying job. As tasks changed, new job descriptions were written together with their skill requirements, and salaries were set again according to external market conditions and internal parity for similar levels of job tasks and skill requirements. Usually, the highest salaries were paid to those in supervisory and management positions; within broad job categories, salaries increased only if the number of individuals supervised increased.

The assumption underlying these job-based pay systems was that individuals' contributions to the organization were bounded by the parameters of the specific jobs they occupied.

More recently, changes in the structure of all types of work organizations suggest that it is difficult and costly to maintain a job-based pay system that reflects the contributions that individuals are providing to work organizations. In schools as in businesses, workers are increasingly asked to contribute in myriad ways to the achievement of organizational goals. These contributions are rarely bounded by a specific job held by the individual. Often, moreover, teams of employees work synergistically, pooling their knowledge and skills in ways that enable them to contribute more to the organization than they could working separately in narrowly defined jobs; paying for the job in this type of organization is, at best, complicated and, at worst, counterproductive (Heneman et al., 2000).

In addition, and as vexing, individuals in many organizations are being asked to move in and out of job roles as needed to meet organizational goals. For each move, a job-based pay system requires that a job description be written and that the system grade the job for equity across the system, then set pay ranges, and, finally, recruit, select, and place an individual correctly in the pay range. Organizations have found that doing this as often as they want to change job categories has become enormously expensive; the bureaucratic effort to maintain equity in this environment both increases costs at a time when organizations are pressured to do more with less and impedes the speed with which organizations, again including the schools, need to respond effectively to changing environmental pressures and system demands (Crandall & Wallace, 1998; Hammer & Champy, 1993; Katzenbach & Smith, 1993; Lawler, 1986, 2000a; Ledford, 1995a, 1995b; Mohrman, Cohen, & Mohrman, 1995).

As a result, numerous organizations are replacing steeply hierarchical organizational structures with flatter, more egalitarian structures; school-based and shared-decision management are the counterparts in education. When they do so, they move away from identifying tasks and pay associated with specific jobs and toward identifying and managing the competencies needed within the organizations to accomplish goals and performance targets (Crandall & Wallace, 1998; Heneman et al., 2000; Lawler, 1990, 1995, 2000a; Ledford, 1995b).

In the process of implementing these changes, many nonschool organizations are discovering that managing skills and competencies is a key management challenge (Zingheim & Schuster, 1995a, 2000). Some suggest that the human resources management role for creating high-performance organizations centers on developing organizational and individual competencies, often called *core competencies* (Lawler, 2000b). Indeed, Ledford (1995b) argues that the new "atom" of human resources management is "competencies" and no longer "jobs." The argument is at least twofold: (a) that in many organizations the nature of work is changing so fast that it is literally impossible to write, grade, recruit, select, place, and induct people into individual jobs; and (b) that work increasingly is being conducted by teams for which each individual performs many jobs over the course of the day, week, and year, so that the mere notion of a job has become obsolete.

As the notion of *job* is replaced by the notion of *competencies* or *knowledge and skills,* knowledge and skills also begin to replace the job as the basis of compensation. Organizations are shifting away from the old way of paying knowledge workers for a job and toward sophisticated, and quite elaborate, knowledge- and skills-based pay systems (Crandall & Wallace, 1998; Lawler, 2000a; Ledford, 1995a, 1995b; Zingheim & Schuster, 2000). Knowledge and skills include those needed for the technical aspects of the work—instructional knowledge and skills in education—as well as teamwork, collegial, managerial, and other sets of expertise.

Education systems and teacher pay strategies are also generally following the above pattern. School systems initially identified different education jobs—teacher, principal, supervisor, and superintendent. Teachers were paid a salary according to a fixed schedule, with steps and lanes. To be hired, a teacher needed only the initial skills required for licensure. As education problems and diverse student needs expanded during the past 30 years, the education system's approach was not to require teachers to learn a set of expanded skills but to identify new and specialized teacher positions—special education, Title I, bilingual, gifted and talented, guidance counselor, psychologist, family outreach, professional developer, curriculum developer, and so forth—and to pay these individuals according to a similar but somewhat higher-level salary schedule. Each teacher and specialized staff member had a narrow job; problems outside the job definition were the responsibility of a different person. As a result, over time, the level of staffing in schools expanded quite dramatically (Odden, Monk, Nakib, & Picus, 1995). Indeed, in many districts, the bulk of significant new money provided to schools over the past 30 years has been used to hire specialized staff members (Rothstein & Miles, 1995).

As Chapters 1 and 2 concluded, this might not be the most productive way to structure, organize, and manage schools—or to pay teachers—as we make the transition into the 21st century, with the goal of teaching all but severely disabled students to high academic standards. Schools accomplishing this goal seem to be organized differently, in a much more decentralized manner and with much broader roles and responsibilities for teachers (Darling-Hammond, 1996; Miles, 1996; Newmann & Associates, 1996; Newmann & Wehlage, 1995; Odden, Wohlstetter, & Odden, 1995; Robertson, Wohlstetter, & Mohrman, 1995; Wohlstetter, 1995; Wohlstetter, Smyer, & Mohrman, 1994).

Just as in private-sector organizations seeking to produce higher performance, teachers in such schools no longer just have the job of teacher. Teachers teach, counsel, plan, manage, create curriculum, train colleagues, evaluate practice, develop budgets, monitor progress, run meetings—in short, engage in a wide range of jobs, each of which requires expertise to perform well. Even for the technical-core instructional program of schools, many new educational strategies require teachers to have expertise in at least two related areas, for example, elementary education and reading or mathematics and learning disabilities (Odden & Archibald, 2000). Thus these schools also need to manage expertise, knowledge, and skills—to develop knowledge and skills for each individual and for the school as a whole so that the teachers within the school have the combined professional competencies needed to accomplish all the school's tasks and purposes.

Because a central element in the management of knowledge, skills, and professional expertise is pay, it might also make sense to shift teacher compensation to a knowledge and skills basis to align the education pay structure with the new focal points of what should be the human resources strategies in education systems. Such a new compensation approach would seek to link teacher pay to expertise and skills that can be applied widely across the many specific job tasks in which teachers will engage, as well as to provide rewards for accomplishing school goals (Zingheim & Schuster, 1995a). Such a new approach to teacher compensation structures could also be used to communicate the new form of work organization in the evolving flat, more democratic, self-managed but highly accountable team-based schools. As Zingheim and Schuster state,

> Traditional pay has failed to meet the challenge of communicating values, directions, and priorities that give the proper messages to people upon whom the [organization] depends for results. New pay is changing and evolving continuously as [organizations] seek competitive advantage. (1995b, p. 12)

Interest in aligning teacher compensation policies to the needs of the broader educational system suggests a belief in the ability of compensation policies to support other education reform strategies. Research evidence suggests that compensation policy can provide this support by serving a variety of organizational functions. As Lawler (1995) argues, compensation can be used to do the following:

❖ Attract and retain employees
❖ Promote skills, competencies, and knowledge development
❖ Motivate particular types of performance
❖ Shape organizational culture
❖ Reinforce and define organizational structure
❖ Determine the cost of compensation to the organization

These six functions of compensation are carried out through a combination of different approaches to, or elements of, pay. Some of these compensation approaches apply to the traditional goals of job-based pay, which could remain even if knowledge and skills became the cornerstone of a new pay structure. Others have become embodied in new ways to pay individuals, perhaps teachers, as well. The pay elements discussed below include traditional approaches, such as pay for membership and longevity, and new approaches including knowledge-and-skill or competency pay, performance pay, gain sharing, and contingency pay.

Traditional Pay: Pay for the Job

Pay for membership in the organization is the entry level of compensation offered to new members. Traditionally, businesses have calculated pay for membership by incorporating information about the value of a particular position to the organization and about employment markets. Education organizations do this, too, for example, by providing pay incentives to induce teachers into hard-to-recruit areas, such as bilingual education and low-performing, high-poverty schools. Starting salary should be set at levels to allow the organization to attract an adequate number of appropriately skilled applicants away from other opportunities in the market and to provide sufficient compensation to retain new employees until they can increase compensation through other elements of the pay system.

Beginning, or membership, salaries determine the competitive pool for new entrants to the organization. If beginning wages are insufficient, then an insufficient number of employees as well as inadequately skilled employees are likely to be hired. In the late 1970s and early 1980s, research showed that the quality of teachers along with their salaries had declined in the 1970s (Schlechty & Vance, 1983). Some researchers and policy-makers today, including the authors, have expressed concern that non-competitive starting salaries for teachers are failing to attract sufficiently skilled entrants to the teaching workforce to meet current and future demands (Darling-Hammond, 1994; National Commission on Teaching and America's Future, 1996). Economists have argued that the combination of a primary female teaching force and increased opportunities for women in the broader labor market means teacher pay either needs to rise or only a declining quality of individuals, particularly women, will be attracted to or remain in teaching (Manski, 1987; Rosen & Flyer, 1994).

The high-standards, high-involvement model of schooling described in Chapter 2 suggests the need for competitive membership pay—beginning teacher salaries—to attract individuals who can develop into the content and pedagogical experts required of teachers for the more effective schools of tomorrow. As shown in Chapter 1, beginning teacher salaries today are modest, below those of liberal arts graduates, substantially below those of all college graduates, and even more significantly below those of technologically oriented college graduates.

States and local school systems should take seriously the importance of beginning teacher salaries and set policies that target beginning or membership pay at a level so that education can compete successfully for new entrants into teaching. Setting a policy that the average beginning teacher salary should be at the average for *all* college graduates would position education to more effectively recruit the number and quality of individuals into the high-standards, high-involvement, high-performance education system needed for the 21st century.

Moreover, as the nation faces the need to hire millions of new teachers over the next two decades because baby-boomer teachers retire and more teachers are required for class size reduction policies, a competitive beginning salary is all the more important. Inadequate beginning teacher salaries, and thus a lower-quality beginning teacher corps, will have a long-lasting negative impact on the quality and performance of the American education system.

But raising beginning teacher salaries will require substantially enhanced teacher salary budgets. Federal, state, and local governments can contribute to this fiscal imperative. In an era of large federal surpluses and a growing economy, if these significant investments are not made now, they will be more difficult, if not impossible, to make later, as surpluses decline and economic growth slows.

Moreover, previous efforts to entice new individuals to enter teaching, such as loan forgiveness programs, have been shown to have very limited impact. On the other hand, fellowships with service paybacks, in which districts, states, or the federal government pay costs up front, are much more successful (Odden & Conley, 1992). The latter should be enacted if policymakers want to be serious about having a solid impact on the number and quality of individuals who decide to enter teaching over the next decade. Such enticements for teacher training, combined with higher beginning salaries, would have a strong, positive impact on the quality of individuals who enter the teaching profession.

Furthermore, as discussed further in Chapter 5 on knowledge- and skills-based pay, the time has come to pay teachers in high-demand areas a salary premium, not only at the beginning but also throughout their career. Thus beginning salaries for teachers in shortage areas, such as mathematics, science, and technology, should be even higher, for the education system to compete more effectively in the market for teachers with these high-demand knowledge and skills.

If these fiscal incentives at the front end were followed by various pay-for-performance elements discussed in this chapter and the remainder of the book, the salary side of education would be much more attractive to the current generation of individuals whom the education system needs to entice into teaching (Ballou & Podgursky, 1997).

Pay for longevity or seniority-based pay, the other component of job-based pay, provides additional compensation, based on years of experience or seniority, to employees for remaining with the organization or in the profession over time. The single-salary schedule's pay increments or *steps* for years of experience are education's form of longevity pay. Longevity pay is sometimes confused with skill-based pay, because some might think of experience as a proxy for increasing skills. However, traditional longevity pay provides all employees with the same pay increases for each year of experience, whether or not they increase knowledge-and-skill levels, and thus is best conceived as membership rather than competency pay.

This pay element is quite dominant in education. The steps in most teacher salary schedules account for the vast bulk of teacher salaries above the beginning salary figure. One study in Boston found that years of experience accounted for 90% of the salary above the beginning base, with education units and degrees accounting for just 10%. A cursory look at most teacher salary schedules suggests that the importance of years of experience is typical of how most teachers earn a salary increase after they are initially hired. Although this practice was considered fair when the single-salary schedule was initially created, the fact that experience after the first 3 years is linked only loosely, if at all, to student learning shows that the way we pay teachers does not reinforce the system's imperative to improve student performance (Hanushek, 1997; Murnane, 1983).

In education, caps on the number of years of experience recognized as teachers move from one district to another illustrate the notion that in some education systems, years of experience are not necessarily considered to be equivalent to years of increasing value of the employee to the organization.

As we discuss in Chapter 5, there may be arguments for longevity pay in education even with a drastically altered teacher competency system. One model we discuss in Resource A provides longevity increments but only for teachers who have attained a comprehensive array of professional expertise and high professional standards; the notion is that the system may want to exert financial effort to retain teachers, but only the most skilled and accomplished teachers. However, no state or district has adopted that approach. Districts adopting knowledge-and-skills pay programs generally have some years of experience element, but teacher performance to a higher level of practice is still the factor that produces higher salaries and is the key to the highest salaries. As the Cincinnati model is designed, years of experience increase salary but only modestly and only within a particular performance category.

Kerchner, Koppich, and Weeres (1997) discuss the notion of the "electronic hiring hall," which they proffer as a new role for unions designed to provide career security for teachers even if positions in particular schools or districts change more than they do today. In the past, longevity pay was also an element in the pay structure that contributed to stability and security, but new strategies need to be invented for the ever-changing nature of education and schools in the future.

New Approaches to Pay: Pay for the Person

As discussed at different points above, new approaches to compensation seek to pay the person rather than link pay just to a particular job. This approach to pay attempts to identify the attributes of individual employees and then to link pay increments to the attributes that the organization needs in order to accomplish its goals. It is a way to use the pay system to encourage employees to continually increase their knowledge, skills, and competencies.

In the past, *skill-based pay* has been used as a generic term to describe compensation of individuals for the skills they demonstrate rather than for the particular job they occupy. More recently, skill-based pay in the private sector has been limited to describing this type of compensation "in settings where the work tends to be more procedural and less varied" (Zingheim & Schuster, 1995b, p. 11), such as manufacturing or blue-collar work.

Again, in the private sector, competency pay has become the new term used to describe pay for the development of "more abstract knowledge or for behaviors that are less easily observable than most skills in skill pay" (Zingheim & Schuster, 1995b, p. 11). Thus the term *competency-based pay* is more often applied to workers in managerial and executive positions, for professionals, or for knowledge workers more generally.

The use of skill and competency pay is growing rapidly in the private sector and is also being experimented with in the school setting, where it is called knowledge- and skills-based pay because competency pay connotes merit pay to some. Knowledge- and skills-based pay in education provides an excellent match for the needs of the school organization because it supports the development of a "culture of concern for personal growth and development and a highly talented work force" (Lawler, 1995, p. 17)—what some have referred to as the development of a "learning organization" (Senge, 1990; Zingheim & Schuster, 1995b).

Because knowledge- and skills-based pay encourages career-long development of professional expertise, it provides an excellent match for the high-standards, high-involvement school of the 1990s described in Chapter 2. Knowledge- and skills-based pay can be used to provide incentives for teachers to continue to develop their knowledge, skills, and competencies in new and more effective forms of pedagogy; deeper and more conceptual subject matter—knowledge needed to teach consistently with the ways children learn advanced cognitive expertise; and the leadership and management skills needed to engage in effective school site management and decision making.

Another advantage of knowledge- and skills-based pay is that it can provide a clearer career development path for teachers who want to enhance their professional practice to make their own instruction and the collective instruction of their school's faculty more effective. Moreover, to a certain degree, it is both strategic and incumbent upon organizations, including schools, to identify a knowledge-and-skills career path, because the organization (education system) will meet its goals only if its workers (teachers) develop the requisite expertise to do so.

By this logic, the standards-based education environment in education means that the education system should identify the knowledge, skills, and expertise teachers require to be more successful in teaching all students to high performance standards. These compilations of professional expertise are now called *teaching standards* and are discussed at more length in Chapter 5. This teacher expertise would both expand and deepen over a teacher's career and should serve as the vision for teacher preservice training, recruitment, induction, development, evaluation, and compensation—that is, should anchor the overall, education human resource system, including the way teachers are paid. In this sense, knowledge- and skills-based pay in education becomes not only an interesting new way to pay teachers but also an integral part of the strategic changes required to accomplish the country's education goals and implement standards-based reform.

It should be noted that research on skill-based pay in the private sector suggests that it tends to increase pay for individuals, because it increases flexibility of the workforce and productivity of the organization. It also is associated with higher worker morale. In addition, organizations that use skill-based pay as an element of pay tend to invest more in employee training programs and are more likely to implement decentralized, worker involvement in organizational management (Jenkins, Ledford, Gupta, & Doty, 1992; Lawler, 1995, 2000a; Lawler, Mohrman, & Ledford, 1995; Welbourne & Mejia, 1995).

Skill or competency pay, like any other element of compensation, may be paid out to employees as an increment to base pay, or as a lump sum bonus. Early research on skill-based pay suggested that it should be paid as an increase in base pay because the additional skills and competencies developed increased the long-term value of the individual to the organization (Lawler, 1990, 2000a). More recently, companies have been moving toward using bonuses to reward the development of specific skills and competencies, to reflect the fact that some skills provide short-term value to the organization, but need to be replaced by other skills over time. Bonuses enable companies to reward employees for development of these critical skills and competencies without locking themselves into future payments for skills that may become outdated. Bonuses also provide a stronger incentive for continuous skill improvement (Ledford, 1995a). As a result, schools may want to consider some combination of base and bonus pay to reward increases in skills and competencies.

As discussed further in Chapter 5, Douglas County, Colorado, began to implement forms of knowledge- and skills-based pay in 1995. They began modestly with a bonus for skills in computer software packages—word processing, spreadsheets, and so forth. The places that converted career ladder programs into career development programs, such as Arizona and, for a while, Charlotte-Mecklenburg, North Carolina, also developed versions of knowledge- and skills-based pay. As discussed in Chapter 1, pay increments for certification from the National Board for Professional Teaching Standards is a knowledge- and skills-based pay element; increasingly, the practice is to provide permanent pay increases to National Board-certified teachers and not just a one-time bonus. Chapter 5 shows that more recent knowledge- and skills-based pay programs provide permanent pay increases for the expertise identified, thus changing teacher base pay more to knowledge and skills rather than years of experience.

Pay for Behaviors or Outcomes

Performance pay represents another element of pay and compensation. Performance pay can reward specific behaviors or outcomes at the individual, team, or organizational level. At the individual level, performance pay is usually called merit pay. Performance awards are usually offered as additional pay for high or improved performance. As with skill and competency pay, they may be added to base salary or provided as bonuses, but bonuses provide a stronger incentive for continuous improvement in performance. Indeed, organizations that add performance awards to base pay discover over time that the highest-paid employees are those with the most seniority, not necessarily those who are the most productive. Although the tendency is to add performance awards or merit awards to base pay, it is much more strategic to provide them as a bonus so they need to be re-earned each year (Lawler, 1990).

Individual Merit Pay

In the past, the most common form of performance pay in education, as in other sectors, was merit pay. Merit pay provides rewards to individuals and is most appropriate in organizations in which individuals can control their own work and be readily evaluated on individual performance—circumstances that exist in fewer and fewer of today's organizations (Lawler, 1981, 1990).

There have been many problems with how merit pay has been developed and used in all organizations, and today its use is declining (Lawler, 2000b). Merit pay often is used in annual evaluations of individuals, and the merit award is added to base pay, thus rewarding the workers for the rest of their life for behaviors that earned a merit increase in a single year. The annual merit award thus turns into a long-term annuity. Such an approach to pay is not wise; if individuals are to be rewarded because of performance in one time period, it is better done as a one-time bonus than a lifetime annuity.

But the most problematic aspect of individual merit pay, especially in education, is designing and implementing a plan that can work. The track records for individual merit pay in both the private sector (Lawler, 1990, 2000b) and in education (Hatry, Greiner, & Ashford, 1994; Murnane & Cohen, 1986) are dismal; few work, and most are abandoned after 2 or 3 years, thus causing more hardship than improvements in organizational performance.

Merit plans in education have conceptual, strategic, technical, and political shortcomings. Individual merit plans are conceptually flawed because there is widespread agreement that the best schools are characterized by collaborative and collegial work both between teachers and administrators and among teachers. Individual merit plans seeking to reward the top teachers work against the development of a collaborative, professional school culture (Johnson, 1986).

Merit plans in education would also not be strategic. To be sure, the education system needs to keep its most able teachers. But the skills, knowledge, and effectiveness of all teachers need to be enhanced for the system to teach more students to higher standards. Thus a strategic pay plan seeks to reward all teachers for increasing their expertise and effectiveness and does not focus on just the top 10% to 20%. And as Chapter 5 shows, appropriately designed knowledge- and skills-based pay programs can provide the highest salary to the most expert and effective teachers.

Technically, it also is difficult if not impossible for an education system to design an individual merit plan that covers all teachers. Although most merit plans in the past—in both education and the private sector—failed in part because the criteria for identifying individual merit were unclear, that shortcoming can be in part resolved in education by using test scores. With value-added approaches, analytic techniques are available to identify the impact individual teachers have on improvements in student learning over time (Jordan, Mendro, & Weerasinghe, 1997; Wright, Horn, & Sanders, 1997). The problem is that no education system has test scores for the students of all licensed staff members. A system might have reading and mathematics test scores; it could even have test scores for history and science. So a merit system could be designed for teachers of those subjects. But that would still leave out of the system large percentages of other teachers—art, music, vocational education, family and consumer education, physical education, library—as well as nearly all other licensed professionals—guidance counselors, psychologists, nurses. Separate strategies would need to be developed for these other staff members, which means the system would have multiple merit programs, a recipe for program failure (Lawler, 2000a, 2000b).

Individual merit programs in education are opposed by most educators—teachers and administrators—and will likely cause controversy, adversarial relationships, and disruption. If the goal of a merit program is to improve organizational performance, such political opposition does just the opposite.

Thus the education system would be wise to postpone any movement on individual merit pay and experiment with all the other forms of pay for performance, which can gain the support of educators (Urbanski & Erskine, 2000), and only revert to new forms of merit pay when and if none of the multitude of other new ways of paying teachers work.

Group Performance Awards

Team- and organizational-level incentives, by contrast, are useful in organizations in which no single individual is responsible for meeting organizational goals, but the service or product relies heavily on the work of many individuals and on interactions among them, a characteristic of many organizations today including schools. Indeed, the most rapidly emerging new form of pay in organizations outside of education is group or team-based performance awards. These organizations continue to struggle with how best to design and structure such bonus programs, but the focus on the organization or team rather than the individual is becoming the clear norm (Crandall & Wallace, 1998; Heneman, 1992; Heneman et al., 2000; Lawler, 2000a; Lawler, Mohrman & Ledford, 1995; Zingheim & Schuster, 2000).

We argue that these two compensation elements—knowledge- and skills-based pay and group performance pay—appear to be the cornerstones of a new compensation system that better reflects the needs of standards-based education reform and the type of new school organization it requires. Lawler (1995) describes two different organizational styles that align compensation with the core values, processes, and practices of the work organization. The first describes the historical management and compensation styles in education (the scientific-management model of schooling, and the single-salary schedule with merit pay, as described in Chapter 2). This model maintains a top-down, decision-making style, a centralized structure, a steep hierarchy, and a stable set of job skills. The compensation system that matches it includes job-based pay and individual performance or merit pay.

The second, which Lawler (1995, 2000b) calls an employee involvement, organizational design, maintains wide employee involvement in decision making, a decentralized organizational structure, a more egalitarian approach rather than a traditional hierarchical approach, continuous knowledge and skills development, and a relentless focus on results. This structure is much more like the high-standards, high-involvement model of schools described in Chapter 2. According to Lawler, the compensation system that matches this organizational style incorporates group-based pay— for performance based on organizational results—and base pay, which is based on knowledge, skills, and expertise (Lawler, 1995, 2000b).

In creating group-based performance awards, one key issue is the nature of the group. The group could include all employees in an organization, all employees in a unit of the organization, or individuals in various teams (including only teams that provide a full service and make a complete product). In the private sector, profit sharing is a type of performance award provided companywide; plant bonuses are for just a particular subunit; and team performance awards are provided to groups within a plant or discrete organizational unit. Research shows that the employees' line of sight, or perceived connection, between work effort and a performance award is strongest for team awards and weakest for companywide awards (see Chapter 4). Organizations often provide performance awards for nonfinancial results including both quality improvements and customer satisfaction.

In education, the analog to these group units are the district, the school, and some subschool units, such as multiage teams in elementary schools as well as houses or departments in secondary schools. As education implements performance awards, it will need to understand the power of performance awards provided at these different levels. We guess that district-based performance awards would, as in the private sector, have the least impact; teachers might feel that they are able to directly influence little outside of their own school. We expect school-based performance awards to be the most appropriate. The education system will also need to discover whether school-based performance awards are the lowest workable level for such incentives or whether subschool, team-based performance awards can also be constructed.

During the past few years, a number of districts have created performance awards for district administrators based on improvements in student performance for the entire district. Los Angeles, New York, and Minneapolis are examples of districts that have taken this approach. As Chapter 6 shows, however, performance awards for teachers and administrators in schools tend to be site based and provided on a schoolwide basis. In small rural areas, with only one or two schools, a district-based performance program could work, but in larger districts, the line of sight between the efforts of teachers and principals is strongest at the school and not the district level.

Gain sharing represents another approach to compensation. Under gain sharing, individual, team, or organizational bonuses are paid as a reward for identifying improvements in organizational processes that lead to increased efficiency. Gain sharing provides increments or bonuses for identifying ways to reduce costs and maintain or improve the quality and quantity of work produced (Lawler, 1990).

Gain sharing may be a useful concept in education and could be used to pay individuals, teams, or whole schools for identifying ways to improve efficiency (money savings) or to provide improvements in organizational outcomes at the same costs (Lawler, 1990). In other organizations, gain sharing often is implemented after performance awards for improving results, particularly in organizations where the need to improve results is more important than the need to cut costs (Mohrman, Mohrman, & Odden, 1996). We argue that education fits this organizational scenario; although education might not see revenues rise beyond inflation over the near term (National Center for Education Statistics, 2000), it certainly faces pressures to increase results (Odden & Clune, 1995). Resource reallocation to produce higher student learning without spending more is a strategy to implement this goal (Odden & Archibald, 2000). At the same time, gain sharing could induce education systems to think more about reducing labor intensity, as individuals retire and move, and increase the use of computer technologies to provide learning experiences. A gain-sharing system that allows the remaining teachers to use that salary money to buy technologies while also restructuring their own work, as a strategy to boost results, seems appropriate, because such a program provides both a salary bonus and further increases in student achievement without an increase in costs.

Contingency pay makes a portion of pay contingent on the undertaking of specific activities. Contingency pay has been used successfully in the Saturn plant in Tennessee to encourage employee participation in training programs. At Saturn, a portion of pay (approximately 5%) is held back and paid out only if employees participate in 80 hours of training activities each year. The total payout is contingent on group participation in training, not just individual, so if only 95% of employees participate in the required number of hours of training, only 95% of the withheld pay is paid out (Geber, 1992).

Chapter 6 of the first edition of this book discussed possible applications of contingency pay in education (Odden & Kelley, 1997), but we do not include a chapter on contingency pay in this second edition. As discussed in Chapter 2, contingency pay is a more accurate label for the so-called merit pay programs that have weathered the test of time, that is, those programs that essentially pay teachers for engaging in extra tasks (Murnane & Cohen, 1986). But providing pay bonuses for engaging in professional development; for conducting any number of schoolwide improvement tasks; for developing new curriculum programs or units; for producing own-school, quality reviews; or for doing a host of other potentially valuable activities is a strategy that could have some merit in education.

Benefits as Part of Compensation

Although we do not discuss benefits at much length in this book, a comprehensive view of teacher compensation would include benefits as well as salaries. Indeed, teacher benefits constitute 20% to 35% of salary in states and districts where benefits include the federal social security. Moreover, several years ago, Lawler (1990) noted in his compensation book that employees rarely value benefits at the same level as the actual cost, in part, because benefit packages often include elements that individuals do not need or want.

This is particularly true in today's world of double-income families; for example, families rarely need health coverage from both spouses. But there can be many other mismatches in what benefit packages offer and what employees want. Young employees rarely want life insurance, especially if they are not married. Young employees would rather have more income than outlays for retirement. Workers with children highly value benefits for child care, but such benefits are all too seldom offered. Older employees would rather have more spent on a health care package that includes prescription drugs and the beginnings of longer-care programs.

The point is that benefit plans with standard offerings might match the needs of the average employee but might not match the individual needs of each individual employee. Shifting to a cafeteria benefit program helps relieve this mismatch. Under such a program, employees are able to "spend" a fixed amount of money on the benefits of their choice, thus helping to match how the benefits dollars are spent with the specific benefit an individual needs.

Cafeteria plans do not have to provide full choice of all benefits. Each organization or school system would need to decide how much of the benefit package would be standard and how much could be provided on a cafeteria or choice basis. Lawler (2000b) argues that in the 21st century, when all organizations are competing for high-quality talent, to include a varied benefits package in the organization's approach to compensation can give certain organizations the competitive edge they need to recruit and retain quality workers. School systems should seriously consider taking this approach. Almost all teacher benefit packages are standardized across all teachers in the school district. Providing some type of choice could very well enhance the economic value of what school systems spend on teacher benefits, thus improving the compensation package offered at no additional cost (at least for the benefits part of the package).

A final issue that should be placed on the teacher compensation change agenda is the pension program. Nearly all teachers are part of public pension programs that provide a defined benefit at retirement, which is usually some multiplier times the number of years worked times the average of the salaries (usually, of the highest-paid 3 years). In Wisconsin, for example, the multiplier has been 1.6. So a teacher with 30 years of experience would multiply 30 times 1.6, to produce a retirement salary of 48% of their highest 3 years of pay. If that was $60,000, the retirement salary would be $28,800; in Wisconsin, social security would be added to this figure but paid by the federal government.

Although there is still debate on the issue, increasing numbers of analysts argue that defined-contribution pension programs could provide retirement salaries for teachers that would be at much higher levels but cost the same in terms of annual contributions. Although any public system would need to make a transition over time to such a program, and some constraints would be needed on the investment instruments that the system allowed, educators should seriously investigate shifting to a defined-contribution system. It has the potential to actually double teacher retirement salaries. Furthermore, because many teachers, particularly female teachers, move from district to district and from state to state, they often do not qualify for a full pension in any place. Shifting to a defined-contribution system with immediate vestment, and making the pension portable across all districts and states, would eliminate this serious inequity in the way current teacher pension systems work (see Odden & Conley, 1992).

In sum, after designing and implementing changes in teacher salary structures to enhance the economic attractiveness of education, the education system should take a serious look at the benefit systems as well. Large amounts of money are now spent on teacher benefits; there are ways to significantly increase the perceived as well as the actual economic value of benefits by shifting to more of a cafeteria approach generally and a defined-contribution strategy for the pension part of benefits.

Conclusions

In education, as in other sectors, organizations "often initiate pay changes when they realize they are not getting the expected results from techniques that proved successful in the past" (Zingheim & Schuster, 1995c, p. 34).

New, high-performing school organizations, such as the high-standards, high-involvement school described in Chapter 2, are making significantly enhanced demands on teachers for increasing knowledge, skills, performance, commitment, and results. Traditional school organizational structures do little to focus teachers, after licensure, on the development of specific skills identified by the school as important to improve the educational success of students. Traditional school organizations demanded less of teachers and, therefore, could afford to have teachers concerned mainly with just their own classroom and to pay them in uniform ways. Traditional schools were content with little coordination between the instructional efforts of teachers and the management efforts of administrators (Bacharach & Conley, 1986).

But public and labor force requirements for better school results, increases in educational standards, and a more complex student body no longer allow for the luxury of that more relaxed school environment. Evidence suggests that teachers and administrators must achieve closer communication and that teachers must develop new knowledge, skills, and professional competencies for the tougher curriculum that needs to be taught, for their new roles in school organization and management, and for the ambitious student achievement results that their efforts must produce (see, for example, Ball, Cohen, Peterson, & Wilson, 1994; Conley, Schmidle, & Shedd, 1988; Newmann & Associates, 1996).

To send a more consistent message to teachers about what knowledge, skills, behaviors, and outcomes the schools value and expect, a new set of compensation elements could be developed for schools and the education system. One such approach would provide membership or beginning pay that is much more competitive with highly skilled college graduates entering other professions. Competitive membership pay is needed because new school organizations expect new teachers to have high levels of content knowledge and pedagogical skills and to be able, throughout their careers, to continue to develop increased knowledge and skills in these areas as well as the requisite skills to engage effectively in broader leadership and management of the school organization.

Knowledge- and skills-based pay is also critical for an education system and a school culture that value continuous knowledge-and-skill development. In addition, knowledge- and skills-based pay would reward intellectual and clinical skills growth and development in an occupation that can require many years to develop expertise to the breadth and depth required in new school organizations. Moreover, knowledge- and skills-based pay would be consistent with the professional initiatives to license teachers on the basis of a beginning set of knowledge and competencies and to certify experienced teachers on the basis of an advanced set of knowledge and competencies, both strategies linked to evolving curriculum standards (see Chapter 1). In this more professional system, knowledge- and skills-based pay would function as a bridge from beginning teacher status to certification from the National Board for Professional Teaching Standards and would provide the incentives to continuously work at acquiring professional expertise.

Group or school-based performance awards also seem increasingly appropriate to the emerging school organization, as businesses, communities, and the nation call on the collective efforts of teachers within schools to dramatically raise student achievement in order for all students to have a fair shot at participation in economic, civic, and family life.

Gain sharing and contingency pay could also contribute to a more effective pay package for teachers. Public schools need to be accountable for public expenditures; gain sharing provides an additional incentive for employees to look for ways to provide the same or improved services at reduced costs. Furthermore, as discussed above, gain sharing also could induce schools over time to trade some school resources for computer technologies, as nearly all high-performance organizations exploit the full potential of computer technologies to restructure the workplace in the process of improving results at the same or even lowered cost structures.

Although not discussed at any length in this book, contingency pay can be used to better focus organizational attention on quality staff development and training programs or on efforts to collect and analyze data to monitor and improve school performance as well as to develop additional approaches for continuous school improvement.

In the chapters that follow, we explore these elements of pay and compensation more closely and identify ways in which the education system could successfully incorporate them into new human resources and compensation policies for teachers.

But teacher benefits should also be on the agenda for analysis and change. As argued above, some choice of benefits would probably enhance the economic value of teacher benefits, and a defined-contribution pension program has the potential for doubling teacher retirement salaries without increasing annual pension contributions.

What Is the Relationship Between Pay and Motivation?

4

B efore moving to specific proposals for redesigning teacher compensation, it is important to have at least some understanding of the theories underlying worker and teacher motivation, their connection to compensation, and the empirical research that shows to what degree and in what context they work. That is the purpose of this chapter. Readers with little interest in theory could move on to Chapter 5, as this chapter provides the theoretical motivation underlying the material that follows.

The fact is that many previous attempts to change teacher compensation were ineffective at motivating higher teacher performance because most of those programs were implemented with flawed understanding of the psychological theories of worker and teacher motivation and poor understandings of the school organizational context (Hatry, Greiner, & Ashford, 1994; Murnane & Cohen, 1986; Shedd & Bacharach, 1991). This chapter addresses the general issue of teacher motivation and how work conditions, as well as salary structures in general, and performance incentives are related to teacher motivation. To set a theoretical and organizational context, we begin with the broader literature on human motivation in work organizations. We then apply these broader understandings of motivation to teachers in schools and potential new ways to structure compensation that reinforce other elements that motivate teachers.

Theories of Motivation

Several theories have been formulated to explain how employees are motivated, and the roles incentive programs—such as compensation, which is the largest formal incentive in any organization—can play in motivating workers. Rather than contradicting one another, the various theories are best understood as approaching the issue of motivation from different angles and, combined, offer a more comprehensive understanding of how and why workers are motivated to higher performance, and the contexts in which various compensation programs work. Contingency theory (not to be confused with contingency pay) addresses incentive pay from an organizational perspective, whereas other theories—expectancy, goal setting, social dilemma, and participatory management—approach the issue from the perspective of the individual. Each theory supports notions of both intrinsic and extrinsic motivation.

Contingency Theory

Contingency theory postulates that compensation and incentive programs work when they fit well with the basic strategies and characteristics of the larger organization, including more specifically its human resource practices. The more closely design elements of the incentive plan match the key strategies and overall vision of the organization, the more effective the incentive plan will be at motivating employees and increasing productivity (Lawler, 1990; Welbourne & Mejia, 1995). For example, an incentive plan that targets employees throughout the organization as well as sub-teams within the organization, first through a profit-sharing plan and second through a team-based, gain-sharing plan, would fit an organization that desires high levels of teamwork across divisions, with employees working toward a single goal—profits. As an alternative, an organization emphasizing quality or customer satisfaction would provide performance awards for quality improvements or customer satisfaction, as several organizations now do. Organizations structured with self-managed teams would provide incentives to the teams, not to separate individuals.

In an expansion of contingency theory, Cumming (1994) states that the organization must support the processes the incentive plan is emphasizing. To continue the above examples, the same organization that desires teamwork across divisions must provide for open systems of communication among teams and provide training in teamwork and decision-making skills. An organization emphasizing quality and customer satisfaction must have clear quality benchmarks and feedback from customers. If organized through self-managed teams, the teams must have the means to get the job done (Lawler, 1986). Substantial empirical research generally supports contingency theory (Welbourne & Mejia, 1995).

Goal-Setting Theory

Goal-setting theory was first proposed as a psychological theory of employee motivation by Locke (1968). According to the theory, goals motivate employee behavior when they are specific, challenging, and accepted as worthwhile and achievable. Indeed, research shows that simply setting clear and measurable goals motivates employees to higher performance (Mento, Steel, & Karren, 1987; Mohrman & Lawler, 1996; Rowan, 1996).

Incentive pay is easily imbedded within goal-setting theory, simply by adding a financial award to the attainment of goals. Wright (1989) demonstrated that incentive pay increases employee commitment to goals. Other empirical research shows that larger incentive rewards can be provided when employees set more challenging or multiple goals, thereby reinforcing the importance of goal setting (Heneman, 1992). Finally, Heneman (1992) concludes that motivation will be greatest when goals and rewards, which largely include financial rewards, are coupled through a performance award rather than separated as two solitary issues.

Expectancy Theory

Expectancy theory is the most prominent theory used to explain employee motivation and the design of effective compensation programs. Expectancy theory draws from psychology to provide insight into compensation plan elements that are effective in motivating individuals. Expectancy theory postulates that individuals will respond favorably to an incentive program if three conditions are met (Cumming, 1994; Heneman & Schwab, 1979; Heneman, Schwab, Fossum, & Dyer, 1989; Johnson, 1986; Lawler, 1986, 1990; Welbourne & Mejia, 1995). First, individuals must believe that they can accomplish the goal embodied in the incentive plan and that doing so is substantially within their control, that is, successful goal accomplishment must be seen as realistic, and workers must believe that they have the ability, skills, competencies, and authorities to accomplish the task being rewarded. This is called expectancy. Second, employees must perceive a connection between their individual efforts and receipt of an award. This is called *line of sight* or *instrumentality*.

Third, employees must value the reward itself enough to put forth the effort to achieve it. This is called valence. Expectancy includes having sufficient resources to achieve higher performance, including time, energy, and peer support, that is, having sufficient control over their work environment to mobilize their efforts toward goal attainment.

This theory does not encompass all aspects of the organizational or individual context for motivation and incentive programs, however. For example, Lawler (1971) describes a situation in which employees can see the link between their performance and pay, and they also value higher pay, and yet they cannot be motivated to improve performance if there also are strongly negative consequences for working harder, such as rejection by peers or exhaustion.

There is considerable empirical research supporting compensation programs based on expectancy theory. Because the line of sight between an individual's effort and an award is potentially the most direct, incentive programs closer to individuals, such as competency-based pay or team performance awards, have the strongest empirical support for their effectiveness in stimulating motivation (Blinder, 1990; Heneman, 1992; Heneman et al., 1989; Kennedy, Fossum, & White, 1983; Lawler, 1971, 1990; Wanous, Keon, & Latack, 1983; Welbourne & Mejia, 1995).

Social Dilemma Theory

Social dilemma theory addresses motivation and behavior under *group* incentive programs. Based on economic perspectives, social dilemma theory proposes that in group situations, individuals have an incentive to become free riders, that is, to shirk in their work effort and still receive incentive pay for the extra effort put forth by coworkers. In other words, some workers can benefit from the efforts of the group without contributing to that effort. This complements expectancy theory in that the line of sight between individual effort and group rewards is somewhat less clear, thus potentially reducing the motivation to work harder for the incentive award.

In reviewing the literature on the social dilemma, however, Richards, Fishbein, and Melville (1993) concluded that the free-rider issue is more theoretical than actual. Furthermore, the structure of the work team can function to mitigate the free-rider problem; the fact is that the work team has enormous influence over the work behavior of each individual on the team. When group effort is coordinated and workers understand how everyone's effort is interdependent, the social dilemma can largely be eliminated. Runge (1984) asserted that free riding can be minimized when the group communicates expectations about fair individual contributions to group effort. When individuals know what level of performance is expected, they generally contribute according to those expectations, a behavior in line with goal theory—the goal being the expected level of effort and performance.

Participative-Management Theory

Finally, participative-management theory suggests that when employees, particularly highly educated employees, have a voice in important decisions on both organizational objectives and job-specific duties, they are more likely to be motivated to work and be committed to the organization. Vroom (1964) explains that when employees are involved in decision making, the decisions become theirs, and they have a greater stake in making those decisions become successful. Both Lawler (1973) and Welbourne and Mejia (1995) review the rather extensive literature on how participative-management systems affect group behavior and motivation. These reviews found that participative management works when group norms support participation and, generally, that participative management works as the theory suggests.

Job involvement is a modern aspect of participative-management theory. Job involvement connotes a situation in which employees are formally asked to make important decisions about the nature of the work tasks; such involvement can take the weak form of a quality circle or the strong form of high-involvement management. Quality circles are relatively weak because they exist outside the regular organization and too seldom have a lasting impact on the regular organization. High-involvement management, by contrast, reflects a substantive management decision to restructure and decentralize substantial decision-making authority (Lawler, 1986). Nearly all research on job involvement shows that it increases both individual motivation and organizational results (Blinder, 1990; Lawler, 1986, 1992; Lawler, Mohrman, & Ledford, 1995).

Implications of Motivation
Theories for Compensation

These motivation theories have implications for the ways in which organizations can enhance worker motivation through both intrinsic and extrinsic factors. Goal-setting theory suggests the importance of setting clear and measurable goals for organizational results as well as for individual and group performance. Expectancy theory suggests that motivation can be enhanced when incentives are tied directly to goal attainment; when employees are given the opportunity to expand and develop new work skills through training, thus enhancing their capacity to accomplish work tasks; and when employees are given more control over their work structure, thus allowing them to decide how best to accomplish goals. Participative-management theory suggests that employees are more satisfied and motivated to work when their jobs are enlarged to include management tasks, such as involvement in decision making, thus providing more worker involvement in determining both immediate work conditions and work processes. Overall, motivation theories suggest employees are more likely to be intrinsically motivated when they have control over the quality of their work and are given ample opportunities to create a sense of professional efficacy through goal setting, professional development, job enlargement, job involvement, and goal attainment.

Extrinsic variables, including salary structure and performance incentives, also emerge as elements that can motivate higher work performance. For example, so-called soft extrinsic items, such as reward programs, dinners, or trips, can be successful at recognizing employee achievements and making employees feel more valued by the organization. Small cash awards or dinners, for example, can have the advantage of immediately linking performance to an award (Lawler, 1990).

Moreover, certain specific compensation structures use extrinsic motivators to support and reinforce intrinsic motivation. For example, knowledge- and skills-based pay can reinforce the development of expertise, which is crucial in order for goal-setting, expectancy, and participation theories to work. Development of skills and competencies become an intermediate objective that provides the line of sight to accomplish the goal. Knowledge- and skills-based pay offers employees compensation not for the specific jobs they perform but rather for the sets of skills they bring to the workplace. For example, an autoworker paid under a skill-based pay plan would be compensated for the ability to complete any number of assembly tasks rather than for simply knowing just one task—such as attaching the door to the car.

Under this compensation scheme, employees are encouraged to develop multiple competencies and skills to become more flexible workers for the organization, and then they are compensated more for having the wider array of talents. The emphasis on professional development and learning new job skills is intrinsically motivating and is then reinforced by the compensation system, the formal, extrinsic reward in nearly all organizations.

A knowledge- and skills-based pay system also follows contingency theory, in that organizational objectives and human resource practices are aligned; here, pay supports professional development and employee flexibility, both of which lead to higher rates of productivity. Nearly all studies show that skill-based pay plans for both knowledge and production workers enhance employee motivation and productivity (Heneman et al., 1989; Heneman & Ledford, 1998; Jenkins, Ledford, Gupta, & Doty, 1992; Ledford, 1995a, 1995b; Schuster & Zingheim, 1992; Zingheim & Schuster, 1995a).

Certain forms of performance awards can also be used to support intrinsic motivation. Group-based bonus plans reward organizational teams for meeting stated goals. These reward plans typically focus on measurable, quantitative outcomes to determine rewards—but the results can be financial as well as service quality or customer satisfaction. Therefore, as contingency theory predicts, the alignment of bonuses with goal setting and collaboration can lead to productivity increases and improved employee motivation (Blinder, 1990; Lawler, 1990; Schuster & Zingheim, 1992). Group incentives, such as salary bonuses and gain sharing, all signal the importance of teamwork and collaboration, which have been shown to enhance worker motivation (Blinder, 1990; Lawler, 1990; Welbourne & Mejia, 1995).

But Lawler (1990) also shows how some group performance award programs inherently contain a line-of-sight problem. In a system with many organizational units (such as a school district with several schools), individual employees may not see how their individual performance directly affects the performance of the entire system, thus diminishing the potential of a systemwide performance award to motivate greater work effort. Furthermore, nonmanagement employees typically have little control over the larger management decisions that can lead to better results (Lawler et al., 1995). Thus systemwide performance awards are less likely to have a motivational impact on employees than organization or team awards as well as gain-sharing plans, all of which include the important direct-participation component and a more direct line of sight between work effort and award.

Gain-sharing plans distribute bonus awards when goals are met while costs are cut, relative to some baseline. Gain-sharing plans typically include employee participation in decision making as part of the system, which participative-management theory and job involvement have shown to be effective at raising motivation. Furthermore, gain-sharing plans specifically set targets for productivity increases, which lead to receipt of the bonus. By setting these targets, employees have clear goals and expectations for their work, which goal-setting theory has demonstrated is effective at enhancing intrinsic motivation. When nonmanagement employees are encouraged to use their expertise about the work process and make changes to increase productivity, gain-sharing plans give employees opportunities to expand their jobs, become more involved, collaborate with colleagues, and improve the quality of their work, all of which increase intrinsic motivation. In a review of 71 studies on gain sharing, Welbourne and Mejia (1995) reported that nearly all showed positive effects on firm productivity, as well as improved quality, lower costs, better attendance, and higher employee satisfaction on the job.

But not all extrinsic incentive plans are successful at motivating employee performance; in fact, some are downright detrimental to job satisfaction and intrinsic motivation. Most of the ineffective plans involve either individual incentive or merit pay plans, which award bonuses to employees based either on subjective supervisor ratings of their performance or on financial or quality targets linked to the individual. The problem with most individual incentive systems or merit pay plans is that they are inappropriate for work organized into teams or groups, the work form increasingly dominating most workplaces (Lawler, 1992). Merit pay plans foster competition among individuals and thus work against collaboration on the job. Individual performance awards create incentives for employees to do what is best for them and not necessarily what will benefit others. Lawler (1990) concludes that individual incentive plans can only work in very specific circumstances, with employees who do very simple and well-defined tasks that are easy to evaluate—such as piecework and sales—and in organizations where employee flexibility and collaboration are not needed, which clearly excludes the public education system.

Summary

The numerous theories of motivation identify several variables including compensation structures that motivate workers to high or improved performance. Empirical research demonstrates that contingency theory offers valuable insight into organizational practices that can support motivation, whereas expectancy, goal-setting, and participative-management theories all help to explain individual psychological responses to incentives. Employees rely on both intrinsic and extrinsic motivators to maintain job satisfaction. Effective intrinsic motivators include clear goals and expectations, opportunities for professional development, job enlargement and involvement, and achieving efficacy through attainment of reasonable performance targets. On the extrinsic side, sufficient salaries, soft extrinsic rewards, and new compensation systems, such as knowledge- and skills-based pay and group-based performance awards, can all support high levels of employee motivation; indeed, these forms of extrinsic rewards can reinforce intrinsic motivating factors as well.

Critiques of Extrinsic Incentives

Despite the rather consistent and positive research results on new forms of compensation, a few opponents of performance pay continue to criticize the use of incentive pay in the workplace. Two of the more publicized criticisms are those of Alfie Kohn and of traditional adherents of the total quality management (TQM) movement.

Kohn's (1993) main argument is that incentive pay, an extrinsic factor, manipulates employee behavior so that people lose intrinsic interest in their work and stop cooperating or collaborating with coworkers, thus destroying work relationships and reducing organizational performance and productivity. The theoretical basis of Kohn's criticisms derive mainly from McGregor's (1992) Theory Y perspective on workers (that workers are inherently motivated) versus the Theory X perspective (that workers need to be controlled) but ignores most of the more recent theoretical postulations discussed above. Furthermore, the bulk of the studies on motivation that Kohn cites are laboratory experiments, sometimes with children, rather than studies of the behavioral responses of adults in real work settings with actual incentive plans. The negative findings Kohn cites from the workplace generally pertain to individual merit pay or individual incentive plans in organizations that require more team than individual work. In these settings, Kohn's findings are not surprising; merit pay plans rarely work, a conclusion also reached by many proponents of group performance awards (Heneman, 1992; Heneman & Young, 1991; Lawler, 1990; Schuster & Zingheim, 1992).

Some TQM adherents, such as Scholtes (1994a, 1994b, 1995), suggest that use of compensation for employee motivation is antithetical to the total quality management approach for a variety of reasons. First, TQM argues that performance problems in organizations are caused by improperly functioning *systems,* not poorly performing *individuals.* Second, TQM operates on an assumption that all employees are intrinsically motivated. Thus TQM adherents argue that performance assessments of individuals blame or credit *individuals* for poor or good *system* performance. Use of compensation to motivate employees, therefore, too often prevents organizations from addressing the systemic problems that are central to an organization's poor functioning.

TQM supporters also argue that performance assessments, which are at the root of most merit pay plans, tend to be made on the basis of anecdotal evidence or personal relationships rather than on any objective measure of employee performance. Linking compensation to individual performance assessments thus pays some individuals more than others on the basis of inaccurate information, thereby demotivating rather than motivating employees.

Advocates of performance pay and group incentive plans would agree with Kohn and TQM supporters such as Scholtes that in many situations, such rewards do little to improve productivity or enhance employee motivation. Individual merit and incentive plans are culprits to avoid, particularly for settings that require collaborative work. But as the preceding section showed, several other new pay systems, including knowledge- and skills-based pay and group performance incentives, can work with and reinforce other intrinsic factors that motivate employees to work harder for greater organizational results.

Mohrman (1989), moreover, shows how carefully designed performance appraisal and pay plans can overcome many if not all the concerns of Kohn and TQM adherents, particularly if they focus on enhancing employee knowledge and skills; signal continuous improvement of skills, competencies, and organizational results; avoid individual awards and competition among workers; and exist in new organizations that have changed the system of work by significantly involving workers in organizing and managing their activities. Furthermore, even Scholtes (personal communication, 1995, Fall) supports the notion of knowledge- and skills-based individual pay and group performance awards through a gain-sharing plan—if the workplace is restructured to strongly involve all workers, the TQM management processes are firmly in place, and costs and firm results are clearly measured.

Another analyst—Frederick Herzberg—is also often quoted by people who argue that money does not motivate. Herzberg's most widely known research concluded that money was a *dis*satisfier and not a satisfier

(Herzberg, Mausner, & Snyderman, 1959). The research identified two categories of factors that affected individuals' satisfaction with work: satisfiers and dissatisfiers. Satisfiers included such intrinsic elements as challenging work, goal accomplishment, and some work independence. The presence of these factors led to satisfied and more motivated workers. Dissatisfiers, called hygiene factors, created problems, lack of motivation, and dissatisfaction when not present. Hygiene items included such things as food, rest, and money. If individuals did not have a sufficiency of these items, they were dissatisfied; but the items' presence did not lead to satisfaction. By claiming that money was a dissatisfier and not a satisfier, Herzberg has been widely cited as an authority who found that money does not motivate and that intrinsic factors were the primary motivators of workers (Herzberg, 1968).

However, Herzberg's work has been widely criticized and countered by numerous empirical studies, as discussed below. Furthermore, Herzberg incorrectly equated satisfaction with motivation. Satisfied workers are not necessarily motivated workers, and motivated, high-performing workers may not be the most satisfied. The fact is that individuals are motivated by a variety of intrinsic and extrinsic factors including money. And as we show in the next section, this later conclusion is also what has been found in the research on teachers, motivation, and money—that teachers are just like other workers in that they are motivated by a mix of intrinsic and extrinsic factors, including salary and salary levels.

An example is a meta-analysis of dozens of carefully controlled empirical studies on the positive and negative impacts of financial incentives on worker performance in the private sector (Gupta & Mitra, 1998; Jenkins, Mitra, Gupta, & Shaw, 1998). The goal was to summarize and synthesize the research evidence on whether financial incentives could be valuable tools in influencing employee behaviors and organizational performance or whether they punished employees and thus reduced organizational performance. The studies covered the use of financial incentives in three settings: laboratory experiments, experimental simulations (which were laboratory settings but designed to portray actual work situations), and controlled field experiments in real work settings.

The meta-analysis found that financial incentives have a strong positive impact on employee performance. Overall, the effective size (average standard deviation impact) across all settings was 0.34, although the effect size for field settings was a full 0.48. These results showed that financial incentives had a significant impact on employee behavior in terms of increased performance. They also analyzed whether the effect of financial incentives was different for tasks that were intrinsically motivating or interesting versus tasks that were more mundane. They found that the effect size was the same for both kinds of work tasks.

According to the authors, their findings counter several myths about whether employees value money. One myth is that financial incentives do not motivate. The results show the contrary. Employees need to be more motivated to produce greater results. Thus the link between financial incentives and employee performance indicates that incentives impact motivation as well.

Another myth is that people do not value money. This belies the study's findings that financial incentives had a systematic link with both performance and motivation. To be sure, the authors said that intrinsic factors also motivate workers, but the study showed that so does money.

A third myth is that financial incentives undercut workers' attitudes toward intrinsically motivating tasks. If this were true, the impact of financial incentives on intrinsic versus extrinsic tasks would be different, but the study found the same impact across both types of tasks. Other meta-analyses have reached the same conclusion about the inaccuracy of this myth (Wiersma, 1992).

In sum, this meta-analysis found that money can and does motivate higher performance, that it does so most strongly in the real work setting, that it does so for both intrinsically interesting work tasks and more mundane work tasks, and that there is no systematic evidence that financial incentives undercut intrinsic factors that might also be operating in the workplace. The fact is that workers are motivated by a variety of intrinsic and extrinsic factors including money.

Applications to Education

The above theoretical and empirical research on motivation can serve as a framework for considering the work conditions, pay, and performance awards that can affect teacher motivation in schools. This section examines the literature on teacher motivation, first, applying the general theories of motivation to teachers in schools and second, discussing the key financial variables that impact teacher motivation and behavior. The studies discussed provide insight into potential new teacher compensation structures that could reinforce intrinsic motivators just as they do in organizations outside education.

Theories of Motivation
Applied to Teachers in Schools

This section summarizes research knowledge about how the four different theories of motivation discussed previously have worked in the education setting.

Goal-Setting and Expectancy Theories

Teachers are primarily motivated by two major factors—helping students achieve and collaborating with colleagues on teaching and learning issues. Collaboration helps teachers develop a set of effective instructional strategies that, when they are deployed, positively impact student achievement. When these connections occur, teachers develop a sense of professional efficacy or confidence that students in their classrooms will learn, which over time motivates teachers to higher performance. These conclusions about teacher motivation align with goal-setting and expectancy theories (Conley, 1991; Little & McLaughlin, 1993; Lortie, 1975; McLaughlin & Yee, 1988; Rosenholtz, 1989; Smylie, 1994).

A good example of these phenomena was Rosenholtz's (1989) study of effective schools in Tennessee. The schools Rosenholtz identified as effective, called *moving* schools, had established clear, specific, and measurable goals for student achievement. Teachers shared these school goals and were committed to accomplishing them. These schools were also characterized by a high degree of teacher collaboration. Teachers collaborated for the purpose of developing a set of teaching strategies that were successful in improving student achievement. Teachers in these schools believed that their own professional learning was an ongoing, never-ending process. Success in producing student achievement not only served as an ongoing motivator for teachers in these schools but also helped them develop a sense of professional efficacy—they were confident of succeeding when they entered their classrooms. In moving schools, the entire organization worked together to enhance student welfare and learning; superintendents, principals, and teachers all saw their work as interdependent.

Rosenholtz also identified a number of ineffective or *stuck* schools. These schools had either grandiose, immeasurable goals, such as teaching all students to their maximum potential, or just unclear, fuzzy goals. Teachers in stuck schools did not receive support from superintendents and principals for their professional development efforts. Teachers felt isolated from one another and found little time for collaboration. Their teaching strategies were the product of their own individual work. In these schools, most teachers were uncertain about their technical teaching abilities, felt that teaching skills were predetermined and inflexible, and were uncomfortable with others watching over and evaluating their work. Rosenholtz (1989) found that the goal for teachers in stuck schools often had little to do with student learning; instead, teachers simply wanted to get through each workday.

Rosenholtz's findings align with expectancy and goal-setting theories. Teachers in moving schools had specific, measurable, and attainable goals for student achievement. They were given the tools necessary to accomplish the goals, including time for collaboration and resources to engage in ongoing professional development focused on instructional strategies. As a result, teachers in moving schools had and believed they had the capacity to produce student outcomes and actually did so. And as expectancy theory would predict, they were thus motivated to help the school organization succeed in its mission. Rosenholtz's research, however, did not include analysis of how changes in compensation, such as competency-based pay and group performance awards, could be used to enhance teachers' motivation even further.

A wide variety of additional research in school settings supports the motivating influence of high-quality professional development. McLaughlin and Yee (1988) interviewed 85 teachers in five districts in California to study their conceptions of a satisfying career. Nearly all (94%) reported a desire to remain in teaching rather than move into administrative positions; advancement for these teachers meant the chance to continue to grow in professional skills, particularly through collegial interaction. McLaughlin and Yee (1988) state that "teachers with rich opportunities to grow and learn are enthusiastic about their work and are motivated to find ways to do even better" (p. 28). Numerous other studies report similar findings on how opportunities to engage in professional development contribute strongly to teacher motivation (Firestone & Pennell, 1993; Hart, 1994; Lieberman & Miller, 1991; Little, 1982, 1993; Little & McLaughlin, 1993; Rosenholtz, 1989).

In a series of studies, Miskel and colleagues have found that teacher expectancy is related to student achievement, perceived organizational effectiveness, and job satisfaction (Miskel, 1982; Miskel, DeFrain, & Wilcox, 1980; Miskel, McDonald, & Bloom, 1983). These findings in education are consistent with results in other sectors, where expectancy has been consistently found to be positively correlated with both job satisfaction and job performance, although a significant amount of performance variation is left unexplained by the models (Bandura, 1997; Heneman & Schwab, 1972; Mitchell, 1974).

In addition, a number of research studies on school-based performance award programs have found expectancy and goal-setting theories to be useful frameworks for examining and explaining teacher motivation under school-based, performance award programs (Chan, Galarza, Llamas, Kellor, & Odden, 1999; Heneman, 1998; Heneman & Milanowski, 1999; Kelley, 1998; Kelley, Conley, & Kimball, 2000; Kelley, Heneman, & Milanowski, 2000; Kelley & Protsik, 1997; Leithwood, 2000).

Social Dilemma Theory

Social dilemma theory is only beginning to be tested within the educational setting. Today, several states and districts have just begun to implement group plans, usually school-based performance awards, to which social dilemma theory and the free-rider problem applies. South Carolina, Kentucky, and Dallas, Texas, are examples of places implementing performance awards that accrue to all the individuals in a school if student achievement meets or exceeds some performance improvement target. These programs have not been subject to a free-rider analysis but have been shown to help improve student performance (Clotfelter & Ladd, 1996; Kelley & Odden, 1995; Milanowski, 1999; Poggio, 2000; Richards & Sheu, 1992; Smith, Rothackerand, & Griffin, 1999).

Data collected from teachers in the Kentucky school-based performance award program between 1995 and 1997 (Kelley, 1998; Kelley & Protsik, 1997) are consistent with Richards et al. (1993) finding that the free-rider problem may be more of a theoretical than an actual problem. Particularly in the early years of implementation, teachers in the assessment grade levels did express concern that they were investing themselves more heavily in improving student performance than teachers in other grade levels. However, over time, the continuous improvement design of the Kentucky program forced schools to look beyond a narrow group of teachers to develop whole-school strategies to improve student performance. Improvements in feedback data on student performance at the classroom level, combined with an incentive for teachers to examine and reflect on the data, encouraged schools to move toward strategies of involving all teachers in the improvement effort. In the sample of schools in Kentucky, the free-rider problem seemed to be more significant at the high school level, where decentralized organizational structures, specialized course offerings, and professional norms provided greater opportunities for free riders than at the elementary level. However, across all grade levels, the free-rider problem exists whether or not a performance award program is in place. In some schools, the program provided a vehicle for enhanced collaboration, support, and a concerted effort to change existing norms to discourage shirking.

Participative-Management Theory

Participative-management theory also seems to hold for teachers. Research is clear that teachers want to be involved in decisions affecting the curriculum and instructional program (Conley, 1991; Conley & Bacharach, 1990; Shedd & Bacharach, 1991). Research has been mixed on whether teachers also want to be involved in other issues—broader organizational and management issues—that are involved in running a school. More recent research suggests that many—and particularly the best and most professionally oriented—teachers want this kind of involvement (Hart, 1994, 1995). Furthermore, teachers in places that have provide real, school-based management want control over budget, personnel, and other management issues so they can fully implement new educational strategies (Wohlstetter, Mohrman, & Robertson, 1997; Wohlstetter, Van Kirk, Robertson, & Mohrman, 1997).

Teachers who are highly involved in restructuring schools are able to influence multiple aspects of the school organization. In these schools, teachers frequently work in teams, where the team is responsible for every aspect of service delivery to students. Their involvement includes setting goals for student growth, determining how best to achieve those goals through new curriculum and instructional strategies, applying resources toward that end, and working collaboratively to attain those goals. Job involvement can include working on teacher professional development and teacher evaluation by peer teams. In some cases, teachers are asked to make decisions on budgets and facilities.

Mohrman and Lawler (1996) and Mohrman, Lawler, and Mohrman (1992) argue that participation in job involvement activities enhances intrinsic satisfaction because teams of teachers have the authority to use their expertise to create the working conditions that most influence service delivery and student performance. In many cases, teachers who lack these opportunities to influence their work environment and who have little control over schoolwide decisions feel frustrated and discouraged (McLaughlin & Yee, 1988).

Hart and Murphy (1990) identified a sample of high-promise and low-promise, early career teachers (less than 5 years of experience) and conducted interviews to test how they responded to restructuring, work redesign, and job involvement. Teachers were labeled high- or low-promise based on undergraduate grade point average and principal ratings of their performance. Based on this sample, Hart (1994) reported that teachers at all levels expressed a desire to take on more responsibilities, use greater authority, and participate in professional development activities. But high-promise teachers were significantly more likely to value opportunities to take on extra, schoolwide responsibilities and claimed that long-term school leadership positions enhanced their job satisfaction.

Shedd and Bacharach (1991) similarly reported that teachers who worked in coordinated and cooperative teams described feeling more motivated at work and were more successful in achieving improved educational outcomes such as higher student achievement. Other studies and literature reviews show the same results; teachers want to work in, and are more highly motivated by, an atmosphere that promotes professional collaboration. In short, research strongly supports the assertion that teachers want more job involvement opportunities and find enhanced motivation from these expanded roles (Conley, 1991; Darling-Hammond, 1996; Hart, 1994; Johnson, 1986; Lortie, 1975; Louis, Marks, & Kruse, 1995; Malen, Murphy, & Hart, 1987; Smylie, 1991; Talbert & McLaughlin, 1994).

Emerging research on teacher involvement also shows how the combination of the above theories can work to enhance not only teacher motivation but also education system performance. A 5-year study of school restructuring found that teacher empowerment (teacher involvement in schoolwide strategic and operational decisions) by itself did not directly produce improved student achievement or motivation. Teacher empowerment worked when it was (a) targeted toward improving the curriculum and instruction program to meet high standards, and (b) used to produce a professional community of teachers characterized by collaboration in developing effective instructional strategies and teacher responsibility for student achievement. The research showed that the result of these efforts was greater student achievement, a key teacher motivator (Louis et al., 1995; Marks & Louis, 1995; Newmann, Marks, & Gamoran, 1995; Newmann & Wehlage, 1995).

In sum, education research supports the more general theories on worker motivation as applied to schools. Clear, measurable goals enhance teacher motivation. Opportunities to collaborate enhance teacher motivation. Using collaboration to expand one's professional expertise, particularly toward an expanded set of instructional practices, motivates teachers. Involvement in schoolwide decision making outside of the classroom, particularly if it is focused on enhancing the curriculum and instructional program to produce high levels of student achievement, also enhances teacher motivation. When all these processes work together, moreover, student achievement improves, which in itself is a strong teacher motivator. Finally, the combination also produces enhanced teacher commitment not only to the goals of the school but also to the teaching profession itself.

One important effect of school-based performance award (SBPA) programs is the extent to which teachers are motivated directly by the potential to receive a salary bonus. But it is also important to consider other effects that may be related to participation in the SBPA program. The Consortium for Policy Research in Education (CPRE) identified teacher perceptions of outcomes related to the SBPA programs in Kentucky and in Charlotte-Mecklenburg, North Carolina (Kelley, Heneman, & Milanowski, 2000). Consistent with other research findings, teachers indicated that they valued intrinsic rewards the most, although 74% of the teachers in Kentucky and 92% of the teachers in Charlotte-Mecklenburg indicated that receiving a pay bonus was desirable or very desirable.

Interestingly, *intrinsic* rewards—satisfaction from seeing student performance improve and from meeting school goals, and the opportunity to work collaboratively with other teachers on curriculum and instruction—were also the most likely positive outcomes of the SBPA program. These data suggest that SBPA programs may facilitate the strengthening of professional communities within schools, helping to develop and focus teacher collaboration on curriculum and instruction (Kelley, 1998).

Hall and Caffarella (1997) found similar results in a study of the group incentive pay plan in Douglas County, Colorado. Their third-year implementation evaluation found that

> The Group Incentive has emerged as the most powerful and widely accepted part of the [Performance Pay Plan]. . . . The survey data and teacher interviews clearly document that the Group Incentive part has wide teacher participation and support and is making a number of significant differences. Each school's Group Incentive plan is designed to affect some aspect of student learning. All reports indicate that for most plans and for most years, this is indeed the case. Student learning is being affected positively. Additionally,

the Group Incentive process is breaking down the individual class-room isolation so common in schools. Teacher collegiality is in-creasing across grade levels and subject areas too. (p. 53)

These data suggest that compensation can be used to align extrinsic and intrinsic rewards by providing clear goals for teachers to work toward; incentives for collaboration around these goals; enhanced, more mean-ingful, and more relevant professional development opportunities; and the opportunity for satisfaction from seeing student performance improve.

Compensation Factors That Motivate Teachers

Compensation can also influence teacher motivation and behavior. This section discusses the research on money, salary levels, and the poten-tial of new approaches to compensation, specifically knowledge- and skills-based pay and group performance incentives to motivate teachers.

Money and Teacher Motivation and Values

There is widespread research that shows that money matters to teach-ers. By saying this, we do not mean to imply that only money matters. We know that individuals do not enter teaching to earn "big money." And working conditions, professional development opportunities, and in-structional leadership by principals and central office administrators are also highly desired by teachers (Farkas, Johnson, & Foleno, 2000). In fact, working conditions and good leadership matter for all workers, public and private, inside and outside of education.

But it would be a mistake to claim that money does not matter to teach-ers. Two recent studies reinforce this comment. First, in research on school-based performance awards in education, Consortium for Policy Research in Education researcher Kelley and colleagues (2000) listed 17 potential outcomes for teachers, one of which was the salary bonus for meeting the performance improvement target. They asked teachers to rank order how they valued all the potential outcomes, which ranged from the bonus to intrinsic satisfaction in seeing improvements in stu-dent achievement. A factor analysis showed that teacher responses could be grouped into four categories. The top, most valued outcomes included the pay bonus as well as satisfaction from seeing students learn more. In short, teachers valued money but they also valued other, intrinsic and extrinsic outcomes.

Similarly, the Public Agenda sponsored a series of focus groups with teachers on how to improve teacher quality (Farkas et al., 2000). They asked teachers to identify and rank order the most effective ways to improve quality. Reducing class size was the number-one item, followed by four other items, each of which was identified by between 50% and 60% of teachers. Higher pay was one of these items.

The next section provides even more information on how money matters for teachers. The point here is only to note that it would be as inaccurate to say that money does not matter for teachers as it would be to say that only money matters. Like nearly all other workers, teachers are motivated by a multitude of factors including pay. A mix of extrinsic and intrinsic factors motivates teachers as it does nearly all other workers. And like nearly all other workers, the particular mix of motivational factors for any individual teacher can vary significantly. Money should not be ignored.

Salary Levels

Salary levels are important to teachers. Goodlad (1984) found that teachers did not enter the profession for the money but rather for the intrinsic satisfaction of working with children. Yet when they left the profession, teachers reported low pay as the second most important reason for leaving, following the lack of efficacy. The combination of discovering teaching both difficult and financially unrewarding discouraged longevity in the profession. In a review of the empirical research on salary and behavior, Ferris and Winkler (1986) found that higher beginning salary levels attracted more able individuals into teaching and that higher average salaries reduced teacher turnover rates. Similarly, Spuck (1974) found that extrinsic rewards were important in attracting and retaining teachers. Baugh and Stone (1982) provided evidence of widespread teacher movement from district to district in search of higher salaries. Nearly all recent surveys of teachers who leave the profession identify low salaries as the key factor (Harris & Associates, 1995).

Even though having a positive impact on student achievement is a major motivator of teachers, it turns out that salaries also play important roles. Research shows that teacher behavior is strongly affected by salary levels, including the decision to enter the profession, the decision to stay in a school district (versus moving to another district with higher salaries), and the decision to remain in or leave the teaching profession.

In other words, just as in other professions, money matters. Money is not the only thing that matters, but it is an important factor that does influence teacher motivation and behavior.

Knowledge- and Skills-Based Pay

Knowledge- and skills-based pay (KSBP) is just beginning to enter the structure of teacher compensation. From a conceptual and system-aligning perspective, such elements of teacher compensation make sense. If opportunities to engage in professional development motivate teachers, and if the actual expansion of professional expertise motivates teachers, then a competency-based pay system that provides financial rewards to teachers who expand and deepen their professional practice would merely add an extrinsic reward to what already are intrinsic motivators, thus reinforcing their strength.

Hart (1994) reports that high-promise, early career teachers in the Hart and Murphy (1990) study described earlier wanted a compensation system that tied rewards to the core tasks of teaching rather than one that separated pay from what teachers actually did each day in the classroom. In fact, only the lowest-performing teachers believed they could make positive career progress under the single-salary schedule. McLaughlin and Yee (1988) reported that an "investment-centered" environment that rewarded teachers for growth, risk taking, and change would provide the incentive for teachers to continue their own professional learning and keep them interested and involved in students' learning throughout their careers. Darling-Hammond (1996) suggested that skill- or competency-based pay for the advanced expertise teachers developed in learner-centered schools also would make sense. These findings point to the potential of a competency-based pay model to effectively support teachers' professional growth and, therefore, reinforce their intrinsic motivation as well.

Under a knowledge- and skills-based compensation system, indirect measures of teacher skills, such as years of experience and education units used in the single-salary schedule, would be replaced with more direct measures of teacher knowledge and skills (Conley, 1994; Firestone, 1994; Kelley & Odden, 1995). Teachers could be rewarded for developing expertise in three broad areas: depth of knowledge in content, curriculum and instruction; breadth of skills in nonteaching functions such as curriculum development and counseling; and management skills necessary to work in site-based-managed schools. As the Hart and Murphy (1990) study and the job enlargement literature show, teachers not only perform a wide variety of tasks throughout the workday but also desire that their rewards be tied to these core tasks. A knowledge- and skills-based pay system would make this direct link. As teachers grow professionally in the three skill areas, their level of pay would increase to recognize their new level of expertise.

Knowledge- and skills-based teacher compensation would provide opportunities for the education system to formally recognize, through salary increases, activities that other research demonstrates to be motivating to teachers—collaborating and engaging in professional development to enhance professional skills, particularly those related to curriculum and instruction (Firestone, 1994).

Research on knowledge- and skills-based pay in education is just beginning. One of the earliest efforts in education was a program developed in Douglas County, Colorado, in 1993 and 1994. The plan includes two forms of knowledge- and skills-based pay. The first is a skill-based pay element. The district identifies skill blocks that they would like every teacher to develop (examples to date have included technology, assessment, and diversity). Teachers receive between $250 and $500 for completing the skill block. The second form is an outstanding teacher award, in which teachers volunteer to participate in the program. They develop portfolios to demonstrate knowledge and skills. The materials are reviewed by building principal; outstanding teachers are awarded a $1,000 bonus. The plan has received extremely high levels of support from teachers, who have approved district contracts with the new pay plan with as much as 99% approval.

CPRE research on the knowledge- and skills-based pay program in the Vaughn Next Century Learning Center (described in detail in Chapter 5), a charter school in Los Angeles, also shows that such a pay strategy can gain teacher support (Milanowski & Kellor, 2000a). The plan initially caused some controversy, with veteran teachers more skeptical of the new structure. And in the first year, the criteria were unclear for determining whether teachers had the knowledge and skills and thus created perception of program unfairness. For the second year, however, the school adopted a set of teaching standards with more specified performance review criteria; these changes reduced negative perceptions, and most senior, as well as all newer, teachers signed on to the new system. Teachers also stated that the program stimulated schoolwide discussion of good instruction, which they felt was helping the school improve teaching practices in the classroom. Finally, anecdotal evidence suggested that the new way of paying teachers was helping the school both to recruit and retain good teachers.

CPRE also conducted formative assessment (Milanowski & Kellor, 2000b) of the first-year pilot of the Cincinnati performance assessment, teacher evaluation system (again, see Chapter 5 for a fuller discussion of the district's overall KSBP plan). The pilot was conducted in 10 of the district's 80 schools. About 75% of the teachers interviewed expressed support for the new teaching standards that the district had adopted, although positive ratings were higher among newer and midcareer teachers than among veteran teachers. Furthermore, although most evaluators felt comfortable applying the scoring guides to assess teacher practice to 16 different standards, there was wide variation in the capacity of administrators to implement the system well and to provide useful instructional feedback to teachers. Not surprisingly, teachers with evaluators implementing the system well generally supported the system, whereas teachers with evaluators having more difficulties had a more skeptical attitude toward the system. Because implementation was so mixed in the pilot, the district decided to spend 2 additional years getting the performance evaluation system working before using the results in its new knowledge- and skills-based pay structure.

Group-Based Performance Awards

Through three eras of implementation, in the 1920s, 1960s, and 1980s, individual merit pay plans for teachers have failed to improve schools or motivate teachers to higher performance. The well-documented problems with merit pay include lack of fair performance evaluations, creation of competitive work environments, distrust between teachers and administrators, and unstable funding (Bacharach, Conley, & Shedd, 1990; Bacharach, Lipsky, & Shedd, 1984; Hatry et al., 1994; Heneman & Young, 1991; Johnson, 1986; Murnane & Cohen, 1986; Shedd & Bacharach, 1991).

However problematic *individual* merit pay plans have been, *group* or *collective* performance awards have the potential not only to overcome the problems with merit pay but also to motivate teachers to higher performance. The education system has only begun to experiment with these new versions of performance incentives. The new version of incentive plans tends to award the entire faculty when schoolwide student achievement reaches or exceeds expected levels of improvement. Programs in

Kentucky, South Carolina, and a dozen other states and districts share these features. An analysis conducted by Clotfelter and Ladd (1996) found that the Dallas program had a positive impact on test results when scores were evaluated against comparable school districts in Texas.

These and other similar group and schoolwide performance awards in education need further analysis. Preliminary and anecdotal evidence by the mid-1990s suggests that they are far superior to the old and ineffective merit pay plans. They seem to be aligned with other intrinsic factors that motivate teachers, especially a focus on student achievement and success in improving student achievement (Firestone, 1994; Kelley et al., 2000). Although there continue to be skeptics about the viability of any type of performance awards in schools (Cohen, 1996), the arguments in this and later chapters imply that group, that is, school-based, performance awards are different from individual incentive programs and are worth trying.

To reiterate, in theory, compensation incentives provide a way to cut through the multiple, competing goals of schools in order to provide clear performance objectives for teachers to work toward. By allocating a small portion of pay to reward group performance, school-based performance awards encourage collaboration among teachers. This corrects an important problem created by individual performance pay plans. Individual performance pay produces competition among teachers, which tends to encourage teachers to close their doors and lock their files rather than share successful ideas and strategies with their colleagues.

A significant amount of research supports the idea that schools that succeed are schools in which teachers engage in professional dialogue with one another. SBPAs provide a potential vehicle for fostering such dialogue.

There is a growing body of evidence about the effectiveness of school-based performance award programs. For the most part, the evidence from theory-driven, empirical studies of the actual workings of these programs in schools is consistent with expectations. SBPA programs do the following:

❖ Provide clear goals for teachers, administrators, and policymakers

❖ Leverage other resources to support these goals

❖ Produce outcomes many teachers view as positive, including the monetary bonus, opportunities to see student performance improve, and opportunities to collaborate with other teachers and to participate in meaningful professional development (Heneman & Milanowski, 1999; Kelley et al., 2000; Kelley & Protsik, 1997; Milanowski, 2000)

The research suggests that program design and implementation processes are critical to the success of school-based performance pay (Hatry et al., 1994; Leithwood, 2000; Odden & Kelley, 1997). These findings are further elaborated in Chapter 6.

Conclusions

The primary teacher motivator is improved student achievement. Thus an education system organized and structured to increase student achievement will be one that also enhances teacher motivation. Within this type of system, several factors can individually and as a group improve teacher motivation. Clear education goals focused on student achievement are characteristic of successful schools and foster teacher motivation. Teacher involvement in schoolwide activities, including both the instructional program and the overall management of the school, is motivating. Teacher motivation is also positively impacted by having opportunities to engage in professional development; having those experiences actually enhance professional expertise boosts motivation even further. In short, several intrinsic variables are positively connected to teacher motivation.

Salaries and compensation also are important. Overall salary levels matter to teachers; lower relative salaries are associated with a decline in the quality of individuals attracted to teaching, loss of teachers to higher-paying districts, and loss of teachers to other professions. Higher relative salaries have just the opposite effect.

In terms of the structure of compensation, research is clear that individual merit and incentive pay programs do not work and, in fact, are detrimental. On the other hand, new ideas for teacher compensation—which have begun to be tried and researched in education—offer high promise and are addressed in subsequent chapters.

New compensation components should not be viewed as motivators by themselves but rather as part of an overall set of education system strategies designed as a whole to advance teacher expertise and educate students to high standards. The new pay structures—competitive salary levels, knowledge- and skills-based pay, and school-based performance awards—would work to reinforce the larger systemic bundle of overall goals and motivational strategies.

5

Rewarding Individual Teachers for Developing and Deploying Needed Knowledge and Skills

Knowledge- and skills-based pay is useful in organizations such as schools, for which the knowledge, skills, and professional expertise needed are sufficiently complex that it takes years of training and experience for their full development. It is also useful in organizations in which the needed expertise evolves over time, is unique, or needs to be tailored to the local context—conditions that certainly apply to many schools. In these cases, university preservice training programs only begin the process of developing the required knowledge and skills; ongoing professional development, training, and continued skill acquisition are needed throughout the career of individuals in the organization or school.

In addition to providing extrinsic rewards for the continued development of professional expertise, knowledge- and skills-based pay reinforces the creation of an organizational or school culture that values employee growth and development (Crandall & Wallace, 1998; Lawler, 1995, 2000a) and provides for an explicit career path linked to increasing professional competence (Crandall & Wallace, 1998; Heneman & Ledford, 1998; Heneman, Ledford, & Gresham, 2000). Over time, knowledge- and skills-based pay also enables an organization to enhance overall capacity by investing in its people and thus expanding its human capital. Some analysts consider human capital to be an organization's most important resource (Lawler, 2000b; Pfeffer, 1994). In service industries such as schools, this is certainly the case, as demonstrated in previous chapters. Thus knowledge-and-skills pay in education would focus key organizational resources on enhancing the future productivity of the school through the continuous improvement of the capacities of the teachers who work within it.

Knowledge- and Skills-Based Pay

The single-salary schedule currently provides pay increases for years of experience, education units, and university degrees. These variables are indirect indicators of knowledge and skills; under this system, a teacher with more education units and more experience in the classroom is assumed to have developed a greater array and depth of professional expertise. Unfortunately, many of the credits used as a basis for salary increases are only loosely—if at all—connected to teaching responsibilities, to emerging notions of challenging subject matter instruction, or to site-based leadership and management skills. And research has not found strong connections between these salary parameters and student learning (Hanushek, 1994, 1997; Murnane, 1983). A knowledge- and skills-based pay system would supplement or replace these indirect indicators with more direct measures of teacher knowledge and skills. Teachers would be paid for what they know and can do.

Such a system could reward the development of four types of professional knowledge and skill. The first and most critical would be depth of expertise in the areas of content, curriculum, and instruction. This would represent the instructional skills needed to be successful in teaching a wide variety of students to high-performance standards. A second set could be those important to nondirect instructional functions, such as curriculum development, professional development, guidance counseling, student advising, and parent outreach. A third set could be management expertise required of teachers in schools engaged in site-based management—for example, running meetings, gaining consensus, developing and monitoring budgets, strategic planning, and program evaluation. A fourth would be involvement in professional communities and activities, such as local or regional professional network engaged in curriculum development or instructional improvement, state and national professional associations—for example, Association for Supervision and Curriculum Development (ASCD) and its state affiliates, and content associations such as the National Council of Teachers of Mathematics and its state affiliates—and advocating for students who need social services (Ladsen-Billings, 1997).

Classroom Instructional Knowledge and Skills

The first set of knowledge and skills relates to teaching and learning. Recent research findings document both the shortcomings of teaching across America—for example, the instructional tapes from the Third International Mathematics and Science Study (National Center for Education Statistics, 1995)—and significant advances in what is known about how to teach all students to higher performance standards (Bransford, Brown, & Cocking, 1999). The information from the latter—one of the best summaries of research on how students, particularly those in the middle and bottom, learn complex materials—plus craft knowledge from effective teachers need to be compiled into knowledge and clinical practice compendia and serve as a guidepost for the kind of teaching expertise needed, the development of which could be rewarded in a knowledge- and skills-based pay structure.

Instructional knowledge and skills reflect levels of expertise in a particular teaching area. For teachers, such broader and deeper skills would reflect increasing competence both in teaching itself and in the subject area taught. The current practice is to use educational units, certificates, and degrees as indicators that the teacher has achieved knowledge and competency levels beyond those required for initial licensure. The knowledge and skills represented by these indicators are likely to be uneven in quality, general in nature, and probably not specific to current education needs. Knowledge- and skills-based pay would require more specific and focused assessment systems for measuring depth of skills and knowledge in subject matter, curriculum, and instruction.

Furthermore, these curricula and instructional knowledge and skills should be linked quite closely to the content knowledge and pedagogical skills required to teach ambitious new curriculum frameworks to all students; such a linkage should potentially enhance student, school, and education system performance. An important element of standards-based reform and of current notions of teacher professionalism is the need to link teacher training and compensation to the knowledge and skills required by new curriculum standards (Darling-Hammond, Wise, & Klein, 1995; National Board for Professional Teaching Standards, 1995; Smith & O'Day, 1991). Because both the Interstate New Teacher Assessment and Support Consortium (INTASC) project and National Board for Professional Teaching Standards (NBPTS) certification are linked to these developing curriculum standards, as are district and state adaptations of the Danielson (1996) Framework for Teaching, their assessment strategies could be used by districts and states to build the knowledge-and-skills career paths from professional licensure to Board certification. Board certification itself could constitute an advanced level of instructional expertise. Rewarding development of enhanced instructional knowledge and skills throughout a teacher's career would, then, provide an additional strategy for continually improving teacher capacity in this important area.

The specific nature of instructional skills required would need to vary by education level: elementary, middle school, and high school. Indeed, INTASC and the National Board have different standards for teachers at different education levels. This development level appropriateness would need to be added to the more general Danielson (1996) Framework. Furthermore, some form of advanced-subject-matter knowledge is appropriate for each level. Indeed, elementary teachers in Korea, for example, are required for certification to have depth knowledge and skills in one of seven identified content areas, and schools hire teachers to ensure a full mix of depth skills. By adding advanced knowledge and skills for all level of schools, the education system could signal that in-depth knowledge of content areas such as mathematics and science is important for elementary as well as middle and secondary school teachers. One way this could be done, for example, would be to reward in the salary schedule a master's degree but only in the subject matter taught, or for at least one content area for elementary teachers.

Knowledge and Skills for Other Educational Functional Tasks

The second set of knowledge and skills refers to educational tasks that are distinct from classroom instructional skills. For instance, many house concepts in new schools require teachers to act as advisors and counselors to students (Darling-Hammond, 1996), as do many new comprehensive school designs (Sizer, 1996; Stringfield, Ross, & Smith, 1996). Someone who has mastered a set of counseling and advising skills, in addition to teaching skills, must conduct such roles properly. A knowledge- and skills-based pay approach would encourage the acquisition of such expertise by attaching pay increments to counseling and advising competencies. There are several possibilities for such additional knowledge and skills: content knowledge and pedagogical skills in a second subject area (especially for schools stressing multidisciplinary approaches or needing teachers qualified in more than one content area); additional knowledge and skills could also include expertise in professional development, curriculum development, instructional materials evaluation and assessment, assessment development, and skills related to the specific design a school might be implementing (such as a Comer Development School, a nongraded primary school; a Coalition school; or a technology-oriented school such as the Co-NECT Design of the New American Schools).

Knowledge and Skills in School Management and Leadership

The third series of knowledge and skills are those related to managerial and leadership expertise, including those needed for schools functioning under site-based management. Budgeting, running meetings, operating in a team, collegial structure, evaluating programs, developing school improvement plans and the like are all knowledge and skills needed by school faculty for local leadership and management to work effectively.

Again, specific knowledge and skills would be used in the pay structure only if they supported the organizational arrangements and core educational purposes of the particular school. Some skills that are important in schools may best be considered as separate jobs and paid for as such, such as coaching and club advising, if they are considered to be extracurricular.

Knowledge and Skills for Professional Activities

Skills and activities representing broader involvement in professional activities is a fourth arena and one reflected in nearly all teaching standards that have been developed. As mentioned above, this could include documentation of interactions with parents; advocating for student social, psychological, and other noneducational needs; and involvement in professional activities outside a teacher's classroom and school. Such involvement could include participation in local or regional networks of teachers engaged in developing standards-based curriculum units (Adams, 2000), participation in national or state ASCD or content professional organizations (National Council of Teachers of Mathematics, National Science Teachers Association, International Reading Association, etc.), or in other professional involvement or outreach. This set of activities and skills connotes that a professional teacher works on issues beyond the individual classroom.

Summary

A knowledge- and skills-based pay system with all these elements can more directly relate compensation to the range of knowledge and expertise most teachers need to acquire and apply within their job setting. As discussed in Chapter 1, the country has produced several examples of teaching standards that incorporate in different ways and to different degrees the above four sets of professional expertise for teachers. The four most prominent are (a) the PRAXIS III standards developed for the first-year teacher (Dwyer, 1994); (b) the INTASC standards developed for the second- or third-year teacher, which explicitly include some measures of content-specific pedagogy (Moss, Schutz, & Collins, 1998); (c) the 30 or so standards created by the National Board for Professional Teaching Standards (www.nbpts.org); and (d) Danielson's (1996) Framework for Teaching, which provides a teaching framework designed to cover novice, midcareer, and experienced teachers, and which can be made to align with the previous three standards. Both states and districts have taken various aspects of these standards and have adapted them to their own use for teacher licensure (Youngs, Odden, & Porter, 2000), teacher professional development, performance-based teacher evaluation, and, in the past few years, new compensation systems. In subsequent sections of this chapter, several of these district and state initiatives are described (longer case descriptions can be found at www.wcer.wisc.edu/cpre/tcomp/research/ksbp/studies.asp).

Although the above standards can be adopted or adapted by districts and states, knowledge- and skills-based pay plans should also seek to fit and reinforce the local school organizational and instructional arrangements. By providing for site-based management and local control, and by focusing on results, standards-based reform is creating a situation in which schools can differ from one another in their specific organizational and instructional designs. Knowledge- and skills-based pay plans might, therefore, need to differ, at least to some degree, from school to school even within a district or state. Different schools might need to specify specific sets of knowledge and skills to fit their instructional and organizational strategy, particularly if they have adopted a specific, comprehensive school design (Stringfield et al., 1996). On the other hand, the specification of knowledge and skills cannot be completely idiosyncratic. Some basic commonalties must be maintained across schools so that the system has some professional coherence and teachers have a reasonable ability to move among schools. A workable balance needs to be created between systemwide uniformity—state or district—and local site variation. The system could require knowledge and skills in core areas, tracking core curriculum standards; the core also could be aligned with, and constitute a bridge between, initial licensure under an INTASC standard and certification by the National Board. This is the approach that Cincinnati, Iowa, and the Vaughn Next Century Learning Center (a charter school in Los Angeles) have taken, as discussed below. The common knowledge and skills would then constitute the skeleton upon which personnel in local schools could build customized knowledge and skills by defining and measuring additional skills.

Linkage to Career Development

Knowledge- and skills-based pay encourages educational careers formed by a continuous focus on knowledge-and-skill acquisition. By acquiring additional expertise, individuals increase the number and kinds of roles they can perform in the organization. This flexibility and depth enhances their value to the organization and thereby offers opportunities for salary growth not available in a job-based pay system. As employees acquire new knowledge and skills and begin to perform more effectively in traditional roles and extend to new roles, they, in essence, move through a career in the school. Each career move, and the accompanying acquisition of a new array of knowledge and skills, and the opportunity to perform the tasks and roles, brings with it increased stature and value to the organization, as well as a larger salary. Although we traditionally tend to think of careers as moving hierarchically up the organization, knowledge- and skills-based careers are defined by the growth of knowledge and skills, not by the limits of a narrowly defined job. Employees advance by developing expertise in four directions or combinations thereof: instructional skills, instructional-support skills, leadership and management, and professional skills (Mohrman, Mohrman, & Odden, 1996).

A knowledge- and skills-based pay structure could nicely fit the developmental stages of a teacher's career (Conley & Odden, 1995). Teachers begin their teaching career with a focus on developing and perfecting a limited set of instructional and classroom management skills. Over time, they broaden and deepen this professional expertise and become more effective in teaching. The next step includes engagement in broader schoolwide tasks that include collegial efforts in creating even greater curriculum and instructional expertise, as well as various school improvement activities. Over time, engagement in these broader roles can include managerial tasks as well (see also Huberman, 1995). As the professional expertise and contribution to school effectiveness expands over these career developmental stages, a knowledge- and skills-based pay structure could provide a financial reward as well, thus reinforcing the intrinsic satisfactions that also accrue (see Chapter 4).

In short, a knowledge- and skills-based teacher salary structure could reinforce the natural career stages of most teachers, aligning the financial elements of a teacher's career with the expansion of his or her professional expertise. Indeed, the performance levels that are included in the four major existing teaching standards actually describe a career development path that is accurate for most teachers. First, an individual would begin teaching with a provisional license granted at the completion of a teacher preparation program. Many states not only require successful completion of a preservice training program but also a passing score on a test of content knowledge as well as a test of professional and pedagogical knowledge.

The next stage of professional competence could be described as basic, which in Danielson's (1996) Framework for Teaching is meant to indicate a do-no-harm level of practice. *Basic* reflects a level of practice for the brand-new beginner who might have one to two basic classroom management strategies and a set of more general effective teaching strategies but who is just beginning to develop competence in content-specific teaching. Many claim that the PRAXIS III assessment seeks to determine whether a teacher meets at least this level of clinical practice.

The next level, one that could be the level for providing the professional license and a performance level that could be captured in the INTASC performance assessments, could be described as beginning, content-specific pedagogy. A teacher at this stage would be consciously seeking to integrate knowledge of content with knowledge of how students learn that content, together with appropriate curriculum and pedagogical strategies. At this level of performance, a teacher would be deploying a solid array of content-specific teaching practices, but this level of sophisticated teaching would not yet permeate every day's or unit's instructional strategies.

The next level, perhaps that indicated by *proficient* in the Framework, would indicate solid, day-to-day implementation of content-specific instruction. Teachers at this level of teaching are well-developed professionals with a broad array of both classroom management and pedagogical strategies who could, with some ease, adjust instructional strategies to the needs of their students and the cognitive goals of each curriculum unit. The goal would be for all teachers to reach this level of practice.

A next level could be called *advanced*. This could indicate some extra type of expertise, such as insight into student assessment and linkage to curriculum strategy. Districts and schools could identify other types of emphases, which could qualify a teacher for an advanced status. It could be linked to special instructional, curriculum, or pedagogical expertise or to some other focus of high concern to a state, district, or school.

Finally, there is also the national level of practice represented by teachers who earn certification from the National Board for Professional Teaching Practice. National Board-certified teachers show that they have met the Board's high and rigorous *national* standards for accomplished teaching. Although the Board's standards are high, districts or states could choose to set performance levels that are lower or higher than that required for Board certification. Nevertheless, Board certification represents an independent, national, and rigorous performance level for teachers, the results of which can and are being used in many different ways in new teacher incentive plans.

In sum, the teaching standards that exist already can be cobbled together in ways that provide a natural career development path for teachers (see also Steffy, Wolfe, Pasch, & Enz, 2000). If used as the basis for a knowledge- and skills-based pay structure, the result could marry an external incentive—higher pay—with a career development and expertise development path that nearly all professional teachers easily could follow.

Knowledge- and Skills-Based Pay Is Different From Individual Performance Pay

Knowledge- and skills-based pay should be clearly distinguished from individual performance-based pay. *Individual performance pay* has traditionally been used to describe systems that evaluate teachers against one another for a fixed pool of funds, often using subjective measures of performance from annual classroom observations. The objective of individual performance pay is to identify the "best" teachers and to reward them with additional pay (Hatry, Greiner, & Ashford, 1994). In contrast, knowledge- and skills-based pay rewards teachers for developing and using knowledge and skills described by external, professional standards and identified as being valued by the school—such as the ability to teach all students the mathematics in state or district standards. Skill attainment is assessed relative to predetermined, clear-cut standards—mastery of the particular knowledge or competency. Knowledge- and skills-based pay does not create competition among teachers but signals the types of knowledge and skills the school would like its faculty to acquire. Knowledge- and skills-based pay systems thus focus individual teacher skill development on the knowledge and expertise necessary for the school to accomplish its goals and for the teacher to develop along predictable career paths.

Examples of Knowledge-and-Skills Pay Structures

A knowledge- and skills-based salary component could be added to the current salary schedule, replacing either the education or experience component of the current salary schedule, or both. For example, salary increases could be tied to professional licensure or certification being developed by INTASC, the PRAXIS system from the Educational Testing Service, or the National Board for Professional Teaching Standards (see Odden, 2000). Teachers could start their teaching career with a Provisional License (a temporary permit to enter the classroom) at a beginning salary level and earn significant increases in pay when they received a professional teaching license and certification from NBPTS (Conley & Odden, 1995). A local, state, or national knowledge-and-skills system developed by the teaching profession, such as the Danielson's (1996) Framework for Teaching, could identify and assess additional milestones in skill, knowledge, and competency development in between professional licensure and Board certification, with locally as well as state-determined minimum salary increases linked to this assessment (Odden, 2001). Several new strategies developed at the school, district, and state levels for using knowledge and skills to pay teachers are presented below. Further information, and, in some cases, detailed case study reports, can be found at www.wcer.wisc.edu/cpre/tcomp/research/ksbp/studies.asp.

Add-On Examples

Of course, the most common add-on approach is represented by states and districts that provide a salary increase for teachers who become Board certified by the National Board for Professional Teaching Standards.

States employing about 50% of all teachers in the country provide such incentives. The salary increments vary from a one-time bonus of $1,000 to a 5-year stipend of $10,000 annually. North Carolina raises the salaries of Board-certified teachers by 12%; Florida provides a salary increase for Board-certified teachers of 10% of the average statewide teacher salary and an additional 10% if the teacher works with other teachers in a mentoring type of role. Several local districts provide similar incentives for Board-certified teachers. Cincinnati adds to the state's $2,500 increment an additional $1,000 annually. Los Angeles provides a 7.5% overall salary increase and an additional 7.5% hike if the Board-certified teacher mentors other teachers. Many states and districts also pay all or some of the $2,300 assessment fee. See the National Board's Web site for the most current state and local Board certification incentives (www.nbpts.org/state_local/where/index.html).

Several districts have gone beyond pay for National Board certification and provide additional pay for locally developed knowledge and skills. Douglas County, Colorado, was one of the first districts that added knowledge-and-skills increments to its salary schedule. One of the most recent plans is in Menomonee Falls, Wisconsin.

Douglas County, Colorado

Douglas County is one of the fastest-growing districts in the country. Located between Denver and Colorado Springs at the foothills of the Rocky Mountains, the district enrolls about 30,000 students, which is about three times its enrollment of the late 1980s. It is a relatively high-income district, and its students do well, but the district spends at one of the lowest levels in comparison to other Colorado districts; operating expenditures per pupil were about $4,860 in fiscal year 2000.

The district adopted its performance pay system for the 1994-1995 school year, after a lengthy development process, with wide participation by teachers, union leaders, administrators, and the public. The goal was to have some type of performance pay as a backdrop for going to the public for a tax increase to build new schools and, over time, to increase spending. As the program was implemented and Colorado initiated its standards-based education reform program, the pay program adopted elements that reinforced those educational directions as well. Although the program has changed modestly over the past several years, its basic elements have remained the same.

The plan includes the following seven elements:

1. Base pay
2. Pay for years of proficient experience
3. Pay for educational units and degrees
4. Skills-based pay
5. Responsibility pay
6. Outstanding teacher bonus
7. Group incentive pay

Base pay refers mainly to beginning salary. For the 2000-2001 school year, the beginning salary for a teacher with a teaching license was $27,000. Although teachers also receive step- or years-of-experience-based salary increases, the difference is that these increases are not provided automatically. To earn the annual step increase, a teacher must have a proficient rating on their annual evaluation. The district has identified several indicators of performance for each teacher that are embodied in standards of performance. Teachers must earn a satisfactory in each area to be deemed proficient; one unsatisfactory rating is sufficient to have the teacher fall below the proficient level and not earn the annual step increase.

Third, the district retained salary increments for education units and degrees. Salary increments based on years of proficient experience as well as education units and degrees are determined by a formula. Base pay is multiplied by 1.03 raised to a power determined by the teacher's level of education units and degrees. For the specific formula, see www.dcsd.k12.co.us or www.dcft.net.

Fourth, the skills-based pay components have evolved and expanded over time. In the first year, the district had one skill block for teachers who were trained in the Claris Works software package, which included word processing, districtwide communication, desktop publishing, and spreadsheet analysis. If they passed a performance-based assessment of those technical tools, they earned a one-time $250 salary bonus. Since then, the district has added skill blocks in Authentic Assessment I and II, Diversity I and II, and the Internet in the classroom. The bonuses now range between $250 and $500, with an average of about $350 per skill block, still paid as a one-time bonus. Response from teachers has been positive and strong, so training demands on the district also have been high (Hall & Caffarella, 1996, 1998).

The fifth pay element includes two types of responsibility pay, one for site responsibilities and one for the district. Each school receives $5.50 per pupil for site-identified extra responsibilities, such as extracurricular activities, committee work, mentoring or leadership, or other defined school needs. Schools decide which activities count, which teachers assume them, and what the pay level is. Because the amount of money is low, sometimes the teacher receives only $25 to $100 for such site responsibilities. Another budget pays teachers for participating in district activities such as the pay-for-performance implementation team, group incentive award (see below), and evaluation committee. Stipends for these activities range between $500 and $700 per teacher.

The sixth pay element is an annual bonus for the outstanding-teacher award. This is a volunteer program that requires teachers to submit a portfolio on their instruction and their achievements. Initially the bonus was $1,000, but it was increased to $1,250 for 2000-2001. After the first year, the district specified three types of portfolios. Type A addresses district criteria in three areas: assessment and instruction, knowledge of content and pedagogy, and collaboration or partnership. Type B focuses on standards-based instruction and highlights teacher efforts and successes in implementing the district's academic standards. Type C is the portfolio submitted for National Board certification. In 2000, a fourth type of portfolio was added; the portfolio simply needs to provide evidence of the teacher's producing "outstanding" growth in their students' achievement over the course of the year. For the first 5 years, teachers had to submit a portfolio each year to earn the annual bonus, but teachers stated that the annual portfolio was too burdensome. Thus, beginning in 2000-2001, teachers earn the bonus for a 2- to 3-year period.

The last pay component is a group performance incentive. This element, also voluntary, provides a bonus to all participating teachers in a school, or a group of teachers in a school, who undertake a specific plan to improve student achievement. The plans must focus on school and district goals, produce above-average achievement gains, and have clear timelines and responsibilities. The district provides a fixed pot of money, so the payout is determined by that budget total divided by the number of teachers in all groups that accomplish their goals. In 1998-1999, 36 groups participated in the program; 33 groups successfully accomplished their objectives; and the bonus was about $400 per teacher.

Although the latter four elements have been quite popular among teachers, the dollars supporting them constitute only about 1.5% of the total teacher salary budget and so does not constitute a large component of the pay. Nevertheless, the program has garnered strong teacher support, contracts have been approved by very large teacher majorities, and the program has been continued, enhanced, and improved each year (Hall & Caffarella, 1996, 1998; www.dcft.net).

Menomonee Falls

Menomonee Falls is a suburban district of about 4,000 students just northwest of Milwaukee. Its knowledge-and-skills, add-on compensation program was designed both to enhance the state's and district's standards-based education reform program and to increase the teacher salary budget for expertise the school board believed was crucial in producing better student achievement.

The core of the new salary elements is part of a broader effort to expand and focus the district's professional development program, to make all training activities—including those rewarded in a higher salary—more linked to the district's strategic instructional directions. First, the district adapted standards for teaching; they took the standards developed by the National Board for Professional Teaching Standards and modified them for use in the district. Then, the district required that all teacher assessment and professional development, including that for new teachers, be linked to the teaching standards. Third, teachers with at least 3 years of experience can take a district-provided, 3-unit mentoring course, which provides instructional assistance linked to the teaching standards. The district is trying to encourage an institution of higher education to provide this course, but according to district guidelines. Compensation for completing this course is equal to 5% of the beginning teacher salary in the district.

Fourth, teachers with at least 5 years experience in the district can take another district-provided, 3-unit course on action research. This course is designed to help teachers develop a personal instructional improvement plan and to move toward earning the district's Professional Development Certificate (see below). Action research must focus on classroom instruction and assessment. The goal is to help teachers set learning goals, understand their instructional practices, and assess the degree to which their instruction actually produces improved student learning. The goal is consciously to have each teacher and the district as a whole develop instructional strategies that are effective in producing student achievement gains. The district hopes to entice a higher education institution to offer this course as well.

Fifth, the district is encouraging experienced teachers to earn the district's Professional Development Certificate (PDC). To do so, a teacher needs to take and pass both of the above courses, and complete another 3 units of education in a master's degree program. When the PDC is earned, the teacher is eligible for a $1,500 salary supplement for each of the next 5 years. The district is hoping to entice a higher education institution to offer a master's degree linked to its (and thus the National Board's) teaching standards, so even the full master's degree would be related to the district's strategic instructional goals.

Finally, the district provides $2,000 annually to every teacher who earns certification from the National Board for Professional Teaching Standards; this incentive is in addition to a similar amount from the state of Wisconsin.

Although the overall program does not represent a shift in the overall structure of the teacher salary schedule, as Menomonee Falls retains its traditional single-salary schedule, the above elements signal both that compensation in the future will be likely to be more fully linked to the district's strategic and instructional directions and that salary money over and above inflation will be likely to focus on knowledge and skills and not the traditional steps and lanes.

Comprehensive Change Plans

Until 2000, most states and districts chose an add-on approach as a new way of paying teachers by keeping the old single-salary schedule and providing various incentives for some specific professional expertise, such as National Board certification or variously identified knowledge and skills, as the above examples indicate. These changes represented steps in the direction of paying teachers in new ways but did not dramatically change the way teachers were paid. But the new pay plans in the Cincinnati Public Schools and the Vaughn Next Century Learning Center, a charter school in Los Angeles, represent teacher salary systems that are substantively and structurally different.

The Cincinnati Plan[1]

The teachers' union and the administration jointly designed the new teacher salary system in Cincinnati. The plan includes a knowledge- and skills-based pay (KSBP) structure together with a school-based performance bonus and was created as part of implementing the district's strategic plan (Kellor & Odden, 2000; Odden & Kellor, 2000).

The KSBP structure represents the most dramatic change. First, the district adopted teaching standards for all its teachers; specifically, it adapted teaching standards from the Danielson (1996) Framework for Teaching and made explicit reference to the Ohio and Cincinnati content and student performance standards. These standards complimented the state's use of the PRAXIS III standards for its new, performance-based teacher licensure system.

Second, it restructured its teacher evaluation and professional development systems around those standards. In fact, it replaced its previous, traditional teacher evaluation system with a yearlong performance assessment linked to the new teaching standards.

Then, using the results of teacher performance evaluation to both sets of standards, it created a new salary schedule that included five categories of teachers—apprentice, novice, career, advanced, and accomplished. To be placed in each higher category, teachers need to demonstrate a higher level of professional practice through the new performance assessment system.

The goal for the salary schedule was to provide large salary increases for movement from lower to higher categories, that is, from lower to higher levels of expertise and teacher instructional performance. Indeed, salaries are capped at the salary within a category if teachers do not improve their practice to the performance level of the next higher category. And teachers have a fixed number of years to move out of the first two (the lowest) categories or they lose their job. So beginning teachers must enhance their professional practice to at least the third category (about equivalent to the Danielson proficient level) to remain teaching in the district. This level of practice also became the new tenure requirement, as individual teachers cannot retain a teaching job in the district if they do not improve their practice to this level within the first 7 years in the district.

The proposed schedule makes increasing one's professional expertise serious business. But it guides the process with explicit standards and expectations for teacher performance and supports the process with professional development linked to the standards.

Table 5.1 provides several of the details of the new Cincinnati salary structure. The numbers shown are those that would have been used to pay teachers for the 2000-2001 school year. But the district and the union decided to postpone use of the schedule until the 2002-2003 school year so that it could make sure the new performance evaluation system, the results of which are used in the new schedule, was being implemented in a

Table 5.1 Cincinnati's Proposed 2000-2001 Knowledge-and-Skills
Salary Structure

Teacher Category	Performance Required	Salary Range	Conditions
Apprentice	Must be entry level with teacher license.	$30,000	Teachers who fail to advance to novice level within 2 years are terminated.
Novice	Must be rated 2 or better on all knowledge-and-skill categories (on a scale of 1-4).	$32,000-$35,750	Teachers who fail to advance to career level within 2 years are terminated.
Career	Must be rated 3 or better in all categories.	$38,750-$49,250	No maximum limits number of years in category.
Advanced	Must be rated 4 in two categories, including instruction.	$52,500-$55,000	No maximum limits number of years in category.
Accomplished	Must be rated 4 in all categories.	$60,000-$62,000	No maximum limits number of years in category.

valid and reliable way. The schedule shows how teacher performance is
linked to higher pay; each higher teacher category reflects a higher rating
on the new performance assessment system as well as a commensurate
higher pay range. The salary levels in the accomplished category were substantially higher than the previous top teacher salary in the district—and
will take *new* salary money to fund.

The schedule provides additional pay increases for other knowledge
and skills, such as National Board certification ($1,000), a master's degree
($4,600), and a doctorate ($9,375), but only in the area of a teacher's
license. It also includes pay supplements for teachers in shortage areas,
such as science ($750), and stipends for teachers who are licensed in two
areas ($1,250). It further provides stipends for teacher leadership roles
such as being a team leader within a school, a schoolwide instructional
leader, or a peer evaluator that is part of the new teacher evaluation system
($5,000 to $5,500).

In addition, the new structure includes a school-based performance award program, also designed by a joint union-management committee. The improvement benchmarks are linked to the performance goals of the district's strategic plan and use Ohio's proficiency tests as key measures of student performance. In schools that qualify, that is, make sufficient improvement, teachers and the principal receive a $1,400 salary bonus; classified staff members receive a $700 bonus. Schools that consistently fail to improve performance are redesigned.

The Vaughn School New Salary Structure

In September 1998, the Vaughn Next Century Learning Center, a charter school in Los Angeles, began implementing an equally impressive new pay plan (Kellor, Milanowski, & Odden, 2000). Vaughn enrolls about 1,200 students, nearly all of whom have limited English proficiency and are eligible for free and reduced-price lunch. The new salary schedule includes several knowledge- and skills-based pay elements, contingency pay, and a school-based performance award.

First, the school pays for specific skills and knowledge needed for the instructional program in the school. For 1999-2000, it structured these pay elements into three tiers. It used a customized version of the Danielson (1996) teaching standards to review a teacher's proficiency in the various knowledge-and-skills areas, rating a teacher from low to high on a 1-to-4 scale. For tier 1, teachers could earn an additional $3,500: $1,300 for literacy expertise, $1,300 for English as a second language (ESL) or language development skills for their multilanguage student body, $400 for technology skills, $300 for special education inclusion, and $100 each for classroom management and lesson planning. Three evaluators (self, peer, and administration) assessed each area; an average score of 2.5 or higher was required to earn the salary increase for each knowledge-and-skills area.

Tier 2 first required a score of 3.0 or higher in each tier 1 area, and a full California teacher license. Tier 2 then provided for a potential extra $5,600 in pay: $2,500 for English language learner support, $1,000 for math, $800 each for science and social studies, and $500 for the arts. Teachers need to be rated 3.0 or above in each of these areas to earn the salary increment.

Tier 3 provided an additional $4,000 if the teacher's average overall rating for all areas in tier 1 and 2 was greater than 3.5. If the teacher earned the total in all three tiers, salary was increased by $13,100.

Second, the school had four contingency pay elements (i.e., pay increments contingent upon some task or activity occurring). The schedule included $250 for each of certain levels of student attendance and student discipline and $150 for each level of parent partnerships and teaming efforts. The point of this pay element was to provide an incentive for teachers to engage in certain activities or to help cause certain behaviors.

Third, the school had several outcome-related pay elements. Each teacher received an additional $1,500 if the school increased schoolwide performance. A statewide program, which was implemented in 1999-2000, uses the results from the statewide student achievement test as the measurement of improvement.

Fourth, the schedule included several additional elements for managerial and leadership skills. For example, pay increases of $500 each were provided for being a school committee chair, a school *clan* leader (which is leader of a small team within the school), a faculty chair, and a teacher mentor.

Fifth, under a gain-sharing program, each teacher shared in any cost reductions produced. They provided a bonus of up to $250 each for teachers who reduced expenditures for substitute teachers for their own absences. In the future, the school hopes to have gain-sharing plans to reduce costs for other areas, such as building insurance and workers' compensation.

Finally, the above pay elements were on top of beginning pay, some years-of-experience increases, and credential-based pay. Starting salary for 1999-2000 was $31,500. For the next subsequent 5 years, an extra $1,000 is added each year to base pay if the teacher's annual performance review is 2.0 or higher, using the customized ASCD standards. The system also included three categories of pay for teacher credentials: $1,000 for a full-professional, California teaching credential; $2,000 for a master's degree; and $4,000 for National Board certification. Table 5.2 shows how most of these elements appeared in the school's salary schedule.

The overall salary package provided more potential money than teachers would have been able to earn through the salary schedule for the Los Angeles school district.

Vaughn is very pleased with its new salary system. The school met the student performance improvement targets the first year, so all teachers earned the performance bonus. The new salary system has nearly all teachers participating in efforts to improve their skills in areas rewarded by the school and also has nearly all teachers opting into the new system.

Table 5.2 Vaughn Next Century Learning Center's 1999-2000 Salary Schedule

Teacher Category	Knowledge and Skill	Salary Increment
Beginning teacher	No full teaching license	Beginning salary, $31,500
	Full teaching license	Beginning salary, $32,500
Years of experience	1	$1,000
(If average rating is	2	$2,000
at least 2.0 on scale	3	$3,000
of 1-4)	4	$4,000
	5	$5,000
Level 1	Literacy	$1,300
(Average rating	ESL or language devel-	
score of 2.5)	opment	$1,300
	Technology	$400
	Special education	$300
	Classroom management	$100
	Lesson planning	$100
Level 2	Support English lan-	
(Average rating	guage learners	$2,500
score of 3.0)	Mathematics	$1,000
	Science	$800
	Social studies	$800
	The arts	$500
Level 3	Rating of 3.5 or above	$4,000
(Average rating		
score of 3.5)		
Other knowledge	Master's degree	$2,000
and skills	National Board	
	certification	$4,000
Schoolwide per-		
formance bonus		$1,500

And a survey conducted by the Consortium for Policy Research in Education found that most teachers felt motivated by the knowledge-and-skills elements and that 75% wanted the overall program to continue.

Other Strategies for Paying for Knowledge and Skills

Cincinnati and Vaughn provide two good but very different examples of how fundamental changes in teacher salary structures can be created that emphasize pay increases linked to professional knowledge, skills, and expertise. In both cases, larger salaries are earned only as broader and deeper instructional expertise is developed and demonstrated in a performance assessment of the teacher. The greater the instructional expertise, the more the individual teacher is paid. Both places have redesigned the core features of the single-salary schedule.

But in addition to creating a new, core knowledge- and skills-based salary structure, districts and states could add other important knowledge-and-skills elements to new salary schedules as well. One controversial issue is whether to pay a higher salary to a teacher licensed in a subject that has been deemed a shortage area, such as mathematics and science. This issue is controversial because of the long-held norm of *internal pay equity,* that is, paying teachers who have the same general qualifications the same salary, regardless of the specific subject area taught.

This pay norm is also strong in the private sector. For years, large organizations outside of education have graded different jobs across different buildings across the United States to pay the same wage to a job with the same number of points. The idea was to pay all individuals with comparable jobs the same salary in order to have internal pay equity across the company. But companies operate in the general labor market, which increasingly is placing a higher wage premium on individuals with expertise in specific areas, generally computers and information technology. As a result, more and more companies are paying individuals in hot areas a higher salary; those that do not generally lose such employees, and often, as a result, experience declines in organizational performance.

Very few school systems now pay math and science teachers more than teachers of other subjects. But because these teachers are in high demand, both by other higher-paying districts and by private sector technology companies, many school districts are having difficulty hiring and retaining these teachers. Although the custom is not widespread, some districts are beginning to pay such teachers a wage premium; although doing so has been difficult, it has helped them to recruit and retain these talented individuals. As districts around the country experience difficulties in hiring teachers in hot areas, they might simply have to pay some sort of wage premium to acknowledge the realities of both the teacher labor market and the broader labor market.

Another concern around the country is whether teachers know their subject matter sufficiently well to teach it, particularly in ways that allow students to use the content to solve complex and real-world problems. One strategy for providing quality assurance that teachers know their content is to provide a pay increment for teachers who have evidence that they know the content they teach, such as a master's degree in a subject area such as English, mathematics, science, and so forth. At a minimum, a wage increment could be provided if a teacher had, at least, an undergraduate major in the subject taught. This strategy could also be employed for elementary school teachers, a practice deployed in many countries around the world. In creating an elementary school faculty, then, a principal or district would want to ensure that each school had teachers with majors or master's degrees in all the different content areas, thus assuring sufficient subject matter expertise for the school as a whole.

Finally, in this era of comprehensive school reform, school-based management, and charter schools, each school within a district might be deploying a distinctive educational strategy, which, in addition to core content knowledge and instructional expertise, has a set of specific skill sets needed to deploy the strategy effectively. Thus districtwide salary structures could have an element that provided incentives for teachers to acquire the pedagogical expertise needed for the specific school in which they work.

A Proposed, Comprehensive Knowledge- and-Skills Salary Structure

Table 5.3 provides an example of a comprehensive knowledge- and skills-based salary structure. It includes five levels of performance in addition to National Board certification: entry, basic, developing professional, proficient, and advanced. It proposes that the entry salary be the average of all college graduates, thus allowing the education system to compete for talent in the broader labor market. The top salary in the advanced category should be at least 2.0 times the entry level; a district or state could set the salary in each category as a ratio of the beginning salary. A more sophisticated approach would be for each district or state to conduct a market analysis and set a salary benchmark for each category that would allow it to be competitive in recruiting and retaining teacher talent, just as productive private sector companies do. The schedule suggests at least a 15% salary increment for teachers with Board certification.

Table 5.3 A Comprehensive Knowledge-and-Skills Salary Structure

Teacher Category	Criteria for Entering Category	Special Conditions	Salary	Additional Knowledge and Skills
National Board-Certified	National Board assessment	None	At least a 15% increase in salary	Percentage increase for license in shortage area
Advanced	State/district performance assessment	None	At least 2.0 times beginning	License in a second subject
Proficient	State/district performance assessment	None		Master's degree in license area or just in content area
Developing Professional	State licensure assessment	Must possess full professional license		Expertise for specific educational strategy at school
Basic	State/district performance assessment	Can stay in category for only 3-5 years		Specific district expertise, e.g., developing standards-based curriculum units, scoring student work to standards
Entry Level	Completion of pre-service training; could include content test	Can stay in category for only 1-2 years	An average of all college graduates	Specific site-needed expertise, e.g., second language, expertise with at-risk students, etc.

In addition to the above base pay structure, the schedule includes increases for teachers with a license in a shortage area; such salary premiums easily could be 10%. It includes a salary incentive for teachers who are licensed in a second area; districts could set specific subjects for which they would provide this salary hike. This element should include elementary teachers, as their second license could be in reading, learning disabilities, or ESL—expertise needed in most elementary schools around the country. The schedule as proposed includes a pay hike for a master's degree but only in a content area, to reinforce the importance of teacher content knowledge. An appropriate incentive for this expertise would be in the $5,000 range; it essentially replaces all other units and degrees. Finally, the schedule includes placeholders for salary incentives for a comprehensive school design (i.e., expertise for the specific educational strategy being implemented by a school) and for even more specific district and site expertise, such as facility in a language other than English spoken by a significant number of students in the district or school. The schedule is dramatically different from the current single-salary schedule but retains its key feature—paying individuals with the same expertise the same salary—although it expands the indicators used to determine *same expertise.*

Other Issues in Designing Knowledge- and Skills-Based Pay Structures

This section briefly reviews several other design issues involved in creating a knowledge- and skills-based teacher salary structure—measuring and assessing the knowledge and skills, applicability of knowledge and skills to administrators, pricing cells in the salary matrix, and various transition issues (see also Mohrman, Mohrman, & Odden, 1996).

Measuring, Assessing, and Reviewing Knowledge and Skills

Numerous strategies could be used to design valid and reliable structures for measuring, assessing, and reviewing knowledge and skills. In doing so, two issues must be addressed: At what level of the education system—national, state, or local—should the system be developed; and what should be the key elements of the system?

Chapter 1 described the goals of both the Interstate New Teacher Assessment and Support Consortium (INTASC) and the PRAXIS Project of the Educational Testing Service to set standards and develop an assessment system for licensing teachers on the basis of a beginning set of professional knowledge and skills, and of the National Board for Professional Teaching Standards to set standards and develop an assessment system for Board certification for advanced, accomplished practice of teachers to high and rigorous professional standards. Whatever additional assessment systems emerge, these systems, now already largely in place, can serve as anchors for a system of measurement and assessment for knowledge- and skills-based compensation. Research suggests that these systems meet psychometric requirements for validity and reliability (Bond, 1998; Dwyer, 1998; Jaeger, 1998; Klein, 1998; Moss et al., 1998).

Because several of the models discussed in the above section include salary increments for levels of professional expertise between beginning and accomplished status, the logical question a few years ago was how the assessment structure for those interim steps should be constructed and who should develop it. The process we conceived was simply taking the written standards of INTASC and PRAXIS for beginning practice and the National Board standards for advanced practice and then writing standards and creating an assessment process for levels of practice in between these two. As noted earlier, this is precisely what Danielson (1996) did in creating the Framework for Teaching, a set of tools that provides states and districts with a variety of instruments that can be adapted to the design of a state or district knowledge-and-skills pay system—and that includes a performance-based assessment and evaluation system for teachers.

In many other professions that individuals enter soon after earning a bachelor's degree, a *national* system exists for identifying and assessing practice beyond that required for initially beginning practice (Kelley & Taylor, 1995). Actuaries and financial analysts are good examples. In both fields, individuals are allowed to begin practicing these professions after earning only a bachelor's degree. Both of these professions also have developed a national system of knowledge, skills, and assessments, with several levels that are required for more advanced and responsible practice. Moreover, individuals who pass these assessments tend to earn salary increases for each new level mastered. Thus there is a precedent among at least some other professions—namely those in which individuals enter practice before any graduate training—for a national system of measuring expertise as it develops toward that needed for advanced practice. If the federal government wanted to encourage pay for knowledge and skills, it could sanction some body to create such a national system; the teaching profession itself could view this as important for the profession and create such instruments on its own.

The task of developing an assessment system for a knowledge- and skills-based pay structure could also be done on a state-by-state basis. This is exactly the approach taken by Iowa, which in 2000 became the first state to create a statewide, performance-based assessment system (Iowa State Department of Education, 2000). The system embedded performance-based licensing into the system and provided a statewide skeleton for a new knowledge-and-skills salary structure.

There also is an argument that each district should develop its own standards and performance assessment system. Although this strategy has the advantage of allowing tailoring of a system to the exact needs of a local district, it also runs the risk of falling short of the rigor and validity needed for such a complex assessment structure. As Cincinnati is learning, doing this as an individual district is challenging and expensive. However, districts should be encouraged to develop performance-based evaluation systems that are both formative (designed to help teachers develop and improve) and summative (oriented toward personnel or salary decisions). It turns out that most efforts to develop knowledge- and skills-based pay in other organizations use assessment strategies developed by each individual company (Heneman & Ledford, 1998; Ledford, 1995a, 1995b), so if school districts followed this approach, they would be well within the bounds of current compensation practice. Unions could also negotiate the broad outlines of a districtwide knowledge- and skills-based salary structure, identifying which knowledge and skills would be common across all schools, the latitude each school would have to identify knowledge and skills unique to the site, and the pay ranges for the district and site elements (Kerchner, Koppich, & Weeres, 1997; Lawler, 1992).

Because the process for developing such a system would include creating an amalgam of the INTASC and National Board's standards and assessments, the process would engage local educators—administrators and teachers—in the important act of discussing high-quality teaching practice, developing standards for various levels of practice, and creating assessment instruments to measure the practice of each individual teacher and its changes over time. This process itself could provide strong educational benefits to a district and the professionals within it. Again, we suggest that the board and the union create a quasi-independent team to develop both the standards and assessment structure and to require that it be linked to national as well as state curriculum standards and to other structures describing and measuring teaching practice.

Whatever level of the education system creates teaching standards and a related performance assessment system, the assessment system will need to address several common issues (Pearlman, 2001). The goal is to make the assessment fair, valid, and reliable. The system needs to be perceived as fair by all teachers; it must collect the most critical data related to effective instruction, and conclusions about teacher performance must be reliable across assessors and different teacher contexts.

Among numerous aspects of the assessment system that must be considered, we will discuss seven. First, to the degree possible, both the standards and the assessment system must differentiate, to the degree possible, by subject area and school level (elementary, middle school, and high school). Second, the assessment system should provide examples of teacher behavior for each standard and each level of practice, just as examples of student work are used to portray what performance standards for students mean. These rubrics should be widely available to teachers so that they can get a good idea of how their knowledge-and-skill set compares to expectations and so that they can set individual, professional development goals to build toward the standards.

Third, the system should be clear about what evidence will be gathered for each standard and substandard (lesson plans, videotapes, observations, logs of parent contacts, student work, portfolios, etc.) and how that evidence should be used to determine a performance level; the latter requires clear scoring guides, so assessors use the same procedures and criteria to link the evidence to a performance level. A corollary of this point is that all assessors needed to be thoroughly trained and then certified as being able to make reliable judgments about teacher practice to the different performance levels. The training will require several days of up-front work and then several days of follow-through work developing expertise and consistency in scoring tapes of different teachers' instructional practice. Most jurisdictions use at least two assessors when the results are used for high-stakes decisions such as licensure or pay; thus a performance assessment and knowledge- and skills-based pay system are good contexts in which to use peer as well as administrator assessors.

Fourth, although Danielson's system relies heavily on direct observations of teachers (Danielson, 1996; Danielson & McGreal, 2000), conducting those observations is time-intensive and, if it involves individuals from outside the school where the teacher teaches, creates logistical and scheduling challenges. An alternative is to use videotapes of lessons that could be reviewed centrally by a common group of assessors.

Fifth, serious consideration should be given to using videotapes that are part of structured portfolios of a standards-based curriculum unit. Such a portfolio should require the teacher to (a) link the cognitive goal of the unit to a district or state curriculum standard; (b) describe what is known about how students learn this concept, including the common problems and miscues; (c) state how the teacher helped students who were not learning the concept at the beginning of the unit; and (d) include examples of student work and how the teacher scored that work to state student performance standards. Such a unit would also, therefore, provide the evidence to determine how proficient the teacher was at content-specific pedagogy. Because collaboratively developing standards-based curriculum units is a powerful form of professional development, such a portfolio also would reinforce the professional development aspect of an effective, performance-based teacher evaluation system. Over time, such portfolios could be presented as electronic portfolios via the World Wide Web, which also would be a demonstration of the teacher's technology capabilities.

Sixth, the performance assessment system should be aggressive in gathering and using—as part of the assessment—evidence of the student achievement growth that individual teachers produce. Indeed, we argue that over time, we must prove that higher levels of student performance are linked to the measures of teacher effectiveness in the classroom or, over time, the face validity of the system will erode. At some point, one cannot argue that quality teaching is key to student learning (Jordan, Mendro, & Weerasinghe, 1997; Sanders, Saxton, & Horn, 1997; Stronge & Tucker, 2000; Wright, Horn, & Sanders, 1997) and not include evidence of student learning growth in teacher assessment. How to do this in a way that is valid and fair is complex, but no state or district should shrink from this challenge.

Finally, because none of the knowledge and skills can be considered static, and since people can lose skills with inactivity, there must be periodic reassessment of competency areas. As professionals, teachers are expected to constantly update their knowledge and skills over time. If people are found to have lost skills from any specific competency area, then they can be placed on probation for a reasonable period of time to allow time to reacquire the skills before a second reassessment. The salary increment for the specific competency could also be reduced by a small amount (e.g., up to 20%) during this probationary period.

Administrators

Although the proposed knowledge- and skills-based pay system is focused on teachers, similar systems could be developed for principals and other site administrators as well. Particular knowledge and skills would depend on the management roles that emerged in restructured schools. Under depth skills, for example, a new set of knowledge and skills could relate to the broader policy environment of education within a state and to the changing demographic and employment context to which the school must adapt.

If the combination of standards-based reform and school-site management ultimately positions schools more directly with the state rather than the district (under a charter school or state-to-school funding program, for example), a set of skills focusing on these connections would be appropriate. On the other hand, if the principal is positioned as a unit manager in a local system (e.g., a district), principals would need knowledge and skills pertaining to functioning as a leader with more system-wide, district responsibilities.

We should note that knowledge- and skills-based pay is just emerging as a compensation strategy for administrators and managers in the private sector (Heneman & Ledford, 1998; Heneman, Ledford, & Gresham, 2000; Ledford, 1991, 1995a, 1995b; Zingheim & Schuster, 1995a). Although a sound development, only a very few companies have applied this new notion of compensation to organizational or system leaders. Polaroid is a company that has begun to plow this new field. Thus the knowledge base for how to extend knowledge- and skills-based pay to administrators is somewhat limited but is rapidly developing. Nevertheless, the above suggestions appear to be reasonable ways in which a state or district could incorporate administrators at the school site into such a new compensation structure.

Pricing Knowledge and Skills

The dollar values of the different knowledge and skills will vary. Some will be more important and more difficult to achieve than others will. In some cases, certain knowledge and skills may impact the performance of the school, as measured by student achievement, more than others will.

The salary increments associated with the acquisition of the various knowledge and skills should generally correlate with their value to the school. In this sense, the knowledge- and skills-based pay system could become an incentive for people to follow careers that match the skills needed for performance by the school. We guess that the core subject matter knowledge, and the instructional knowledge and skills, would be among the highest priced, as they are the core knowledge and skills for educating children. But the exact prices would be determined through the negotiating process.

Educators should have the opportunity to significantly increase their salaries. At minimum, they should be able, through skill block progression, to match the potential salary growth they presently can expect. As a rule of thumb, this probably means the ability to double their salaries through skill progression. We suggest a structure that allows for more than doubling entry salaries, particularly in restructured schools in which teachers engage in managerial, as well as instructional, tasks.

Starting Salaries

Starting pay refers to the salary a teacher would be paid in a pay system based primarily on knowledge- and skills-based progression. Four issues to consider include (a) what will be the entry-level pay for an inexperienced (licensed novice) teacher; (b) how is pay determined for an experienced educator entering the system above entry-level pay; (c) what, if any, attributes, other than possession of knowledge and skills, warrant adjustment to starting pay, knowing that adjustments will be reflected throughout the tenure of the educator; and (d) how is the pay structure adjusted up (or down) as appropriate through time? It is assumed that the current trend for state teacher licensing will continue to be based on demonstration of knowledge and skills, not just the possession of a degree, such as through the INTASC or PRAXIS system or a similar system (see Youngs et al., 2000).

Entry-Level Pay

The attraction and retention of teachers who can thrive under the increased demands of school reforms require that teacher pay be market competitive (Darling-Hammond, 1994; Odden & Conley, 1992). As stated in Chapter 3, entry-level pay for a licensed teacher with a bachelor's degree should be pegged at the entry-level salary for positions requiring bachelor's degrees in a state or regional labor market in order for education to attract highly competent college graduates. The premise is that once hired, high-achieving teachers will be enabled by knowledge- and skills-based progression to move, within the first 5 years of teaching, well into the top half of the distribution of salaries for college graduates with equivalent years of work experience.

There must also be provision for teachers who enter teaching from nontraditional backgrounds and who may lack the teaching credential. A special provisional status can be created for these individuals, based on surrogates for the elements of the entry-level skill blocks that they possess or do not possess, such as a bachelor's degree without a certificate; substantial completion of coursework pursuant to a credential; or other work experience. Entry-level salaries will be lower than for the entry-level licensed teacher, with the actual salary being dependent upon the qualifications of the provisional teacher. The teacher entering through a nontraditional route might be given 2 years to attain a credential, at which time the entry-level pay for the first skill block will be attained, along with any other skill blocks that the provisional teacher has been able to demonstrate. The key point here is that pay for teachers who enter by an alternative route will be determined by the knowledge and skills they can demonstrate.

Experience Adjustments to Starting Pay

New teachers to a school may be given credit for experience if it qualifies them to enter the knowledge- and skills-based structure at a location other than its starting point. Because years of experience as a teacher do not, in and of themselves, help teachers develop knowledge and skills, they should not, in and of themselves, be assumed to be indicators of attainment of skills and capabilities. Rather, new teachers to a school should have to demonstrate competency on the job. However, a school may not be able to attract experienced teachers with valuable knowledge and skills if the teachers must start at the lowest competency level.

Thus schools could try to ascertain whether a teacher new to the school could demonstrate capability in all or most of the elements of a competency area and give credit in the form of a provisional salary for that knowledge and skill. The provisional salary would stay with the teacher for the first year of employment, during which time certification would be required by on-the-job assessment of the complete set of knowledge and skills for which credit was given. If, at the end of the first year, the assessment showed the teacher's expertise was at a lower level, the salary of the teacher would be adjusted downward, and the teacher would have the same opportunities as other teachers in the school to develop knowledge and skills over time.

Demonstration of knowledge and skills is an important regulator of teachers moving from school to school. On the one hand, it makes the practice possible, but it also makes the process of transfer somewhat formidable. This is not necessarily a disadvantage, because team-based organizations rely on continuity, and thus it is important for people to have an incentive to remain with a school and for new teachers to develop the knowledge and skills needed for that school. But under a statewide system, a teacher could get an endorsement on their license indicating their performance level; this would make it easier for the new district to make a correct placement on a knowledge- and skills-based salary schedule.

Adjustments to the Entire Salary Structure

Adjustments should be based on periodic (perhaps biannual) movements in the labor market, that is, probably the wage market for college graduates and the region's or state's service economy labor market. Although some attention should be given to cost of living, it is presumed that the key factor in retention of employees is equity compared to the market and that cost of living will be reflected in the market movement. Also reflected in market movement will be the general prosperity of a particular state or local labor market, which will directly determine how much money is available to the public schools.

Counseling Individuals to Develop Knowledge and Skills

Mechanisms must be established that ensure a fit between the competency mix needed by the school and the competency repertoires sought by its teachers. For example, each teacher might need to enter into a negotiating process with, say, a school- or district-level competency acquisition steering committee. Teachers would specify their personal career desires. In turn, the steering committee would need to specify the competency mix needed and desired for optimal performance by the school. In this way, teachers could plan their careers interactively with their colleagues, and the school's faculty as a whole could plan, and have some control over, the competency mix available so that organizational and instructional designs could be carried out. Competency areas should be designed so that their acquisition represents a significant accomplishment.

Because knowledge and skills serve both personal and organizational purposes, the cost of acquiring them might be shared by both the individual teacher and the school or district. At the present time, many teachers bear the cost of additional education to move to different columns of the salary schedule based on education units. Many competency areas will require considerable schooling, such as counseling or deeper knowledge of a subject, and the knowledge and skills might need to be tailored to the local school context. For instance, counseling may require considerable knowledge about community resources and the skills to deal with them. These skills and knowledge will best be acquired by cross-training and experience in the school setting. Because such knowledge and skills are directly related to the needs of the school, a strong argument could be made for having the school bear the cost of their acquisition. It should be noted that in the private sector, most training is supported and paid for by the organization.

At the same time, not all knowledge and skills will require extensive training. Districts and unions could develop training guides for some focused set of knowledge and skills or offer training sessions in, for example, new computer skills. Other knowledge and skills would be obtained through workshops or through observing and talking with more experienced and expert teachers, particularly Board-certified teachers. Furthermore, all these competency-development strategies could be focused on developing the expertise required to successfully undergo the Board certification process. All approaches, however, would require district resources, such as released time, perhaps lighter teaching loads at times, opportunities for teaming and mentoring, and funding to engage in formal training opportunities.

Transition to the New Salary Schedule

There are numerous transition issues that would need to be considered: how to place all teachers on a new knowledge-and-skills salary structure, whether any teacher received a salary decrease, how much overall salary increase will be provided as an incentive for all teachers to accept a new salary structure, how quickly to phase in the new salary structure and how to phase it in if not all teachers can be assessed immediately for correct placement, what if any special accommodations will be made for very senior teachers (none, exempting them from the program, etc.), how the system will work for licensed staff members who are not teachers (e.g., counselors, psychologists, librarians, nurses), and so on. Each state or district will need to identify all the appropriate transition issues and determine how they will be addressed. At this point, there are no single right answers to these issues; the key is to identify them and make sure provisions are made so that everyone in the system that is affected knows not only what the new system is and why it is being adopted but also what the rules are for making the transition from the old to the new way of paying teachers.

Note

1. The Cincinnati and Vaughn descriptions are drawn from Odden (2001).

6

School Bonuses
for Improved Student
Performance

A major challenge for educational leaders is how to develop a clear and consistent focus on educating students to high-achievement standards. In the last chapter, we discussed how compensation could be used to create incentives for teachers to develop the knowledge-and-skill set needed to produce student achievement to high standards. In this chapter, we consider linking pay to performance to focus individual teachers and organizational systems on producing key results.

Although the education system has numerous important goals, since the mid-1980s, education reformers have focused on results related to student achievement. In most states, interest is on achievement in the core subjects of reading, mathematics, science, writing, language arts, and some combination of social studies, history, geography, and civics (Pechman & LaGuarda, 1993). Some states also include foreign language, art, music, and health and physical education. Other results are also usually desired, such as higher high school graduation rates, grade-to-grade promotion rates, student and teacher attendance, and parental involvement. Sometimes, increasing enrollments in higher-level academic courses, such as algebra and geometry in high school, also are desired outcomes based on the assumption that students taking these academic courses will learn more than they would in courses that provided a more basic treatment of the subject.

As we argued in Chapters 3 and 4, an education performance award—usually based on performance *improvement*—can make an important contribution to reinforcing these system results. There has been much discussion in recent years about the contribution that individual teachers make to improving or impeding student performance improvement. Although we agree that each teacher's contribution is important, we do not propose individual incentives or individual merit pay programs that have dominated past efforts. The research on individual performance pay is clear and unambiguous: Individual performance pay does not work in educational settings or in other types of organizations that require significant professional team interaction to achieve goals (Hatry, Greiner, & Ashford, 1994; Jacobson, 1987; Murnane & Cohen, 1986). We are proposing that performance awards be provided to a group—the faculty in an entire school or faculty in a subschool team such as a house or department.

Designing group performance awards that encourage teachers to produce the desired results and not just *game* the system (e.g., hold back the lowest achievers, exempt the students with disabilities or with limited English proficiency, teach only the best and brightest, or ignore other important objectives of schooling) is complex and is the focus of this chapter.

Group-Based Performance Awards

Group-based performance awards recognize that student outcomes are the joint product of many people working together in a school. Group performance awards explicitly encourage school staff members to work together toward common goals such as improving student performance. These collective incentives provide an important symbolic focus on outcomes while avoiding the divisive aspects of individual performance incentives.

As we have argued previously, individual merit pay creates competitive rather than collegial work environments. The underlying assumption of individual merit pay is that the individual teacher has control over the achievement of school goals, which we have argued is not the case in collegially run schools. In addition, individual merit pay often creates poor relationships between teachers and administrators.

There has been a significant amount of recent attention to the important effect that individual teachers can have on student performance (Sanders & Horn, 1994; Wright, Horn, & Sanders, 1997). Additionally, advances in data management make it increasingly possible to measure student performance improvement at the individual classroom level. Although it is tempting to use these data to measure and reward individual teacher performance, we believe that the optimal incentive structure is to reward individual teachers for the development and demonstration of teacher knowledge and skills and to reward entire schools or natural subgroups within schools for improvements in student performance.

Collective incentives, such as group-based performance awards, assume that the entire faculty, administration, support staff, and student body must work together to produce achievement results. Indeed, in recent years, researchers have documented examples of school districts that have made impressive improvements in student performance. They have done so by bringing teachers together to solve complex problems of teaching practice and to share curriculum and instructional strategies that work (Elmore, 1997). Compensation systems that reward individual teachers for their excellence provide strong incentives for teachers to focus solely on their own individual teaching practice, rather than "wasting" time helping to raise the quality of teaching throughout the school. Because learning depends on a series of interactions with many different teachers over time, it is critical that educational systems be designed to provide high-quality learning experiences in *every* classroom. Compensation systems that reward group performance provide strong incentives for interaction among teachers likely to raise the level of learning schoolwide.

Group- or school-based performance awards provide a financial bonus to all school employees—faculty, administration, support staff—and even provide additional funds for the student activity fund when, for example, student achievement in core content areas exceeds some predetermined criterion for improvement.

The symbolic significance of group performance awards—the focus on results—might be more important than the fiscal incentives they provide. An important educational goal within each school is to create a collective focus on results and to encourage collaborative actions to improve results. A performance award is a formal, tangible symbol from the system that this goal is important, but the behaviors that such an award motivates are probably more critical than the economic value of the bonus itself. In fact, research on school-based performance award programs suggests that they are an effective mechanism for focusing teacher, administrator, and policymaker efforts. In surveys conducted in 1997, teachers in Kentucky and Charlotte-Mecklenburg, North Carolina, indicated that important outcomes associated with the school-based performance award program included the bonus, satisfaction from knowing student performance had improved, and the opportunity to work cooperatively with other teachers on issues of curriculum and instruction (Kelley, Heneman, & Milanowski, 2000). Similarly, surveys of principals in Kentucky and Maryland suggested that in these programs, the financial incentive promoted changes in individual teaching practice, in teacher teamwork and learning, and at least some modest reallocation of resources to support the reform (Kelley, Conley, & Kimball, 2000).

Designing Group Performance Awards

Compensation incentives are very sensitive to minor changes in program design. Like any compensation incentive, group-based performance awards must be designed carefully, with attention paid to likely incentive effects of each design element. Based on the experiences of states and districts with school-based performance pay programs in the 1990s, Odden, Kellor, Heneman, and Milanowski (1999) identify key design elements that need to be addressed when developing a school-based performance award program. These include the following:

- ❖ Defining and measuring school performance
- ❖ Calculating change or improvement
- ❖ Making the change calculation fair
- ❖ Determining amount of change required to qualify for an award
- ❖ Setting levels and types of awards
- ❖ Funding the program
- ❖ Providing enabling conditions or supports for the program
- ❖ Planning for formative and summative evaluation of the program

In general, performance awards should be provided as a *bonus* for *improving* school results. The size of the bonus should be sufficient to be attractive, given the work required to achieve the bonus, but should not be so much that it deters teachers from striving to achieve important but unrewarded goals of schools. To be motivated, teachers need to believe that the award will be paid if their school achieves the improvement goals. Therefore funding mechanisms should be designed to withstand variations in resource availability over time. But this overview is deceptively simple. In the sections that follow, we discuss in greater detail some of the trade-offs, choices, and important considerations in program design.

The Performance Measure

The key and often most contentious task in creating a performance award is defining the performance measure. The performance measure should include the most valued school goals and be based on improvements in performance. The performance measure should also be adjusted for student mobility, be explicit about the achievement targets for students in special education programs, capture student performance across the full range of achievement levels so that the bottom students are not ignored, and include appropriate modifications for socioeconomic-status (SES) background to ensure a level playing field for participation in the award. To the extent possible, all students should be included in some way in the performance measure.

The performance measure is critical to the success of a school-based performance award. Research on performance awards in education and other organizations is clear. Systems—schools—will get more of what is measured for the performance award and less of other system results. A performance award based on a narrow measure stimulates improved results on a narrow set of outcomes. For example, if the performance measure includes student achievement in only mathematics and reading, teachers will put more emphasis on those topics and less emphasis on other topics, such as writing, science, and social studies.

The Most Valued Results

Thus in creating a performance measure, states and districts need to decide on the most valued school results. Student achievement should be the anchor or major element in any performance measure. All the states and districts we have studied have made this strategic choice. Generally, we suggest that the performance measure include student achievement at least in mathematics, language arts, writing, science, and social studies (or history, civics, and geography). Achievement in these subjects typically constitutes about 80% of the performance measure. This makes the performance measure clearly linked to the key goal of education reform: student achievement to high standards in core subject areas.

Most programs include goals for other desired system results as well. These include high school graduation rates, measures of persistence to graduation, postsecondary attendance rates, student and teacher attendance rates, and rates of parental involvement. Some districts administer periodic surveys of parent satisfaction with their children's school as a measure of school performance. Other goals may be unique to the specific situation. For example, a school-based performance award program in Cincinnati includes the *dropback* rate, which refers to the number of students attending a magnet school who return to the neighborhood school. It is included as a performance element as a way of discouraging magnet schools from directly or indirectly encouraging lower-performing students to leave the magnet school and thus bring up the magnet school's average achievement. The point here is that districts or states may want schools to produce other outcomes and that these, too, could be included in the performance measure (Odden et al., 1999).

In constructing the performance measure, each factor would need to be weighted. For example, a decision would need to be made on whether achievement in the core subject areas would be weighted equally or whether some subjects—for example, writing—would be weighted more. The performance measure could also include measures of achievement within subject areas. For example, if the mathematics curriculum and the testing system were aligned with the standards of the National Council of Teachers of Mathematics (1989, 1991), achievement scores could be obtained for numbers, probability and statistics, geometry, algebra, and the other major mathematical topics. Each of these could also be weighted differentially. A decision would also have to be made on how much to weight the nonachievement topics included in the overall performance measure.

All the weights are value judgments and should reflect state goals, community values, district instructional emphases, and school objectives. There is no a priori correct set of weights. Obviously, the most valued outcomes should be weighted the most, but deciding what measures are most valued should entail significant discussion. States and districts could experiment with different weighting strategies. The weights could even vary by district and school.

Measuring Performance

It is somewhat difficult to separate the question of what performance elements to include from the question of how to measure performance. Cost considerations are likely to influence what performance measures are used, making existing measures an attractive option. But program designers need to be cognizant of the substantive, as well as the financial, trade-offs in selecting an assessment. If the test assesses only basic skills (for example), teachers may spend more time on basic skills and less time on more advanced skills and problem solving, although emerging research suggests that ambitious instruction can improve student performance on both basic and advanced knowledge and skills (Newmann, Bryk, & Nagaoka, 2001).

We suggest using a criterion-referenced test that assesses not only what students know but also what they can do with that knowledge, thus including at least some performance tasks. The dilemma, of course, is that good performance assessments are just now being created (Resnick, 1994; Rothman, 1995), and challenges in producing tests are both valid and reliable (Klein & Hamilton, 1999). Kentucky used a new performance assessment for its performance award program. In 1998, the assessment was replaced with a new assessment to address a loss of confidence in the prior system. Performance assessments designed with an eye toward improving and broadening, rather than narrowing, instruction are difficult and expensive to design and are more susceptible to challenges of reliability and validity.

Given the difficulty of getting statistically reliable and valid scores on performance assessments, some would like to limit tests to multiple-choice items. Others believe that the type of student performance symbolized in performance assessment processes—more complex problem solving—is more important than trying to have a new type of test meet old testing standards. We take the latter position but recognize that reasonable and intelligent individuals can differ on this issue.

Many states and districts will want to use a state test if it exists. This is a natural choice, because a state test—whatever its strengths or weaknesses—represents one official version of what the state values most in terms of education results. But the above cautions hold; if a state test assesses only a limited set of skills, it may encourage teachers to focus more on those items and less on other valued results.

We strongly urge states and districts not to use only norm-referenced, standardized achievement tests—mainly because they do not connote the notion that all students can achieve to high set standards. Such achievement tests are designed to identify which students are smarter or better educated than others. They do not test whether any student has mastered a body of knowledge. Nevertheless, many states and districts might feel driven by public or political pressure to administer norm-referenced, standardized achievement tests and might also be pressured into using them in a performance award as well. If that were to occur, we suggest weighting them less in the overall set of achievement measures and weighting the results of other assessments higher. This has been the approach taken by the Dallas, Texas, school district.

For states or districts that have nothing other than a norm-referenced, standardized test of student achievement, we would strongly urge them to select and begin using a different instrument. Each of at least three possibilities can provide solid measures of what students know and can do in several subject areas. The first is the set of assessments from the New Standards Project, which now includes multiple-choice and performance assessments in mathematics and language arts and soon will provide assessments in science as well. These assessments are available from Harcourt Brace and from Educational Measurement Corporation. The second includes a series of new assessments, some equated to the New Standards Assessments, from the Psychological Corporation (the Stanford Nine, for example), revised tests from CTB, McGraw-Hill, and perhaps other commercial testing companies as well. These assessments often can cover several subject areas, can be scored to criterion levels, and can include performance tasks as well. The third includes state assessment instruments, such as those in Connecticut and Maryland.

In addition to the specific assessment content and design, it is important to select an assessment contractor or to develop administrative support within the state or district, which can accurately score the assessment, in order to maintain public confidence and legal defensibility of the assessment process. The assessment contractor or administrator should also be able to provide detailed feedback on test performance to teachers and schools in a timely manner, so they can evaluate the data and incorporate this feedback into curriculum review, revision, and design. Ideally, these data would be available during the same school year or well prior to the start of the next school year.

Other performance indicators, such as student attendance, can be more difficult to measure than might be expected. For a measure such as attendance to be valid, every school included in the program must use the same method for measuring attendance, and effective ways of ensuring that accurate attendance records are kept must be developed. Depending on the district's size and the extent of its ability to standardize certain types of record-keeping tasks via technology, this type of performance element can be challenging to measure accurately and consistently.

Calculating Change or Improvement

Even after the assessment instrument has been selected and other performance measures agreed on, there are still a number of critical decisions to be made to determine how these performance measures will be used to determine whether a school is eligible for the performance award. One option is to require that the overall performance measure meet some absolute high standard. The problem with such an approach is that it does not recognize improved performance for schools that start from a low-performance base; it would provide performance awards to districts or schools already achieving at high levels. Analysis has shown that such an approach would have skewed the awards to the most advantaged schools with the most advantaged students in school-based performance award programs in South Carolina and Dallas, Texas (Clotfelter & Ladd, 1996).

We also suggest that the change be based on more than a simple comparison with the past year. Schools can game this approach by improving in 1 year, relaxing in the next, and improving in the following year, thus earning half the performance award, on average, over the long run. Changes would be best calculated on the basis of several years of data to ensure continuous improvement over time; the amount of change in any one time period, such as a year, can be adjusted, but the multiple-year time period would show whether that improvement was part of a long-term trend or just a 1-year phenomenon.

Whether one or multiple years of data are used, there are generally two approaches to calculate change. The first is *improvement to a standard*. In this approach, student performance standards are set in advance, and tests or other performance measures are chosen or developed to measure performance relative to that standard. A cutoff score determines the level of performance needed to meet the standard. Specific school goals are set in terms of improvement to that standard.

A good example of the improvement-to-a-standard approach was tried in Kentucky. The goal there was to have all schools teach all students to proficient achievement standards within 20 years. In 1992, a test was given that established each school's starting point. Each 2-year period, each school had to improve 10% of the distance to 100% at or above proficiency to qualify for the performance award. For example, if a school had 20% of its students at proficiency in 1991, it would need to increase that percentage by 8 percentage points (10% times 80% remaining) to a total of 28% to be eligible for the next biennial performance award. In the next biennium, their target would be 28% plus 8%, or 36%. This strategy has the twin advantages of including both an absolute target of high performance and changes over time. Over the 6-year history of the program, performance gains were most evident and consistent at the elementary and high school levels, and in middle school in mathematics. Although there were both gains and declines in the scores over time, the overall trend was for fairly sizable increases in student performance (Poggio, 2000). Teachers working in reward schools recognized that the performance goals were getting more and more difficult to achieve, but they still felt that the goals were attainable (Kelley et al., 2000).

The formula Kentucky used to determine the percentage at proficiency was somewhat more complex. Student performances were scored at four levels: novice, apprentice, proficient, and distinguished. Schools were given credit for student performance at each level, as follows: zero for each student scoring at the novice level, 0.4 for each student scoring at the apprentice level, 1 point for each proficient student, and 1.4 points for each student scoring at the distinguished level. The distinguished level was also considerably above the proficient level and so represented a substantially higher level of performance. We should also note that although this approach included the scores of students along the full range of performance, which we recommend, there was a fairly wide range of achievement in the novice level. Some in Kentucky expressed concern that students at the low end of the novice level could improve substantially but still not to the apprentice level and that their improvement would not be captured in the current scoring structure. An additional level—or two or three—could be added to capture this improvement.

A variation on the improvement to standard model is the *relative improvement* model, in which rewards are paid if schools meet a growth standard, such as a 3% improvement over prior year scores. An advantage of this approach is that standards do not need to be developed as long as there are reliable measures. An important drawback is that the system is unfair to already high-performing schools.

An important question in determining how to calculate the performance benchmark is whether a simpler calculation, such as the one used in Kentucky, is sufficient or whether more complex statistical manipulations should be used. The private sector has tried both approaches (Heneman, 1992). Most would argue for a simpler approach to enhance the possibility that all teachers understand what is in the performance index and thus have a better understanding of what to emphasize to qualify for the award. But simpler measures ignore many adjustments that the more complicated statistical calculations make, which many argue are necessary for the measure to be fair. Both South Carolina and Dallas, Texas, make sophisticated and complex calculations, adjusting for race, poverty, and other biases (Clotfelter & Ladd, 1996).

The approach used in Dallas is an example of the second conceptual model, the *value-added* model, in which the same students are tested in period 1 and period 2, and the scores are compared. Typically, the actual scores in each time period are not compared directly. Rather, a regression analysis is applied to the scores in the first period to determine what scores would be expected in the second period given the makeup of the student population. The actual performance in the second period is compared to the expected performance in that period in order to determine how much more achievement was produced than was expected. The gain is then used as the measure of school performance, and schools that produce a substantial gain in average achievement are then rewarded.

The value-added model has a number of advantages. It is fair to schools with students at lower initial achievement levels. And because the performance of a single group of students is being tracked over time, the value-added approach avoids problems inherent in comparing the performance of different groups of students over time.

The value-added model also has a number of important limitations. Student mobility causes considerable problems with the model because students that move cannot be adequately tracked over time. It can be more costly and time consuming because students must be tested frequently to measure performance gains. Students must be tracked across schools or they will be lost from the comparison base. This demands sophisticated student information systems with capabilities beyond what many districts possess at present. Furthermore, the statistical and measurement technicalities that, in large part, contribute to the advantages of the value-added model may be beyond the capacity of many districts and are likely to make it difficult for stakeholders to understand the system.

On balance, we suggest a less statistically sophisticated approach, but we recognize the merits of the arguments for the more complex approach, and if such an approach is taken, recommend strong consideration of the value-added model now used in North Carolina (Johnson et al., 1999). We are aware that many educators and policymakers in Kentucky would take issue with our calling their approach simple or understandable. The distinction we make is that the Kentucky approach used simple arithmetic to calculate the school score, whereas the Dallas approach uses very complex regression analyses that adjust for several socioeconomic variables. Although the Dallas approach is more complex statistically, neither program uses just a simple change measure, and such an approach would probably be too simplistic and might even be viewed as unfair.

Making the Calculation Fair

For a group-based performance award to be motivating, teachers must view the performance measure as fair. This means that teachers in a variety of school settings, with students from a variety of backgrounds, must view the measure as providing them with an equal chance to earn the award. As we suggest below, having teachers centrally involved in developing the entire performance award program can strengthen the perception of fairness.

To achieve additional aspects of fairness, controls or adjustments need to be made to ensure that the calculations of change in achievement are providing accurate measures, neither too generous nor too conservative, and that it is neither easier nor harder for some schools to succeed. In addition, a fair system minimizes the incentive for a school to reduce the educational opportunities for some groups of students, to improve the scores of other students, and thereby achieve a performance award. This is also what some have referred to as "gaming the system."

School-based performance award programs often include features designed to address fairness and gaming issues, including ways of addressing potential problems associated with the following:

* ❖　Student mobility

* ❖　Inclusion of special education and limited-English-proficient (LEP) students who might not be able to be tested using the regular assessment methods

* ❖　Students in the lower portion of the achievement distribution whom a school might discourage from taking the tests so that they won't bring down the overall achievement level

With respect to student mobility, the issue is how to treat the scores of students who may start school in one site but end it in another, that is, who do not attend school in one site over the duration of the performance award period. One approach is to ignore this problem. The signal is that all schools need to work hard to educate mobile students. With common statewide standards, this is a more feasible approach. But it certainly makes qualifying for a performance award harder for sites that have large numbers of students who end the performance award period in the site but do not start the period at that site.

An alternative approach is to set a minimum number of days that students must be enrolled to be included in the accountability calculations. This approach has been used by a number of states and districts and has the advantage that teachers are not held accountable for the performance of students from other schools or districts.

With respect to special education students, the program should be designed to encourage teachers to focus adequate time and energy on improving the performance of special education as well as regular education students. One approach—which has been tried in some places—is simply to exempt the scores of all disabled students. But this creates a disincentive for teachers to focus on improving the learning of these students. We suggest that the scores of learning-disabled students, who constitute the bulk of special education students, should be required in the performance measure and that appropriate accommodations be made. More severely disabled students could be assessed according to the provisions of their Individual Education Plan.

For limited-English-proficient students, again, some programs simply eliminate the scores of these students, but that seems ill-advised. One approach could be to allow their better score in an English-language-based examination or an examination in their native language. The problem is that few states or districts have sufficient assessments in the native language of all their students. Another approach would be to allow districts to exclude LEP students for a certain number of years and then require that they be included, but this has the downsides of any exemption policy.

To prevent schools from discouraging low-achieving students from taking the test, the percentage of students tested can be included as a performance measure. And to ensure that schools work toward improvement of even the lowest-performing students, schools can be required to reduce the percentage of students in the lowest-performance category in addition to improving overall performance. Alternatively, schools could be required to improve the performance of students across all levels of the performance distribution. These types of measures also help to prevent schools from gaming the system to achieve the award.

Finally, states and districts need to set rules on attendance and promotion. One way to improve test scores without improving instruction is to encourage the lower-achieving students to be absent on the days the tests are given or to hold back lower-performing students and not promote them to the next grade. We know the latter policy is ineffective in producing achievement over time (Shephard & Smith, 1989), and the former is just manipulating scores for any 1 day or set of days. These approaches could be curtailed by requiring that the school could qualify only if a high percentage of students took the test, even 100%. If the test were given at a certain grade level, such as grade 4 or 5, there could also be a requirement that the entire cohort of students who began school in a certain year would have to take the test for the school to qualify.

Setting Achievement Targets

Setting achievement or improvement targets may be one of the most subjective decisions in designing a group-based performance award, but it is also one of the most important decisions. The motivation of teachers and principals depends, in part, on setting challenging but achievable targets. This argues for setting achievement goals at a level that stakeholders view as doable yet high enough that student achievement will noticeably improve.

Factors to consider in establishing reasonable targets include considerations such as historic student achievement trends, the expected availability of support systems to facilitate improvements in student achievement, and political or external considerations. For example, the size of the gain expected may be a function of the extent to which other resources—standards, professional development, site-based management—are available to the school for achieving performance targets. Alternatively, a district with historically low student achievement levels and few success stories might set a relatively low target to enhance early success and thereby stimulate motivation to improve.

The minimum improvement also should exceed measurement error for the school as a whole. If not, then qualification for the award could be due simply to measurement error and not real improvements on the part of students.

Improvements of between 2 and 4 percentile points may be a reasonable target to start with. Because the designs we recommend are based on performance improvement, a relatively small annual percentage increase in any 1 year can result in high levels of performance gain over time.

Setting Levels and Types of Awards

One important aspect of a performance bonus is that it should be a bonus for performance during some specified time period rather than an addition to base salary. Too many organizations have an annual performance review and add the financial reward to the person's base salary. As a result, the person is rewarded every year thereafter for the quality of work performed in a single year. Although workers often prefer this approach because they are rewarded perpetually for one-time performance, the cost to the organization can far exceed the benefits, and the workers reaping the rewards may not be those currently contributing most to organizational performance. Indeed, research shows that in organizations that add annual performance awards to base salary, the people with the highest total salaries are those with the most years of experience, not necessarily those most productive in any given year (Lawler, 1990).

The core idea behind a performance award is to provide a bonus for performance during a specified time period. For this idea to work, the award must be re-earned for each time period it is provided. For example, a school system might provide a performance award for schools that produced predetermined improvements in student achievement, say, at the fourth- or fifth-grade level, over a single year. But because a new cohort of students would be at this grade level each year, it would make sense to provide the award as a bonus so that it must be earned for each new group of students.

As will be discussed, the size of the performance award need not be large. A performance award is as symbolic as it is economically rewarding. It functions as a formal system symbol for producing better results over some time period. But, to motivate improved performance each time period, it must be re-earned each time it is offered and thus must be provided as a bonus.

The Size of the Bonus

When determining the size of the bonus, a general guideline in the field has been that the level of the award must be strong enough to provide an economic incentive for improved performance. The actual value of the performance award varies considerably, both in private industry and in the first generation of performance award programs in education. In private industry, on average, gain-sharing and profit-sharing bonuses were about 9% of base salary from 1980 to 1985 (O'Dell, 1987). In education, bonuses have ranged from a low of about $750 to a high of $25,000 per teacher for performance improvement.

Research in education and other sectors suggests that smaller bonuses may be preferable because large bonuses (set at 30% to 50% of annual salary) provide significant incentives for gaming and neglecting important but unrewarded educational goals. Recent experience with California's bonus program, which provides $25,000 bonuses to each teacher in a school, bears this out. California policymakers have expressed concerns that some schools may be gaming the system to reap this large reward (Sandham, 2001). Recent research suggests that smaller performance awards could be very effective in organizations that provide for substantial employee involvement, which we argued in Chapter 4 was motivating for teachers. In fact, this research suggests that when a performance award is used in conjunction with a decentralized management system that substantially involves workers in designing the nature of work tasks as well as managing the overall operation, performance objectives can be achieved with a relatively small award—in education, the equivalent of $1,000 to $2,000 per teacher (McAdams, 1995).

Research on districts that have implemented school-based performance awards suggests that bonuses in the range of $2,000 are probably sufficient. The actual amount depends on the cost of living, the base compensation conditions, and the difficulty of the goals. Thus we suggest that districts begin designing performance awards at this general level. As shown below, such awards could be financed with a 2% budget set-aside.

To avoid rewarding improvement targets that might be too conservative, two to three levels of rewards might be possible. The first might be a modest but meaningful bonus, such as $1,000 per teacher, based on accomplishing an improvement threshold—just above measurement error. A second or third level could be achieved if the school exceeded its improvement target by additional percentages. For example, if a school had been targeted to increase the percentage of students achieving at the proficient level by 2 percentage points in a particular time period, the first level of payout could be achieved if that 2-point increase were met over that time period. A second level of payout could be achieved if, say, there was a 4-percentage-point gain, and an even higher level if there were a 6-percentage-point gain. The second- and third-level payouts should be larger because they represent a substantial accomplishment beyond what had been minimally targeted. States or districts could set the payouts at $1,000, $2,000, and $3,000 per teacher. Such a strategy would allow the program to reward a higher percentage of schools.

Research on performance award programs in Kentucky and Charlotte-Mecklenburg suggests that program designs that provide awards to a substantial percentage of schools are more motivating to teachers. Teachers in schools that had received awards in the past were more likely to believe that they could achieve the award in the future, and to be motivated to change their teaching practice to achieve program goals (Kelley et al., 2000).

Establishing a Bonus Pool

In the past, performance pay in education has suffered from a number of fatal flaws, one of which is a lack of consistent funding. Most teachers are skeptical about the notion of a performance award. At first, they often assume it will represent just another round of divisive individual merit pay. But when performance pay is designed to reward groups, skepticism centers on whether the funding will be sufficient or long-term. This skepticism is well-earned in education, because performance award funding has often been insufficient and been cut after the first few years.

For example, before Kentucky implemented the performance award in 1995 that we describe below, it had previously promised teachers a $300 bonus for improving results. But that bonus was never funded. In field research on impacts of the current program, we discovered that teachers were skeptical about the current program until they actually received their bonus checks. They simply did not believe the state would actually fund the program and distribute the awards; even after the first years of the program when all bonuses were paid, only about half of the teachers had confidence that the state would continue to come through with the award if school performance improved.

States and districts can ruin for years the motivating potential of a well-designed performance award by insufficiently funding the program or by cutting funding prematurely. In other words, for a performance award to stimulate, motivate, or reward teachers for delivering better student achievement results, it must be anchored by a sufficient, stable, and long-term funding base.

A sufficient funding base is one that is large enough to provide the performance award to all individuals in all schools that qualify—that meet the benchmarks for improved performance. Initially, that might mean that the funding pool should include enough money to reward all schools, if need be. With knowledge gathered over time, a state or district might be able to predict accurately the percentage of schools that would qualify and thus could reduce the overall funding pool. But there would still need to be some type of contingency funding in the event that more schools than predicted qualified. A better option, as we suggest below, would be to maintain the full funding pool but add a second tier, or subschool team award, to the schoolwide award.

A common approach to funding performance awards is to budget a fixed pool of money and let the value of the performance award vary depending on the number of schools, and total number of individuals in schools, that qualify. Another approach is to budget a fixed pool of money and a fixed amount of the award and award schools in decreasing order of improvement reached until the budget pool is exhausted. The advantage of both approaches is that the funding amount is predictable and fixed. The problem with both approaches is that they can undercut the influence of the performance award. As to the former, if individuals are working toward a bonus of, say, $1,000 per teacher, but twice as many schools qualify, and the bonus amount is reduced to $500, the economic worth and incentive power of the bonus is eroded. As to the latter, if a school meets improvement targets but is not rewarded because the bonus pool is not large enough, the motivating force of the program is undercut. In both cases, teachers lose trust in the system and may lose motivation in future cycles.

The reason a set pool of dollars is budgeted for performance awards—and then eliminated after a few short years—is that districts and states rarely view performance awards as permanent aspects of education funding. These awards have been viewed as extras; the rhetoric surrounding initial enactment is robust, but the programs are essentially add-ons. For a performance award to work, it needs to be considered a long-term—if not permanent—aspect of the education program and of funding as well. This means that funding for performance awards needs to be built into the general funding and budgeting systems of states or local school districts.

We suggest the following. The pool for performance awards could be set as a fixed percentage of the budget. This percentage would be set aside each year for the performance award. An estimate could be made of the number of schools (and thus the number of persons) eligible. Given this estimate, the amount of the performance award could be determined.

For example, if a school district were spending $6,000 per pupil (about the current national average), a 2% set-aside for a performance award pool would equal $120 per pupil. Assuming a pupil-to-staff ratio of about 20:1, that would provide $2,400 per teacher or professional staff member, also assuming every school and thus every staff member qualified. If just half the schools qualified, the amount per teacher would double to $4,800, which could be divided between threshold, average, and maximum awards of $1,200, $2,400, and $3,600, respectively, per teacher. As we argued above, such bonus levels would be sufficient to function as a performance award in education.

In short, we suggest that the performance award pool be set at 2% of a district's overall education budget from both the general and special funds (but not including the capital fund). These dollars should be put into a special pot. In the first years, the level of the awards should be set in a way that would allow all teachers to earn them if they were in schools that met benchmarks for improved performance. Annual funds not used for bonuses (if not all schools qualified) could be spent for professional development or for other purposes geared to raising performance levels. Over time, the level of the award could be increased to a level that would be conservatively geared to the percentage of schools estimated to meet improvement targets each year, or additional elements could be added to the award structure.

This approach would provide both sufficient and long-term funding. Of course, at any time, a state legislature or school board could eliminate the performance award. But by financing the award pool with 2% of the budget, the money could easily be made available each year; it would provide sufficient funding for a meaningful award; and it would connote a long-term commitment to school improvement and the use of performance awards.

Philosophy Underlying Distribution of Funds

Different philosophies could guide the distribution of bonus funds. In all the examples given above, the philosophy was that each individual would be given an award of equal amount even if their base salaries differed. Another philosophy would be to link the performance award to the base salary, so that school members got a bonus equal to a certain percentage of their base pay. A lump sum distribution that is equivalent for all professional staff members, regardless of their base salary, would be based on the premise that differentiation of the value of the contribution is captured in the base pay portion of compensation. On the other hand, many organizations choose to deliver bonuses as a percentage of base salary. This also has a compelling logic. Particularly in a knowledge- and skills-based pay system, those with larger salaries will be those with greater depth and breadth of skills and thus, it could be argued, have more pivotal effects on school performance.

Nearly all programs in education have used the equal lump sum approach, and this seems to be the emerging practice in the private sector as well. This approach also can contribute to the cohesion of the team and reinforce its mutual problem-solving efforts. Indeed, in Dallas, one level of lump sum is provided to all professional staff members and another, at half the level, to all classified staff members. Some districts or states might want to experiment with a bonus equal to a percentage of base salary.

Enabling Conditions or Supports for the Program

Enabling conditions include teacher knowledge and skills, instructional methods and techniques, and the organizational conditions that help teachers improve student achievement. These include principal leadership, school-based management, program alignment, district support, professional development, feedback, and the presence of strong professional community.

Enabling conditions can play either or both of two roles to improve student achievement. They can facilitate by having a direct effect on student achievement through improved instruction. They can also have a motivational role in that they may positively influence teachers' expectations as to the likelihood that they will be able to meet the goals. The presence or absence of enabling conditions is a critical factor in the ability of schools to improve performance under group-based performance award programs.

Compensation program design decisions should be made in conjunction with a broader effort to align and focus organizational resources on helping teachers make the desired improvements in student achievement.

Evaluation

Because design decisions are so critical in determining the effects and effectiveness of group-based performance award programs, it is critical to incorporate formative evaluation in the program's design. Evaluation should examine both intended and unintended consequences of the program, and program administrators should be prepared to make changes in design, as necessary, to address problems as they arise. Some things that might need to be reviewed include unintended consequences (such as increased teacher turnover or specific groups of students ignored in the improvement process); whether the unintended consequences are perceived as good or bad; whether the design details are functioning as intended; whether teachers understand the program adequately; and whether program modifications are needed. In addition, the evaluation should review the program's impact on instruction and student achievement. An ongoing evaluation is also an effective means of showing the seriousness of the commitment to the program and ensuring accountability to stakeholders.

School Site Variation

As schools develop their own work designs, it is possible that they may want to develop a bonus distribution system tailored to their work design. In particular, if schools create subunits within the school whereby a defined group of teachers is responsible for the learning needs of a defined group of students, such as an ungraded primary classroom that teachers might have for 2 to 3 years, the school might want to allocate bonus monies partially on the basis of schoolwide performance and partially on the basis of the performance of each subunit. This decision could be made by the school council and might require approval from a majority of the staff members in the site.

In this case, the total bonus pool made available to the school would be determined by overall school performance. Part of the bonus could be paid on an equal basis to all staff members in the school, to reward and motivate schoolwide effort and collaboration. Another part could be paid to staff members in subunits that have exceeded the school target. This system should not put subunits in competition with one another, because schoolwide collaboration is important. Consequently, all successful subunits must be able to receive their performance bonus. The monies budgeted but not paid out to less successful subunits could be used for staff and team development activities aimed at increasing the performance levels of those units.

We recommend that performance awards to subschool units be a secondary objective and implemented after schoolwide performance awards are designed and implemented satisfactorily. The primary goal is to create a simple, straightforward, schoolwide performance award that works— that, in addition to other system strategies, encourages individuals in schools to work hard to improve student performance. Once states and districts have learned how to design and implement effective schoolwide programs, then creation of either second-tier or subschool unit additions could be attempted.

At the same time, we suggest experimentation with subschool performance awards in large high schools, either to houses in restructured high schools or departments in traditionally structured high schools. High schools tend to be large, and the line of sight between house or department membership and schoolwide performance might be too distant.

Again, any subschool award should be contingent on first meeting school-wide performance benchmarks.

Gradual Phase-In

Based on past failures of individual merit pay in education, school performance bonus systems could be met with considerable skepticism by educators and policymakers. We have outlined some of the issues that should be considered and resolved before educators and policymakers adopt such an approach. In the short term, the knowledge- and skills-based component of new pay systems might be given priority for implementation. Indeed, a school system might decide that its best prospects for increasing student learning is an approach that helps ensure a skilled teacher in every classroom. Indeed, there is precedent in the private sector for initially implementing just a knowledge- and skills-based pay approach to show how new skills and knowledge of workers can combine with redesigned work processes to improve organizational results. A subsequent introduction of school performance bonuses could then provide a renewed impetus for performance improvement, often several years after the initial implementation of the altered-base compensation system.

School performance bonus systems can be gradually phased in. During the first year, a minimal bonus could be made available, so that the stakes are not too great as teachers learn how the system works and begin to apply their collective talents to improving school performance. During the following year, the full sum could be made available, based solely on schoolwide performance. In subsequent years, schools could begin a two-component bonus system. Schools that already have a fully developed house or school-within-a-school system might want to begin with a two-component bonus system.

Examples of Performance Awards in Education

During the past 5 years, several states and local districts have been designing and implementing group- or school-based performance awards. The programs in Kentucky and South Carolina have existed for the longest periods of time; the former provides a salary bonus, whereas the awards in South Carolina can be used only for school improvement activities. The Charlotte-Mecklenburg, North Carolina, and Dallas, Texas, programs, which also provide a salary bonus, are the most well-known district-created performance award programs.

Kentucky

In 1989, the State Supreme Court of Kentucky ruled the Commonwealth's educational delivery system unconstitutional. At the time, the performance of students in Kentucky schools was among the worst in the country. In 1990, the state legislature responded by passing the Kentucky Education Reform Act (KERA), which redesigned Kentucky's educational system. Among the initiatives of KERA was the development of an assessment and accountability system (Adams, 1993; Steffy, 1993).

The state created a new performance assessment system—the Kentucky Instructional Results Information System (KIRIS). KIRIS tests students in mathematics, science, writing, language arts, and social studies in grades 4, 8, and 11. KIRIS scores are used as the anchor measure in the performance award program that is part of the accountability system (Kentucky Institute for Education Research, 1995).

Improvements in school performance were assessed based on an accountability index. The index was made up of six equal parts. Five were based on the results of reading, mathematics, social studies, science, and writing scores on KIRIS. Under KIRIS, student performance was rated from lowest to highest as novice, apprentice, proficient, or distinguished. The sixth component was a noncognitive composite score based on attendance, retention, dropout rates, and transition to adult life (Kentucky Department of Education, 1995). Because students were assessed in grades 4, 8, and 11, accountability was measured across cohorts of students rather than as longitudinal performance of a particular group of students. There were no adjustments for student mobility.

The improvement goal was school specific and was equal to one tenth of the difference between the 1991-1992 composite baseline score and a *proficient* rating, which was approximately equivalent to having a weighted average of students score at or above the proficient level. The rationale behind these interim goals was that they provide schools with a reasonable timeline for improvement and set high absolute goals for all schools. Because performance awards were awarded every biennium, the program was designed to provide incentives to bring each school's average performance to the proficient level within 20 years or less.

Every 2 years, schools that exceeded their performance improvement goals received a pool of funds that teachers could distribute as they saw fit.

By law, the funds could be used as salary bonuses, for professional development, or as school improvement funds. In 1994-1995, the awards amounted to about $2,000 per teacher in eligible schools, or a total appropriation of $26 million.

In the first year (1994-1995), 38%, or a total of 480 Kentucky schools, received bonus awards (Harp, 1995). The results at the school level were mixed. At some schools, the question of how to allocate the award money resulted in intense debates over who should get the money. However, many schools found creative ways to use the money to reward a variety of school employees and even to provide incentives and rewards to students for their efforts on the assessments. A case is available on the CPRE Web site (www.wcer.wisc.edu/cpre/tcomp/research/sbpa).

In 1998, public pressure to modify the program led the legislature to vote to replace KIRIS with a new testing and accountability system called the Commonwealth Accountability Testing System (CATS) (White, 1998). CATS includes a new assessment and an attenuated rewards and sanctions program. After a protracted debate, the state decided to continue to allow schools to use reward money for teacher salary bonuses if they so desired.

South Carolina

The South Carolina School Incentive Reward Program (SIRP) was the longest-running state-sponsored, group-based, performance pay plan in the nation. The SIRP was established with the passage of the Educational Improvement Act of 1984, signed into law by then Governor Richard Riley, who became U.S. Secretary of Education in the Bill Clinton presidential administration. In 1998, the state adopted a new performance accountability law; the program has been suspended since that time.

The SIRP awarded approximately 25% of schools with performance bonuses for meeting student-achievement gain goals and for maintaining high levels of student and teacher attendance. Schools had to meet the student achievement criteria to be awarded 80% of the full award for that year; an additional 10% each was awarded to winning schools who maintain teacher and student attendance at or above 96% (Richards & Sheu, 1992).

The reward program placed schools in one of five comparison bands based on four criteria: percentage of students receiving free lunches; percentage receiving reduced-price lunches; average teachers' years of education beyond the bachelor's degree; and percentage of students meeting or exceeding the readiness standard on the Cognitive Skills Assessment

Battery, a test given in all elementary schools. Schools competed with other schools in the same band for awards, and the SIRP rewarded *improvement* in student test scores rather than absolute levels of achievement (Richards & Sheu, 1992).

Award monies from the program were to be used for instructional purposes by the winning schools; awards could not be used for direct payments to teachers. To date, approximate awards of $25 to $40 per pupil have been distributed annually to winning schools, with the typical school receiving from $15,000 to $20,000.

South Carolina's banding system was found to provide a more equitable distribution of funds across schools with very different student socioeconomic (primarily poverty) levels than if the bands were not in place (Richards & Sheu, 1992). However, because the banding system set lower expectations for schools serving lower-SES populations of students, it was also vulnerable to challenges of possible racial bias because high-poverty schools tend also to be high-minority schools.

Dallas

The key component of the Dallas teacher compensation innovation is a school-based performance award that is part of the district's accountability system. A 1990 commission, with substantial representation of the business community, created the system. The performance measure was primarily based on the results of the Texas Assessment of Academic Skills, a criterion-referenced test covering five subject areas, and the Iowa Test of Basic Skills, which is a norm-referenced, standardized achievement test. The weights for each test varied annually. These tests also provided scores for subtopics within each subject area; these subscores were also used and given varying weights. The award was based on gain scores, aggregated to the school level from individual student data. The school gain score was the average gain for each student, which provided an incentive to improve the performance of every student. Each student's gain score was her or his actual score in a given year, minus the predicted score. Through complex, two-stage regression analysis, the predicted score was purged of the influence of any socioeconomic variables including ethnicity, English proficiency, school mobility, poverty status, overcrowding, and a student's race. These achievement gains were supplemented by schoolwide measures of student attendance, grade-to-grade promotion, dropout rates, enrollments in accelerated courses, and SAT and PSAT scores in secondary schools (Clotfelter & Ladd, 1996).

Schools' final-performance gain scores were then ranked from highest to lowest. For the first few years, each principal and teacher in winning schools received a bonus of $1,000, and the nonprofessional staff members received a bonus of $500 each. In addition, the school itself was provided with $2,000.

A fixed fund of money was budgeted for the awards. Awards were provided to staffs and schools by rank order until the budgeted amount was expended. Each year, the number of schools actually receiving bonuses varied, which meant that some schools that produced significant improvements did not qualify for the bonus.

Beginning in 1994-1995, Dallas created a second tier of winners, in which the bonuses were $450 for the professionals and $225 for the nonprofessional staff members. The goal was to provide some level of incentive to the lower-ranked but still-improving schools.

The system initially was funded with contributions from the business community. Today, however, the program is fully funded with dollars from the district's regular budget. A case is available on the CPRE Web site (www.wcer.wisc.edu/cpre/tcomp/research/sbpa).

Charlotte-Mecklenburg

The Charlotte-Mecklenburg program is similar in many ways to the Dallas program. It has evolved considerably since its inception in 1992-1993. In the initial development of the program, first, content standards were developed for the core subjects—language arts, writing, mathematics, science, and social studies; the standards were quite detailed, covering each subject and its subtopics for each grade level. Second, diagnostic tests were developed to allow teachers to gather information at the beginning and throughout the school year on the achievement status of each student. Third, teachers were then trained extensively in how to use the results of the diagnoses to plan curriculum and instructional strategies.

State tests in these content areas were used to determine whether schools qualified for the performance award. The state tested each student in each grade level in each of these subject areas. The performance award was provided on the basis of improvements in schoolwide performance. After the initial scores were compiled in the base year, about 1993, the district set a 5-year target for improvement. The goal was to have each school meet the target over a 5-year period. Schools scoring low in the base year had greater improvements to make. Each year, schools were required to improve 20% of their gap between their starting position and the 5-year goal. Gains were calculated for each individual student and summed across the school to determine schoolwide gains. Schools that had mobile students for at least 100 days during the year included those students' performance in their schoolwide scores. Separate targets were developed for white and African American students, a controversial element but one designed to accommodate the large, different starting positions for these groups of students. Schools that achieved 80% of their improvement targets qualified for the award. The award was a $1,000 bonus for all professional staff members in the school and about $300 to $400 for each classified staff member.

In addition, principals were evaluated on the basis of results. The core elements of their evaluation were whether the school met their improvement targets (qualified for the performance award) and teacher, parent, and student attitudes about the teaching and learning environment. If principals received a satisfactory evaluation, they were not evaluated for 2 years, as long as their school learning gains continued. Principals with unsatisfactory evaluations had to design improvement plans for deficient areas; if improvements were not made within 2 years, they were replaced.

In 1996-1997, North Carolina implemented a statewide performance pay plan that was similar to the existing Charlotte-Mecklenburg program. Some differences between the state and district programs led to concerns about the plethora of different goals that teachers were striving to achieve. Some examples of differences between the two programs included inconsistencies in the level of performance improvement required for reward and differences in scoring. Generally, the state-level goals were somewhat lower than the district goals.

As a result, in 1997-1998, Charlotte-Mecklenburg decided to align its program with the state program. The new program provides additional salary bonuses to teachers in schools eligible for the state awards. The district's commitment to align with the state program means that it will continue to refine the program as the state makes adjustments in its program over time.

In addition to the bonus for staff members in schools that meet the state's goals, Charlotte-Mecklenburg has instituted other pay incentives for teachers to teach in priority schools, which include schools experiencing low levels of student achievement, high principal and teacher turnover, high student mobility, or other risk factors. These incentives are discussed further in Chapter 8. Today, however, the program is fully funded with dollars from the district's regular budget. A case is available on the CPRE Web site (www.wcer.wisc.edu/cpre/tcomp/research/sbpa).

Maryland

The Maryland School Performance Program (MSPP) is a state-sponsored, school-based performance assessment and accountability program that was established following the recommendations of a state commission in 1989. In 1996, a monetary bonus was added for schools showing significant and sustained improvement on the elementary and middle school assessment.

A School Performance Index (SPI) was developed by the Maryland State Department of Education to measure school progress on state standards from a baseline 2-year average. Data generated by the SPI and other performance indicators are used to inform the public, for school improvement, and to gauge statewide progress toward education standards. Each school's or system's performance is measured against its own growth (Maryland State Department of Education, 1997). SPI is the weighted average of a school's relative distance from satisfactory standards for attendance rates and student performance on two test batteries.

Elementary school performance is assessed by MSPAP, a performance-based test that requires students to apply critical thinking skills and integration of knowledge both individually and in groups. Not only is MSPAP intended to monitor school performance, but it is also specifically designed to generate focused instructional change (Koretz, Barron, Mitchell, & Stecher, 1996; Yen & Ferrara, 1997).

Middle school performance is assessed based on both MSPAP performance and performance on the Maryland Function Tests, which are basic skills tests measuring competencies in reading, mathematics, writing, and citizenship. Passage of the Maryland Functional Test is required for graduation from high school.

The Maryland Rewards for Success program provides monetary awards to recognize elementary and middle schools that have made "substantial and sustained" or statistically significant progress on the SPI over 2 years. Funds are paid to improving schools and not necessarily to high-achieving schools where scores may have leveled off. School Improvement Teams are the recipients of the awards and have flexibility in using the funding to build on educational success, but they may not use the award for salaries. The number of eligible schools and the number of students in the award school determine award sizes. In 1998, 83 elementary and middle schools received monetary awards with sizes ranging from $15,740 to $64,605. Since the first award allocation in 1996, a total of $8.25 million has been disbursed as monetary awards.

Schools may also be eligible for performance certificates. These non-monetary recognition certificates are awarded to schools that show 1 year of significant improvement. Schools that receive a certificate and continue significant improvements as defined by the state the following year are eligible for a monetary award.

The Maryland program acts as more of a reward than an incentive program, because the legislature allocates funding for the rewards after the reward cycle has ended. Field research on the Maryland program suggests that the program has a more significant impact on principal motivation; teachers are somewhat less aware of the existence and details of the award (Kelley et al., 2000).

Issues and Recommendations
for Second-Generation Programs

The 1990s versions of performance bonuses, represented by the above examples, avoid the individual focus of merit pay and focus instead on reinforcing collaborative relationships and teamwork through group- or school-based performance awards. This constitutes a major step forward on the performance award front.

So far, all five programs provided both sufficient and long-term funding, although the level in South Carolina was somewhat below the level we recommend. In addition, funds in South Carolina and Maryland were used only for school improvement and not salary bonuses. We recommend allowing the award to be used as a salary bonus for teachers instead of just for school improvement activities. Comparative research in Maryland and Kentucky suggest that the motivational force of pay bonuses is stronger on teachers than school improvement funds (Kelley et al., 2000). Additional comparative research over time is needed to confirm these findings.

One of the most difficult features in designing performance pay plans is developing an appropriate performance measure. The creation of performance award systems brings with it opportunities to carefully design an appropriate assessment instrument; however, there are also large start-up costs and kinks to be worked out of the new system. In these examples, the state or district used both existing tests (in South Carolina, Charlotte-Mecklenburg, and Dallas) and newly created tests (in Kentucky and Maryland). Use of an existing assessment system carries with it risks that the assessment may not have been designed to be a high-stakes assessment, raising questions about the validity and focus of the instrument as the anchor element of a performance award, although ambitious instruction is not at odds with high scores on standard achievement tests (Newmann et al., 2001). Even though Kentucky and Maryland created new tests, they were created as much to provide new kinds of results for more advanced student achievement as for a measure designed for a performance award. Creating new performance assessments is technically complex; questions have been raised about the technical properties of the Kentucky test and about the practice of using teacher-scored student results in a performance award for those teachers (Kentucky Institute for Education Research, 1995). Ultimately, these questions and challenges led Kentucky to toss out their assessment in favor of a newly designed and more legally defensible assessment.

All five examples use improvements in performance as the basis of the final performance index, which is the appropriate strategy. The programs also have made various adjustments to account for bias caused by factors outside the control of local schools; these and other adjustments need to be analyzed over time to determine what are the best approaches for eliminating such bias. Both Kentucky and Charlotte-Mecklenburg (the initial district program) computed each school's performance gain score both relative to past performance and as an absolute standard. Thus schools scoring the lowest initially have the largest gains to produce each year. By incorporating both a change and an absolute standard, this strategy seeks to hold all students and schools eventually to the same high-achievement standard.

The plans also take different approaches to comprehensibility. The complicated banding and statistical adjustments in South Carolina and Dallas, undertaken to eliminate SES bias, also make the performance index difficult to fully understand. But even in Kentucky, Charlotte-Mecklenburg, and Maryland, which use a simpler approach, the performance index is the product of numerous variables, all with different weights, which has led many to say it also is hard to understand. North Carolina uses a value-added approach but makes no adjustments for income and race, thus setting the same goal over time for all students. The fact is that there will be some complexity even in a "simple" performance measure if it includes changes in achievement in several subject areas as well as nonachievement areas, with each variable weighted differently.

Another important assessment issue is which students will be assessed to determine performance levels and performance improvement. South Carolina, Charlotte-Mecklenburg, and Dallas use the scores of all students in a school, but Kentucky and Maryland use the scores of students in a limited number of grade levels (i.e., 4th grade for elementary schools, 8th grade for middle schools, and 11th grade for high schools). When the scores of students in only one grade constitute the overall school performance score, the internal message erroneously may be that only teachers at those grade levels produce the student achievement.

Finally, these examples take different approaches in deciding who or what gets the benefit of the performance award. In South Carolina and Maryland, the bonus can be used only for school improvement activities; this approach assumes that base salary and intrinsic motivation are sufficient for teachers to produce higher and higher results. We believe that a salary bonus would make the program stronger.

In Dallas and Charlotte-Mecklenburg, the programs provide a bonus to all professional staff members and a bonus at about half the amount to all classified staff members; Dallas also provides a bonus to the school as well. This all-inclusive strategy seems to have strong support at the school level; it recognizes that everyone in a school—teachers, administrators, support staff members, and students—must work to produce greater results. In Kentucky, teachers decide how the performance award will be used—whether for school improvement activities, the student activity fund, or for salary bonuses—and who will receive those bonuses. Although this stipulation follows a tenet of social dilemma theory for reducing the shirker problem, anecdotal evidence suggests that this has been a difficult issue to resolve in many schools. Furthermore, teachers decided to use the vast bulk of the dollars for a salary bonus.

We suggest that performance award plans stipulate in advance how the monies can be used. Unlike the current practice in Kentucky, and like the policies in Dallas and Charlotte-Mecklenburg, salary bonuses should, we suggest, be provided to all professional staff members at one level and to all support staff members at another level (probably 50% of the professional level); and some funds should also be provided to the student activity fund. But states and districts need to experiment with alternative structures to see which ones work the best in which different school contexts.

Although these examples have many attractive features, we are not suggesting they are perfect. Although generally strong on some technical factors, they fall short of the process principles we suggest in Chapter 7 for developing new compensation systems. Furthermore, many take significant issue with various features of the above programs, such as the basic-skills focus on the South Carolina tests, the reliability of the Kentucky test, the different gain scores for white and African American students in the initial Charlotte-Mecklenburg program, and the complicated statistical manipulations of the Dallas and the North Carolina performance index calculation. Nevertheless, the above examples represent significant advances from the old merit award programs, and research over time should identify more of their strengths and weaknesses as well as whether they actually contribute to higher school performance.

Gain-Sharing Programs

Currently, the emphasis and pressing need in nearly all districts and states is to improve student achievement. If a bonus system were to be implemented, it would be sensible, as discussed above, to concentrate on achievement outcomes as the outcome worth a bonus. However, cost containment may become of equal importance as school systems are required to improve performance with stable or declining resources. At some point, it may be wise to make a transition to an explicit gain-sharing plan where teachers are rewarded for the cost savings experienced while increasing performance, with a stable or shrinking school budget. In the meantime, the fact that many school districts are encountering severe resource pressures means that bonus systems targeted on school performance are de facto gain-sharing plans.

The core notion of gain sharing is to have work groups—usually schools, but the group could also be a subschool team—not only improve results but also cut costs as well. Three key issues need to be addressed before any type of gain-sharing plan is implemented. The first is the performance measure. The earlier sections of this chapter discussed this issue at length; a gain-sharing program would need to have the same care taken in creating a performance measure. A gain-sharing program also needs to indicate the level of improvement required for a school to qualify for a financial reward if the other component—cost savings—of the gain-sharing program were also met.

Second, there needs to be a baseline measurement of costs that would serve as the comparative benchmark for whether costs have actually been reduced. Both the methodology for calculating the costs and the prices attached to each ingredient in the cost structure would need to be clearly delineated. In addition, there would need to be agreement on whether the cost basis would be inflation-adjusted each year, to determine whether cost reductions have been produced or whether cost reductions have to be made over and above inflation. Furthermore, agreement would need to be made on the categories of costs that would be included in the gain-sharing plan; the goal could be to reduce overall school costs or just portions of school costs, such as utility expenses, specialist expenses, sick leave, and so forth.

Finally, the district and site would need to agree on the portion of the savings that would be retained by the site and the purposes for which such funds could be used. Many private-sector organizations split the costs on a fifty-fifty basis. Because education expenditures are controlled by the district budget, we recommend that school districts consider letting school sites retain all their cost savings. If, as we suggest below, use of all the dollars for a salary bonus seems too generous, a portion (we suggest a large portion) of the gain-sharing cost savings could be used for a salary bonus with the remainder used for school improvement activities, but at the school site that produced the savings. Finally, districts and sites will need to experiment on the motivational aspect of different uses of cost savings, whether for school improvement purposes or for salary bonuses.

We mentioned earlier that a district could include utility costs (telephones, electricity, and heating) in a gain-sharing program. These are small elements of the budget, but careful planning at the site can make significant savings. Because none of these costs include a salary element, it might be appropriate to restrict use of any cost savings to schoolwide improvement purposes. However, a salary element could provide a strong incentive.

If a gain-sharing program included what had been substitute teacher costs, one could argue that the savings could be provided in a salary bonus. A major way to reduce substitute teacher costs is to have teachers in the schools develop different ways of structuring the teaching and learning tasks to reduce the need for substitute teachers. But this usually means site teachers are working harder or smarter, thus making it logical to allow use of cost savings for a salary bonus.

We also mentioned strategies for having some high school classes be quite large and taught by teachers who give excellent lectures. This would reduce costs. Although such a program might also need to be augmented by smaller seminars, faculties could potentially reduce costs with a mixture of small and large classes. Again, because these cost reductions were made by the reorganization of the teaching and learning processes, use of the dollars saved for a salary bonus would make sense.

A third example is cases in which school faculty decided to use salary money to purchase computer technologies to replace some functions now provided by people. Such a strategy would probably be phased in gradually, often when teachers either retire or leave the school for a variety of natural reasons. Each teacher vacancy would present a school seriously considering a restructuring strategy with an opportunity to decide whether they wanted to use the salary and benefits dollars to hire another teacher or to begin a transition to a more technologically infused school in which more technology and fewer people were used to provide instructional services. If such a strategy were chosen, cost reductions could be produced over the medium term, after the initial outlay for computer equipment. Because those saved dollars would derive from savings in the salary budget, use of them for a salary bonus again becomes a logical consequence.

We should note that we are making several suggestions to allow gain-sharing plans to provide teacher salary bonuses. On the one hand, this might strike some members of the public, the board, the administration, and others as unnecessary—regular teacher salaries pay for the ideas and energies of teachers. We suggest, however, that the point of a gain-sharing plan is to create a situation that makes it in the self-interest of teachers to identify strategies that both increase results *and* save dollars. If teachers do not benefit from the saved dollars, particularly if they work harder and smarter in the process, there is no extrinsic self-interest element in the program. We would also note that gain-sharing plans fund teacher salary bonuses with no extra money; dollars saved fund the bonuses. In a sense, this provides a bonus at no cost! Finally, we note that one goal of restructuring schools for high performance and restructuring teacher salary structures as part of that process is to raise the average levels of teacher compensation. Both performance awards and gain-sharing bonuses contribute to this latter goal, the latter without even increasing the district budget.

In short, we hope that the idea of a gain-sharing program and the ability to use the dollars saved for a teacher bonus would be viewed as a positive element for the education system. As we have indicated, we recommend that districts or states first implement competency-based pay plans to signal that an array of new competencies is needed and to provide a salary reward to teachers who develop them. We then suggest adding a group-based performance award for producing improvements in valued educational results. As noted, such an award would be in the $1,000 to $2,000 range per professional staff member. Only after implementing these two compensation changes would we recommend adding a gain-sharing program, which essentially puts an explicit cost reduction focus into the restructuring matrix.

Conclusions

The primary need for the education system is to produce higher student learning and achievement, and we believe the key to that is increasing teacher expertise to be able to teach a high-standards curriculum well to a diverse student body. Knowledge- and skills-based pay provides an incentive for this system element. We believe that a performance award, at a small level, and particularly when combined with real, site-based decision making and restructuring (Newmann & Wehlage, 1995; Odden, Wohlstetter, & Odden, 1995), will also strengthen the focus on improving student achievement results.

The bottom-line question about any educational policy intervention is how does it affect student performance? Overall, the evidence suggests that school-based performance award programs do improve student performance. Students in Kentucky; Dallas, Texas; North Carolina; and Douglas County, Colorado (for example) have all shown improvements in performance following the implementation of school-based performance award programs (see www.wcer.wisc.edu/cpre/tcomp/research/sbpax; Milanowski, 1999; Poggio, 2000; Smith, Rothackerand, & Griffin, 1999). Performance improvement is most evident as measured by the assessment instruments and measures rewarded by the programs, and somewhat less evident using other measures (Klein, Hamilton, McCaffrey, & Stecher, 2000; Poggio, 2000).

Performance improves for at least three reasons. First, the program establishes clear instructional goals that teachers and students can work toward. Thus some improvement occurs as a result of familiarizing students with the assessment process and making sure that the curriculum content on the assessment is covered in the curriculum.

Second, teachers are motivated to encourage students to be motivated to do their best on the assessment. Strategies include invoking school pride, providing a positive test-taking atmosphere, making the test high stakes for students, and rewarding students for their efforts with prizes and parties after the exam.

Third, over time, teachers and administrators implement improvement strategies to meet program goals. These efforts involve both alignment and improvement of curriculum and instructional approaches and can include the following:

❖ Examining prior test scores and revising teaching practice to address areas of identified weakness

- ❖ Strategically aligning curriculum within and across grade levels with the standards and assessments
- ❖ Developing new curricular materials and instructional approaches
- ❖ Investing in professional development related to the goals of the assessment
- ❖ Collaborating with other teachers to improve performance (Kannapel, Coe, Aagaard, Moore, & Reeves, 2000; Kelley, 1998; Kelley & Protsik, 1997; Stecher & Barron, 1999)

Some researchers and practitioners have expressed concern that performance award programs overly narrow the curriculum and divert it from important instructional goals that are not assessed (Kannapel et al., 2000; King & Mathers, 1997; Poggio, 2000; Stecher & Barron, 1999). This also creates potential measurement problems in meaningfully assessing student learning. Most tests estimate student learning by sampling student knowledge. But if the curriculum is carefully aligned to the assessment, rather than representing a sampling of student work, the test may measure a narrow knowledge base developed solely to improve test performance rather than to achieve broader learning goals (Klein et al., 2000; Poggio, 2000). But as noted previously, recent research in Chicago suggests that ambitious teaching should produce gains on both narrower, multiple-choice, standardized achievement tests and performance assessments that assess deeper understanding (Newmann et al., 2001).

It is also worth noting that all these school-based performance award (SBPA) interventions were put in place in dynamic policy contexts, so there is no *pure* experiment to prove the effectiveness of SBPA programs. However, the evidence suggests that teachers working under SBPA programs do change their instructional practices to align them more closely with state learning and assessment goals (Kannapel et al., 2000; Kelley, 1998; Stecher & Barron, 1999).

Cautions

Compensation is not a blunt policy instrument. To be effective, pay systems must be designed carefully, with attention to the assessment instruments used to measure performance improvements, the level of goals established, and the support teachers have to modify instructional strategies in order to achieve program goals. When teachers are put under tremendous pressure to improve, without the resources needed to make the improvements, school-based performance award programs can destroy morale and warp educational objectives.

Teachers need to understand the goals, see them as achievable, feel supported in improvement efforts, and trust that the system will be carried out fairly so they will receive the promised rewards. Although school-based performance award programs can narrow the curriculum, they can also provide goal focus as well as data feedback loops that help teachers to evaluate and improve their own teaching practice. The experience of a number of first-generation programs suggests cautious optimism about the use of these programs. In conjunction with an overall policy strategy to support teachers in improving student performance, school-based performance pay can be effective.

Designing and Implementing Alternative Teacher Compensation Systems

7

Conceptualizing and designing better teacher compensation systems are difficult and are the subjects of the previous chapters. The development and implementation processes for new teacher compensation programs are also complex and are the topics of this chapter. Both research and anecdotal evidence in education and the private sector emphasize the imperative of giving attention to the entire process of development, implementation, and subsequent modification. One reason the entire process is important is that it is the key to building trust, and trust is a critical element in making new compensation systems work over the long haul.

After all, a new compensation structure means that the way people are paid will change. If given the choice, most workers—and probably teachers too—would prefer not to alter how they are paid. Changing compensation structures in a way that gains worker backing over time means convincing people to support something they might otherwise oppose. Trust between workers and managers certainly helps move such a process along.

Thus a process of development and implementation that slowly builds teacher commitment to a new compensation structure will probably be more successful if it can simultaneously build a high level of trust as well. Moreover, because no new compensation design is perfect at the beginning, companies—schools as well—need to make modifications to strengthen the strong points and eliminate or alter the elements that do not work. Trust also helps move forward this part of the implementation process so that short-term design defects don't scuttle the entire effort.

A core strategy for building trust is to involve all key parties—teachers, union leaders, administrators, the school board, parents, and the public—in the entire process. Although the *decision* to change compensation is largely a top-level management and system policy decision, that prerogative of the top stops immediately after the decision is made. From that point on, full involvement of all parties affected, mainly teachers and administrators, is crucial for making development and implementation work and for getting the intended impacts (Conti, 2000; Jenkins, Ledford, Gupta, & Doty, 1992; Milanowski, 2001; Zingheim & Schuster, 1995c).

In the policy brief we wrote for the Consortium for Policy Research in Education, we outlined several principles that should guide development, design, and implementation of new teacher compensation structures (Kelley & Odden, 1995). We include those principles in Resource B and urge districts and states to abide by them as they enter this tricky domain. Changing teacher compensation structures is like playing golf on a course with narrow fairways and small greens together with sand traps, doglegs, trees, and water hazards everywhere. Making mistakes is easy and shooting par is hard. Nevertheless, a solid round is possible. The principles in Resource B provide the broad framework for navigating the teacher compensation change process successfully.

The remainder of this chapter provides additional, more practical and focused guidance for those who have decided to embark on the journey to alter teacher pay systems. The next section summarizes how compensation needs to be linked to the education agenda and how the process of designing the new compensation system can actually function as a communication strategy on both the need for education reform and its key processes and end results. The section that follows suggests three specific activities school systems can deploy to begin the teacher compensation change process. The last section describes roles that different stakeholders in the education system—legislators, schools boards, administrators, unions and teachers, and the community—can play in changing teacher compensation.

Compensation and School Improvement

Teaching students to high performance standards is the key educational challenge of our time. Students need advanced cognitive expertise for effective civic and labor force participation. To meet this challenge, schools and education systems need to design new strategies to produce this higher level of performance. Just as most nonpublic organizations—service providing and product making—are struggling to improve quality, become more productive, and create a competitive edge, so also must schools redesign themselves to teach more students to high standards.

In Chapter 1, we outlined several of the key elements that have been evolving to accomplish this education challenge. They include rigorous curriculum content standards to guide the instructional program, new tests that indicate not only what students know but also what they can do, restructured governance and finance, and a professional development strategy to develop the skills and competencies teachers and schools need to accomplish these goals. We know that when schools put all these elements into place, student performance rises (Newmann & Wehlage, 1995; Pankratz & Petrosko, 2000).

But good execution at the school level depends on individuals, mainly teachers. Teachers need to understand that students must be educated to much higher levels, and then teachers must determine how best to organize the jobs of teaching and the conditions of learning in their schools, how to teach the curriculum, and how to measure performance to produce those results. Even if schools get it right and outline the strategies that would produce the results desired, teachers still need the requisite knowledge, skills, behaviors, and dispositions to effectively implement the strategy.

In other words, for good execution, the overall standards-based education reform strategy needs to be augmented with an intensive, capacity development strategy and a set of incentives—that include a revised compensation structure—that reward both the development of professional expertise and the production of results (Goertz, Floden, & O'Day, 1995; Odden, 1996). Zingheim and Schuster (1995c) argue that the pay structure also can be used both to reinforce these strategic elements and to further communicate about them during the implementation process.

A pay structure can function as a communication device because people listen when their pay structure is changed. Thus communicating what is involved in a new pay structure and why it is being implemented will be very like to get a teacher's attention. However, pay is so important to individuals that communication must emphasize how the new pay system will function, why it was selected, and how it is connected to the strategic elements for implementing a standards-based reform; that is, communication should provide information about both pay and strategy.

We suggest that recognition and reward structures that focus on capacity development and results would be the most advantageous communication and reinforcement strategies for schools attempting to teach students to high standards. A knowledge- and skills-based compensation plan would communicate the core capacities teachers in the school need to teach a high-standards curriculum effectively to a diverse set of students and to engage in the school restructuring process. Indeed, one factor that helped Cincinnati create its knowledge- and skills-based pay system was that identifying teaching standards, or a district consensus on what constituted good instruction, was at the core of their overall effort. Their reason for changing the pay structure was to improve instructional practice, a direct link between pay and reform strategy. A performance award would communicate the performances most valued by the school and signal that producing those results is valued by the system. This also was part of the Cincinnati new pay plan and accomplished the same goal of communicating to teachers the district's most important student performance goals.

We have stated that compensation programs should follow and support broader system change rather than lead such change. In the private sector, however, when companies have misread the market and need to implement strategic changes quickly, they have learned that leading the change effort by redesigning the compensation structure has some advantages (Zingheim & Schuster, 1995c). The changes get immediate employee attention because people are always interested in how they are paid. The pay changes also communicate a new set of values and directions—that new knowledge and skills are key and that better results matter.

The point here is not to suggest that education should lead change with altered compensation structures. We already have a decade of effort invested in standards-based education reforms, which can be undergirded by a revised compensation structure that provides salary increases for developing new instructional expertise and producing results (see Chapter 2).

It is, however, to suggest that a new system of knowledge- and skills-based pay and performance awards could serve as a communication mechanism that change is needed and desirable, that new competencies will be required of all teachers, that much higher levels of student performance must be produced, that future pay levels will depend on these results, and that vigorous attention to these issues is required immediately. Hopefully, this would signal urgency for the need to change; such a pay system would show that it is in the enlightened self-interest of teachers to change toward the core requirements needed to successfully implement standards-based reform.

Again, we hope that the imperative to change schools can precede new teacher compensation structures. And we urge system leaders to develop the trust environment needed to successfully design and implement a new pay strategy. But we also advise leaders—administrators, unions, and policymakers—to forge ahead and change the structure of teacher compensation as a part of both standards-based education reform and rising teacher professionalism. Education needs a dramatic new pay system, and leaders can confidently move forward on that agenda and not worry about incremental change. The next section describes three practical activities leaders can deploy to successfully launch the process of changing teacher compensation.

Three Design Strategies

Designing and implementing a new teacher compensation structure should be considered a major innovation and should be administered through a successful change process. Zingheim and Schuster (1995d) suggest that three common change elements can be used to begin the transition to a new pay structure: readiness assessment, benchmarking, and piloting. These three elements can accomplish several purposes:

❖ Identify current teacher, administrator, parent, and public understanding of the need to change and attitudes toward a new pay system so that transition strategies can start where "people are at" and thus more successfully move them to where they need to be

❖ Ensure that the transition strategies communicate the messages the education system needs to communicate in terms of the importance of new competencies, team management, high standards for all children, results orientation, and other important values that are part of any state's or district's education reform efforts (see www.nbpts.org/Press/exec_summary.pdf)

❖ Collect information and experience from other districts and organizations that have implemented changes in compensation

❖ Provide opportunities to experiment with their own forms of new compensation to devise the best system for a state or district

In general, the first step would be to create a design and implementation team and charge it with creating the process for developing a new teacher compensation structure as well as proposing, by a specific date, such a new structure for the system to implement. This team should include union leaders, teachers, board members, administrators, and members of the public, that is, the major stakeholders for the education system. The design team should comprise about 15 to 20 people, and in the best context, be cochaired by administration members and teachers. If the new system is a statewide structure, state policymakers also should be included. The team could further create subteams to work on specific design elements of new pay structures and thereby involve even more individuals in the entire process.

The design team and its subteams can then implement the following activities.

Readiness Assessment

A readiness assessment is a potentially powerful tool for beginning the transition to a new pay system. When administered well, a readiness assessment helps the implementation team decide what it needs to do to help get the school system ready for a new pay system; it identifies how people might react to a new pay structure, the concerns teachers have, and the kinds of information the team will need to improve the district's readiness to implement a new approach.

Zingheim and Schuster (1995d) strongly suggest that a readiness assessment should be viewed as a two-way communication mechanism. It provides an opportunity for the district, through the compensation design team, to tell teachers and other stakeholders why education change is needed, to communicate new values, priorities, and desired behaviors, and to diagnose where the district and its schools are and where they need to be. Likewise, the assessment asks teachers, administrators, and other stakeholders how to get from here to there on the education reform as well as the teacher compensation agenda.

Thus the readiness assessment needs to be strategically constructed and strategically administered. Zingheim and Schuster (1995d) suggest that the compensation readiness assessment be administered after the following:

❖ The core elements of the overall education reform strategy have been articulated and communicated

❖ Teachers' and administrators' roles in the new school organization are defined

❖ The shortcomings of the single-salary schedule are outlined along with reasons that the new pay structure supports the new education strategies, that is, the reasons that the status quo is not an option

❖ The process for designing the new pay system is described, including how the data from the readiness assessment will be used

The goal of the readiness assessment again is to communicate what the structure of the new pay system will include and to solicit teachers' and administrators' ideas on how to design the specifics of that structure. Thus the readiness assessment should not simply ask teachers and administrators if they want a new pay system and what kind of new pay system they want. The assessment should be very specific. If it includes a knowledge- and skills-based pay element, it should identify issues related to effective teaching strategies and the proposed teaching standards and ask respondents to identify the specific changes or additions they suggest, and perhaps even which of the various substandards are primary and which are secondary competencies. It could also ask for additional competencies that individuals might suggest in different topical areas.

If it includes a performance award, it could seek information on key performance areas (such as achievement, attendance, and parental satisfaction), on key performance measures, and on rewards most valued (such as salary bonuses, opportunities for professional development, certificates, and school improvement resources). If the performance awards include subschool team awards, the instrument should define clearly any subschool teams and delimit the types of results that would be eligible for an award.

The communication purpose of the readiness instrument is to describe to teachers and other stakeholders the general nature of the new compensation structure and to communicate that the design team desires teacher and administrator input into all the specifics of the new system including value judgments where appropriate (e.g., ranking of different types of results, rewards most valued). The technical purpose is to gather the latter data as key information in designing the transition process and the new compensation structure itself.

Benchmarking

The second transition strategy is benchmarking. Benchmarking is the process of visiting or otherwise learning about other school districts and organizations to learn about processes, strategies, and compensation structures they have created. For the purpose of compensation change, the goal is to visit or otherwise learn about other school districts and even private-sector organizations that have changed compensation systems, in order to learn about both design elements and implementation processes. For maximum applicability, the districts and organizations visited or studied should be similar to one's own district.

Districts should prepare all individuals who embark on benchmarking actions. The message should be that this is not just an activity but is an important research task critical to the teacher compensation change process. There should be a general data collection instrument that identifies all the types of information that will be collected. People should be trained in how to interview their peers in these other organizations, how to record the data collected, and how to synthesize findings into a useful report.

The information collected should not be restricted to just the compensation system, as the compensation structure should support overall system goals, management systems, and job structures. Thus information should be collected on goals, curriculum standards, achievement tests, school and classroom organization, related enabling programs and strategies, teacher and administrator roles, and the compensation structure. Data should include not only descriptive information on the above topics but also explanatory data—on why various strategies were selected and, particularly, why specific pay structures were chosen and how they supported the overall goals and programmatic strategies of the district and school. The benchmarking teams should also collect data on results and changes that were made from the original design. The teams will want to know what worked, what did not work, and what effects both effective and ineffective compensation elements had. The team should collect information on future directions and future changes planned. Finally, there must be a plan for synthesizing the data collected and teasing out the implications for the visiting district and then sharing the report not only with the compensation design team but also with other stakeholders in the district.

A related, and perhaps even less expensive, benchmarking strategy is for the design team to send a contingent of teachers and administrators to a compensation design seminar that is operated by the Teacher Compensation Group of the Consortium for Policy Research in Education (CPRE) at the University of Wisconsin-Madison (www.wcer.wisc.edu/cpre/conference/). These 3-day seminars address the conceptual issues as well as the nuts and bolts of designing both knowledge- and skills-based pay programs and school-based performance award programs. During the seminar, the leading state and district knowledge- and skills-based pay (KSBP) and school-based performance award (SBPA) programs around the country are profiled, discussed, and critiqued. Participation in the seminars thus provides the information needed to do the benchmarking but, in addition, exposes the team to expert judgments on the advantages and disadvantages of various approaches as well as to research on their impacts.

Piloting

Piloting is a third transition strategy. States or districts should consider piloting new compensation efforts to test possible options in the exact context in which they will be used. In a sense, this is more feasible in the situation where a state might try different versions of knowledge- and skills-based pay as well as performance awards across districts, but it also could be tried across schools in medium to large districts. Pilots should be full-fledged efforts that have control and experimental groups so that the state or district sponsoring them can learn about effects that are attributable to the new pay systems. Unfortunately, too few pilots are structured in this way, which reduces the learning that can be accomplished from well-designed pilot efforts.

Finally, the results should be widely disseminated within the district or the state, so everyone has access to the results of the pilot. Indeed, secrecy of information at any stage of the process—initiation, readiness assessment, benchmarking, piloting, or implementation—will undermine trust. The best approach is widely and openly to disseminate information at all stages. The ultimate goal is to gather as much information as possible to enhance the chances of success for the final teacher compensation plan that is institutionalized. Gathering and sharing information is crucial to this process; it not only builds and maintains trust but also taps the intelligence of all people and thus maximizes the brainpower devoted to designing the teacher compensation structure a district or state ultimately implements.

The Cincinnati Design Approach

Cincinnati adopted a comprehensive design and development approach that worked well for that district and that we generally recommend for other districts or states as well. First, Cincinnati negotiated into the teacher's contract language a requirement to both change the teacher evaluation system and to develop a new pay structure. Second, the district created a design team of about 20 members, cochaired by an assistant superintendent for the district and the negotiator for the teacher union. The design team then created several subteams to address different elements, first of a school-based performance award program and then of a knowledge- and skills-based pay program. For the SBPA program, it created subteams of measurement and performance improvement calculation, levels and size of rewards, funding, communication, and implementation and training. For the KSBP program, it created subteams of teaching standards, teacher evaluation, pay schedule, communication, and implementation and training. Each subteam was cochaired by an administration member and a teacher union member of the design team, and had 10 to 15 additional members.

The design team met monthly, with each subteam meeting in between each design team meeting. Design team agendas were essentially set by the work of the subteams; each subteam would write short minutes describing the substantive progress they were making in their charge and asking for design team policy decisions when needed. The minutes of both the design team and the subteams, as well as short articles and frequently asked questions, were placed in a special section of the district's Web page to further communicate about the programs. Each program took about a year to develop.

The design team was able to simulate the workings of the SBPA program, using previous years' performance data and so had a pretty good understanding of how many schools would qualify for the awards and what the program would cost. For the KSBP program, the district piloted the new performance assessment system in 10 pilot schools (out of 80 schools in the district) for 1 full year, and then implemented it for 2 full years in all schools before using the results for pay. Use for pay was intended to begin in the 2002-2003 school year.

In both cases, the end result was relatively widespread teacher and administrator involvement in the design process, which led to wider understanding of the programs being developed. But in retrospect, the design team would have been helped in communicating the rationale for, and details of, the programs by administering readiness surveys as well as by a more structured process for informing all teachers in all schools of the design of each of the SBPA and KSBP programs as a prelude to full implementation.

Stakeholder Roles

To improve the likelihood that a new compensation structure will have intended and lasting impacts, there are several key roles that various stakeholders in the education system need to play. It goes without saying that these roles need to be carried out in concert with one another. The key to a successful compensation change process is collaboration throughout the entire process of development, design, implementation, evaluation, and modification. If collaboration breaks down, the plan itself is likely to break down.

State Policymakers

There are several key roles for state legislators and other state policymakers. The early experience of states embarking on compensation reform in the direction of "new pay" suggest two alternative strategies.

Policymakers could develop *comprehensive educational reform models* that are state driven and incorporate standards-based reform, authentic assessment, professional development, preservice training, licensure, site-based management, and a combination of compensation reforms that could include knowledge-and-skills pay and group-based performance awards. The education reform in Kentucky required the state to take this approach, but while developing a school-based performance award program for variable pay, the state was never able to create a knowledge-and-skills program for base pay.

However, in late 2000, state action on new pay strategies began to become more widespread. A proposal for a statewide approach to both knowledge- and skills-based pay and a school-based performance award program was accepted by the governor and legislative leaders in Iowa (Iowa State Department of Education, 2000), and a comprehensive bill was introduced to the 2001 legislature. The states of Maryland, Nebraska, North Dakota, and New York considered at length whether to add new approaches to compensation to their standards-based education reform strategies, but as of early 2001 did not do so. But in 2001, several other states began to create statewide approaches to knowledge- and skills-based pay, with governors and then legislatures in Minnesota, New Mexico, and Washington making proposals for changing how teachers are paid. How these state initiatives will play out over time will only be known in the future, but the issue has now become a valid state policy topic.

The simplest forms of knowledge-and-skills pay are salary incentives and payment of examination fees for teachers taking and passing National Board certification. More elaborate forms would include the approach proposed in Iowa that included the following:

❖ State adoption of teaching standards that include standards for teacher licensure

❖ State development of a performance assessment of teachers to the standards and including three to five different levels of performance, one of which would be for professional licensure

❖ State training of all assessors and certifying of individuals as able to provide fair, consistent, reliable assessments of teachers across various teaching contexts

❖ A state framework using the results of the performance assessment in a new teacher salary schedule

The Iowa Merged Performance Pay proposal indicates one way this could occur (Iowa State Department of Education, 2000).

School-based performance awards could reward schools for improvement on the state's student assessment instruments as well as for improvement in other goals identified as important to creating an educated citizenry. The trend across the country has been for states to create statewide plans when real salary bonuses are provided. In early 2001, about half the states had some version of this program, with the most senior programs operating in California, Florida, Kentucky, and North Carolina, and with proposals for new programs in Colorado, Georgia, and several other states.

An alternative strategy is for state policymakers to enact enabling legislation that encourages readiness assessment, benchmarking, piloting, and adoption of alternative compensation approaches designed at the local level. Such legislation may expand collective bargaining agreements to enable districts to negotiate broader educational policy goals as well as alternative approaches to compensation. Expanding the ability of teachers to negotiate educational policy as well as compensation will give them the ability to obtain the decision-making authority they need to be reasonably held accountable for school outcomes. In 1995, Colorado and Minnesota enacted this type of legislation. California followed suit in about 1996, followed by Florida a couple of years later. In November 2000, voters in Arizona approved a referendum to raise the sales tax by .5%, with a minimum of 40% and up to at least 50% of the dollars dedicated to performance pay plans for teachers, all of which will be designed by local school districts.

Whichever strategy is chosen, state policymakers have a responsibility to stay the course over a long time period, at least 5 years, in order to give a new compensation program a chance to take hold and have its impacts. The history of state efforts to change teacher pay systems is quick abandonment—designing a program and then pulling the funding after the second or third year. This not only blunts any impact the program can have but also creates cynicism and skepticism among teachers, sabotaging levels of trust needed for future attempts of compensation reform to be successful. Particularly for a performance award, states need to identify a *protected* source of funding, such as a 1% budget set-aside, and maintain that funding source over a long time period.

States could also stimulate, help design, and even partially finance a significant, ongoing, capacity development strategy. A standards-based education reform strategy depends on teachers' and administrators' developing a new array of professional competencies. That will only be accomplished through a long-term and restructured professional development strategy (Corcoran, 1995; Darling-Hammond & McLaughlin, 1995). States could ensure funding of such an effort by creating a budget set-aside. For example, when Missouri enacted their education and school finance reform in 1993, they dedicated 2% of the state education budget to ongoing professional development. This has dramatically expanded professional development activities across the state. California, Michigan, and Vermont (Goertz, Floden, & O'Day, 1995) have taken different approaches to developing the teacher and school capacity required for their reform programs. The point is that states can act to strengthen capacity development strategies, which are key not only to education reform generally but also to competency- and performance-based pay strategies more particularly.

Third, states could create and administer a solid student assessment system, which balances basic skills and knowledge with more advanced, problem-solving skills. Policymakers need to be aware that more authentic assessment strategies, such as portfolios, performance events, and open-response questions, may require some trade-offs in levels of reliability for assessing thinking and reasoning skills that are thought to be important if the United States is to achieve international competitiveness.

Finally, states also can create state teaching standards boards, which, in addition to licensing teachers, would create professional standards for teaching practice. Several states, led by Indiana and Minnesota, have created such bodies within the past decade (Darling-Hammond, Wise, & Klein, 1995). Although they have been created primarily as professional ways to *license* teachers, they function for new teachers in much the same way that the National Board for Professional Teaching Standards functions for advanced, experienced teachers—describing teaching practice, providing standards to assess practice, and creating an assessment strategy for measuring an individual teacher's practice with respect to the standards. A key new role for such a state board would be for it to develop standards for teaching practice in between those for beginning and those for advanced, accomplished teachers, standards that could be used for a knowledge- and skills-based pay plan. Iowa is in the process of developing such standards, a state role that also has been discussed in Illinois, Minnesota, Ohio, and Washington.

State policymakers could also consider altering collective bargaining laws to permit more teacher involvement in school management, the various new approaches to teacher compensation discussed in this book, and even new types of union contracts that focus on the teaching and learning environments in schools. Kerchner, Koppich, and Weeres (1997) expand on these issues in some detail. The point here is only that several of the new teacher roles embodied in standards-based reform, including the design of site-based management and the scope of decisions that could be made at the school site, could require changes in state collective bargaining laws. Furthermore, because many of these changes also could be supported by new forms of teacher pay, those state laws that restrict pay to the single-salary schedule would need to be altered to allow enactment of the ideas forwarded in this book.

Districts

Districts—school boards, district administrators, and school administrators—can also play a crucial role in teacher compensation reform.

Indeed, before the Iowa initiatives in late 2000, most teacher compensation reform was undertaken at the district level. Research in the private sector suggests that an important role for management is to determine that changes in the pay structure are needed to improve organizational effectiveness (Heneman, Ledford, & Gresham, 2000; Jenkins et al., 1992; Zingheim & Schuster, 1995c). Once the decision to undertake compensation reform has been made, managers need to work closely with those whose compensation will be affected to develop a reasonable, workable pay strategy.

Even prior to considering changes in compensation, however, districts need to work to develop a climate of trust, professionalism, and cooperation within the district. Most of the knowledge- and skills-based pay cases on the CPRE Web site (www.wcer.wisc.edu/cpre/tcomp/research/ksbp/index.asp) indicate that this task preceded teacher compensation change in nearly all districts. This can be accomplished through a variety of strategies including the use of interest-based bargaining as opposed to the old industrial model. In addition, administrators should work toward strengthening the general conditions of work. The better the conditions of work in a school (teacher involvement in schoolwide, sound facilities; availability of materials; safety, etc.), the more likely a new form of compensation can be implemented successfully. Conversely, the compensation strategy should be developed with the general conditions of work in mind. For example, skills assessment in a high-involvement school should incorporate teachers fully in the assessment process.

Another important role of the district is to commit resources to the design, development, communication, and implementation of the compensation plan. This commitment includes the allocation of resources, such as money for planning, professional development, and salary increments, as well as commitment of human resources. Districts that have successfully implemented new compensation strategies have personnel who are dedicated (both in job description and in spirit) to overcoming the numerous hurdles that will undoubtedly trip up reform efforts along the way. These district-level catalysts need to work closely and energetically with teachers, school administrators, and community members, maintaining strong communication channels and open minds throughout the process.

The process itself should provide for full partnership and participation of teachers, union leaders, and administrators at all levels of the education system. This collaborative effort should begin with identification and agreement of broad educational goals. If the district is adapting its own teaching standards and teacher performance assessment system, it needs to provide the time and resources to fully develop these elements. They cannot be created overnight. At the same time, they do not require a multiple-year development process, either.

Resources also need to be committed to providing training for principal and peer assessors of knowledge and skills, behaviors, or student outcomes where appropriate. Training may also be needed to shift role expectations among district- and school-level administrators and teachers in the development of a school-based management approach. Any effort to make teachers accountable for results must also provide teachers with the knowledge, power, and information needed to focus resources and develop more effective approaches to student achievement. Teachers need to have input on how schools expend their dollars, the focus of professional development activities, and educational policies and approaches. This shift in roles and expectations is made easier through professional development focused on redefining roles and behaviors throughout the organization, in addition to extensive professional development in instructional strategies in a standards-based environment (see Odden & Archibald, 2001).

Finally, districts need to approach compensation reform as an ongoing process. Persistence until the plan is perfected is the key to success. Most plans have initial bugs and are viewed with skepticism by some employees. Much of this skepticism may be overcome by a clear and continued commitment on the part of the district to identify problems that may arise and to revise the plan when needed (Kelley, 1996).

Teachers

Teachers and their unions also have crucial roles in the design, implementation, and improvement of new teacher compensation approaches. Teacher associations and their members need to maintain a positive commitment to the academic goals of the school, good working relations among themselves, and a strategy of working with management to achieve key educational goals. Both district administrators and teacher unions need to work hand in hand to create the level of trust and cooperation needed to enable compensation reform to move forward in a productive way.

In many ways, teachers play the most critical role in compensation reform. Without the cooperation, professionalism, and commitment of teachers to make compensation reform work for them, the likelihood of success is very low. Teachers should be fully engaged in developing and adapting standards for teaching—for licensure, for midcareer, and for advanced practice. Furthermore, teachers should be fully engaged in developing and adapting performance assessment systems that can measure individual teachers in different levels of practice to the standards.

The current teacher compensation system is low-risk and predictable. The single-salary schedule has provided a relatively low-paid profession (teaching) the assurance of regular and predictable salary increases. Furthermore, having worked in the system for some time, many teachers have invested a considerable amount of time and money into obtaining educational credits and degrees to move up through the system.

These teachers are likely to find proposals to abandon the single-salary schedule objectionable and disconcerting. Thus the level of trust between teachers and their unions and between labor and management that is required to reduce fears cannot be underestimated. Teachers need to be willing to take the risk and to work together with administrators and union leadership to create a better system.

Unions could make a considerable contribution by continuing to reconceptualize what it means to be a union in a new system characterized by goals and standards at the top and by substantial decision making by professional teachers in school sites. As labor and management reinvent their relationship, several collective bargaining structures and processes are changing, such as rules governing the application of districtwide agreements to individual schools (Shedd, 1988). Unions and local teacher contracts can be reconceptualized, including the district salary structure, in this new way of organizing and managing school sites within the education system (Kerchner, Koppich, & Weeres, 1997).

Community Members

And finally, the community has a role in supporting experimentation with alternative compensation systems. In many of the districts and states experimenting with compensation reform, direct community interest and involvement proved to be an important catalyst to initiate reform efforts (Kelley, 1996). But beyond providing pressure and input in the need to reform the compensation system, in each of these cases, the community worked to provide constructive input into the design and development of alternative pay plans. In some cases, this input took the form of consulting expertise; in others, the business community provided start-up funds for the design and implementation of the new pay plan.

Figure 7.1. Issues to Consider in Developing Alternative Pay Plans

---

General Questions

Who will be involved in the development process?

Will there be a transition to the new pay plan?

How will the plan be funded?

How will the plan be evaluated?

Knowledge- and Skills-Based Pay

What knowledge and skills will be rewarded or what teaching standards will be adopted or adapted?

Will all teachers be able to be rewarded for obtaining the knowledge and skills?

How will competencies be developed and determined?

How much will each performance level be worth?

How do you retire specific knowledge and skills?

How do you add new, specific knowledge and skills?

How do the knowledge-and-skills pay system and the performance review relate to professional development activities?

Will the school or district provide training in the knowledge and skills desired?

Should it be paid as a bonus or as part of base pay?

Who will evaluate or assess teacher performance to the standards and how?

How often will the assessment process be required for each teacher? What will be the reassessment or recertification cycle?

What is the mix of knowledge and skills in terms of being school-specific or districtwide or determined at the state or professional level?

Performance Pay

What student performance results will be rewarded?

Will awards be provided to teams within schools or to entire schools? (NO QUOTAS!)

How does the plan provide meaningful and timely feedback to teachers?

What measurements of performance will be used?

Will it be high stakes for students? If not, how can student cooperation be ensured?

How will variations among schools and districts, such as SES, human and physical capital, student mobility, or funding, be addressed?

Figure 7.1. Continued

Will performance improvements be based on cohorts or individual-level data?

How will the money be distributed? Only to teachers? Equally to all teachers and educational professionals in each school? To classified school personnel?

What incentives and possibilities are there for gaming?

How much pay is needed to draw attention to the desired behaviors without overly diverting teachers from other, unmeasured but desirable behaviors?

Another important role of the community is the willingness to show support for compensation systems that hold teachers accountable for results. If the community demands improvements in accountability, and schools respond with a new pay system that rewards improvements in student outcomes, the community should be willing to provide resources needed to maintain such a system over time. This fiscal commitment would be especially important for knowledge- and skills-based pay programs that explicitly raise pay levels for the highest performing teachers. Providing these extra salary dollars will show community commitment to fiscally reward outstanding teachers. Not funding these new salary levels would constitute community reneging on what it takes to recruit and retain teachers who are successful at teaching more students to high levels.

Conclusions

The state, districts, teachers, and community members all have potentially important roles to play in the transformation of teacher compensation from a traditional, single-salary schedule to a pay plan that combines elements of knowledge-and-skills and performance pay.

Figure 7.1 provides a list of questions to consider in the development of such an alternative pay plan. Although not comprehensive, this list highlights a variety of issues that have been discussed throughout the book as key design issues.

As we have tried to show throughout the book, compensation reform is not a magic elixir that will cure all education's ills. However, if carefully prescribed and taken in conjunction with other educational reform strategies, it has the potential to strengthen the skills and competencies of the teaching workforce, to develop more reflective and effective practice among teachers, and to focus teacher efforts on improving the most important student outcome measures. Furthermore, teachers may feel more satisfied with their work as schools provide clear directions for performance improvements and reward the most skilled teachers working collaboratively to create more effective school environments.

Finally, over the medium to long term, we hope that these new teacher salary structures will also help provide much higher salaries for teachers. Good teachers are individuals highly valued by many, many organizations—not just schools. To recruit and retain such talented individuals, the education system needs to pay them much more than they are paid today.

Compensation to Enhance Teacher Quality and Supply

8

Compensation is a key formal element of a human resource and organizational-management strategy that affects the quality of work produced by influencing the attraction, development, retention, and attrition of employees. Effective human resource strategies are designed strategically with a clear understanding of the knowledge-and-skill mix needed for an organization to achieve its goals. Compensation designs in education are constrained by a number of factors, such as a lack of control of overall funding; a sometimes awkward, poorly aligned, and inconsistent policy and accountability environment; variations in the quality and focus of preparation programs; and politically challenging, collective-bargaining rules and agreements. All organizations face constraints in the development of compensation designs. The challenge is to work within those constraints to find the right mix of compensation incentives to produce the most desired results.

In the preceding chapters, we have laid the foundation for the beginnings of meaningful teacher compensation reform through the development of knowledge- and skills-based pay and group-based performance pay. We have shown how changes in school organization and context have created a window of opportunity for both widespread and meaningful compensation reforms. Our focus thus far has been on two types of compensation reform that we believe can provide an important boost to efforts to enhance the educational opportunities for all students:

knowledge- and skills-based pay and group performance pay. We believe that knowledge- and skills-based pay can enhance the quality of the teaching force by attracting teachers interested in continuous improvement and reflective practice and by providing meaningful, salient developmental feedback to teachers throughout their careers. It has the opportunity to enhance teacher supply by strengthening teacher skill and support, thereby reducing the number of teachers who opt out of teaching because they lack the skills needed to make their work successful and, thus, intrinsically rewarding. Group-based performance pay can enhance the quality of educational outcomes by providing clear and salient goals to guide decisions about the investment of teacher effort and other resources to support the goals. Although we believe that these two approaches to pay are particularly promising, many other compensation issues and strategies could be used to enhance the supply of high-quality teachers working to educate all students to high standards. In this chapter, we consider a few of these other compensation strategies. (For a more complete treatment of these issues outside of education, see Crandall & Wallace, 1998; Lawler, 2000a, 2000b; and Zingheim & Schuster, 2000.) The chapter first, however, discusses staffing challenges in high-poverty, low-performance districts and the roles that new compensation strategies could play in those places with the most problematic staffing challenges.

Staffing Challenges

Although many school districts must overcome obstacles to identifying, attracting, developing, and retaining a high-quality teaching force, finding qualified staff for some schools and some subject areas can be especially challenging. Overall, current projections are for an impending teacher shortage nationwide. The Department of Education estimates that at least 2 million new teachers will have to be hired in the next decade (Blair, 2001). But school districts with large minority, low-income, and low-achieving student populations tend to have the most difficulty attracting and retaining highly qualified teachers (see also Odden & Kelley, in press). These districts include large urban and some rural districts and are more likely to experience higher turnover, have a more difficult time recruiting replacements, and be staffed with teachers who are less experienced and lack a license. Those with a license tend to have lower pass scores on the license assessments and more failed attempts prior to successfully passing (Allen, 2000; Cunningham, 2000; Haycock, 2000).

Although many highly qualified and excellent teachers teach in hard-to-staff schools, there are also a number of teachers that lack the skills and training needed to serve the many disadvantaged students in these schools. Attention to teacher quality is critical for all schools; it is particularly critical for hard-to-staff schools. Thus policymaker attention has been drawn to using compensation and other policies to enhance both the quality and the supply of teachers in these schools. Although enhancing quality and supply are not necessarily competing goals (Haycock, 2000), teacher quality and teacher supply policies are often at odds with one another. For example, policies designed to address teacher quality include staged, performance-based licensure and pay systems designed to raise the bar for entry into the teaching profession and encourage teachers to continue to develop their skills throughout their careers. Policies designed to address teacher supply may provide alternative certification routes that bring experienced professionals from *other* professions into teaching with little or no training, mentoring, or exposure to research and practical application of effective teaching methods.

But compensation is a major issue that contributes to the difficulty in recruiting and retaining quality teachers in hard-to-staff schools (Walker, 2000; Haycock, 2000). First, the level of compensation tends to be low, and even when higher in urban areas, inadequate to compensate for the increased costs of living in urban areas. For example, the median teacher salary in New York City in 1996 was $45,965, compared to $64,217 for "low need" districts in the state (Cunningham, 2000).

Research on teacher transfer reinforces the problem of inadequate compensation. Research on teacher transfer (teachers moving to other districts) and exit (teachers leaving the profession) in high-need districts in Wisconsin suggests that high-need districts suffer most from higher transfer rates than other districts face. Increasing the wages of teachers in high-need districts relative to other districts can reduce both exit and transfer attrition, but the research showed that a 25% to 33% salary differential would be needed to equalize transfer rates for Milwaukee teachers, compared to surrounding districts. The largest impact occurs for beginning teacher salaries, but for men, increasing maximum salary also would have an important effect on reducing male teacher transfer (Imazeki, 2000). The Imazeki study suggests that a significant investment would be needed if the *level* of compensation were the only policy variable enlisted to attract teachers to high-need districts.

Although this chapter primarily focuses on compensation, other issues, such as working conditions and leadership, are also critical factors that need continued attention from policymakers. Teachers need classrooms that are safe, clean, and equipped with the tools necessary for effective instruction, and they need excellent school leaders who can nurture, direct, and support the development of strong and effective teachers.

Compensation Issues and Innovations

In addition to group performance pay and knowledge- and skills-based pay, a number of other compensation issues and innovations are currently being implemented or considered in order to address critical issues of teacher quality and supply. These include higher beginning or overall salaries; recruitment incentives, such as signing bonuses, loan forgiveness, and housing subsidies; higher salaries for subject matter shortage areas; pay incentives for mobility; and attention to the design of the total compensation system.

Higher Beginning and Overall Salary Levels

A number of states and districts, including many urban districts, are seeking to raise beginning and overall salary levels to make them more market competitive. According to *Education Week,* "at least 29 governors have set teacher pay hikes as a priority this year. . . . And legislators in 28 statehouses from Alabama to Washington have introduced a flurry of bills aimed at increasing pay" (Blair, 2001, p.1). The efforts are aimed at increasing the quality and supply of teachers.

Some states are working to increase salary levels across the board without significant changes in the structure of compensation. Southern states, in particular, have been working to raise salary levels to national or regional averages. In 2001, a number of states—Colorado, Iowa, Montana, Nebraska, New Mexico, and Washington, for example—were considering proposals to link pay to the development and demonstration of teacher knowledge and skills (Blair, 2001).

With a recent infusion of state money from California's large fiscal surplus, many of its districts—including several urban districts—began raising beginning salaries to the high $30,000 level. This should allow them to recruit from a larger and higher-quality labor pool, but over time, they may need to provide higher top salaries to address teacher retention issues as well.

Across districts and across states, there is significant variation in the amount of salary going into payment for experience versus payment for education. Some districts may find it useful to provide a more attenuated schedule, with higher beginning salaries but less growth in pay. Knowledge- and skills-based plans can provide flexibility to raise beginning teacher salaries quickly by rewarding the demonstration of knowledge and skills for teachers at the beginning of their careers. Early evidence on knowledge- and skills-based pay systems suggests that this is exactly what happens. Teachers interested in increasing earnings focus their energies to produce professional growth early in their careers (in particular), to enrich their abilities in rewarded knowledge-and-skills categories, and to move up quickly in salary.

Recruitment Incentives

Many states and districts are providing signing bonuses, moving expenses, home mortgage assistance, and even subsidized housing for teachers as recruitment incentives. These efforts add to the intensity of the competition for good, new teachers. When combined with efforts to raise starting salaries, they suggest that financial rewards for new teachers are much more available today than in the past. To be competitive, districts must offer a competitive beginning salary, which would equal about $35,000 if the national benchmark were the average starting salary for all college graduates. In particular, high-need districts facing environmental limitations (e.g., inadequate facilities, lack of equipment and materials, safety issues) might want to consider offering recruitment incentives such as signing bonuses and moving expenses.

As with any compensation incentive, signing bonuses need to be carefully designed to produce desired results. In 1999, Massachusetts implemented a signing bonus program that provides $20,000, paid out over 4 years, and a fast-track training program for individuals around the country who agree to teach in Massachusetts. The program was modeled loosely after Teach for America. Although the program has successfully recruited new teachers to the state, there is a relatively high attrition rate, and some teachers have expressed concerns about the inadequacy of their preparation and mentorship for the challenges of teaching. In the first year, 63 teachers were recruited into the program; 18% left after the first year of teaching, compared to a national average attrition of 9% for first-year teachers (Gold, 2001). In addition, most of the teachers in the program ended up teaching in affluent communities rather than in the urban districts where they were needed most (Viadero, 2001).

Other states are joining in as well. Legislation was introduced in 2001 in Pennsylvania to spend up to $31 million to pay for signing bonuses for teachers who agree to teach for at least 5 years in Pennsylvania in shortage areas such as math, science, and special education. Teachers would receive, on average, a $6,000 bonus. A program in South Carolina to provide an additional $18,000 per year to teachers who spend 1 to 3 years as mentors in poorly performing, largely rural schools met limited interest. Only 74 teachers applied for the program, despite the recruitment efforts of the state, which extended the deadline for application twice (Gold, 2001). State experiences with pay for National Board certification seem to be more successful, as incentives have encouraged rapid expansion of the number of teachers seeking and receiving certification in states that provide bonuses ranging from $2,000 to $50,000 over the 10-year life of the certificate (Kelley & Kimball, in press).

In addition, many districts now offer salary differentials for teachers in low-performing, hard-to-staff, or high-poverty schools. The Fairfax County, Virginia, public schools extended the school day and hiked teacher salaries by 7% in their 20 lowest-performing schools; they also added more to those schools' budgets to help them implement new and more effective intervention strategies. New York City provides an extra 12% to teachers in its hard-to-staff, low-performing schools. Charlotte-Mecklenburg, North Carolina, discovered that teachers in schools that did not qualify for its school-based performance bonus were leaving them in greater numbers than other schools. So they provided a salary hike of 6% over 3 years: 2% the first year, 4% the second year, and a permanent 6% increase after 3 years in the school.

Higher Salaries for Shortage Areas

It is becoming more and more common for school systems to provide higher salaries for teachers with a license in a shortage area. The most common shortage areas are mathematics, science, computers, and special education. Both Cincinnati and San Francisco provide such salary augmentations in their recent contracts. In most places, these salary differentials are at least $5,000 a year and continue as long as the shortage area exists. States have joined in as well. The current Utah governor has recommended a one-time, $20,000 bonus in exchange for teacher commitment to teach math and technology for 4 years (Blair, 2001).

This behavior mirrors emerging practice in the private sector where companies are providing higher salaries to employees in hot areas such as computer programming and telecommunications. Those organizations that do not pay such salary differentials experience significant turnover in these employees and a drop in organizational performance, just as many school districts—particularly those in technology-impacted communities—lose mathematics and science teachers when they are paid the same as English and history teachers.

Pay Incentives and Teacher Mobility

For many teachers, moving across district or state lines has come with significant financial sacrifice. First, many district contracts recognize only a few years of experience for teachers moving into the district—regardless of how many years of experience those teachers actually have. Although the procedure is changing, common practice has been to credit teachers for only 4 to 6 years of experience, however many years they have actually taught. And teachers who choose not to stay in one district for their entire careers may lose thousands of dollars as a result.

Currently, about 50% of new teachers in *urban* areas leave their jobs within the first 5 years; about 20% to 30% of new teachers in *rural* areas also leave within 5 years (Blair, 2001). A partial cause for these high turnover rates may be that teachers working in high-need urban schools are forced at a very early stage in their career to make career-long decisions about what district they want to be associated with. Even young, idealistic teachers may prefer to move to more comfortable, higher-paying, suburban districts early in their careers rather than lock themselves into a future trade-off between working in challenging conditions throughout their careers or facing a significant, future financial sacrifice if they decide to change districts.

At the state level, teacher mobility is limited by state teacher licensure requirements that often force even experienced teachers to submit to large course loads and hurdles to teaching in a new state. A number of states have begun to provide provisions for licensure portability for National Board-certified teachers to lower the hurdles to mobility for these teachers. Furthermore, there is typically no portability of pensions across state lines, so teachers who move across state lines also lose significant pension benefits (Odden & Conley, 1992).

Barriers to mobility may have made sense in a time when few people changed venues during their lifetimes and fewer still changed careers. But today, most people have more than one career and more than one city they have called home. Facing very real current and future crises relating to teacher quality and supply, it seems counterproductive to continue policies that force experienced teachers to leave the profession or face severe financial sacrifice for movement across state and district lines.

Total Compensation

Total compensation expands the compensation picture to include benefits and pension plans. The lack of portability of pension plans was discussed above, but benefit packages and pension plans in education also tend to be conservative and traditional. New approaches to benefits and pensions provide greater flexibility and greater attention to the fact that individuals at different stages of life are likely to make very different choices about the mix and risk involved in benefits and pensions. Some in business have even recommended developing benefits packages that are integrated with employees' personal lifestyles, to encourage employees to make personal choices that lead to more healthy choices about financial decisions and personal care (Federico & Goldsmith, 1998).

Highly structured benefit plans do not allow employees to make choices about what benefits they desire; as a result, employees typically value fixed benefits packages at only about 70% of their actual value. More flexible benefit plans enable employees to select the benefits they prefer, subject to cost constraints. Flexible benefits packages could be an important component in a compensation strategy designed to help recruit and retain highly qualified and productive workers in education, just as they are in the private sector (Crandall & Wallace, 1998; Lawler, 1990, 2000b; Odden & Conley, 1992).

Pension plans could also be designed to provide greater flexibility for teachers to choose how their money will be invested. Defined-contribution pension plans provide a fixed amount of funding that teachers can choose to invest in the pension program that makes the most sense to them. By decoupling the investment from state pension funds, which are often underfunded and very conservative, teachers could make their own choices about the level of risk and types of investments they choose. Furthermore, when teachers move across state or district lines, the pension would be completely portable, so there would be no penalty for teacher mobility.

Research Findings on Alternative Compensation Strategies

Because our experience with many of these salary innovations is quite new, research findings on their effects are only beginning to emerge. There is substantial research to show that raising beginning teacher salaries enhances the education system's ability to recruit from a broader, higher-quality market. When coupled with other initiatives—for example, signing bonuses, greater overall pay, mentoring or induction, and improved working conditions—higher beginning salaries are even more powerful. Education will not be able to recruit its share of quality individuals unless it pays competitive beginning wages.

The research on the impact of raising overall teacher salaries is mixed. Ballou and Podgursky (1997) offer one of the most insightful critiques of this policy, particularly as it affects recruitment of new, quality teachers. Through longitudinal research, they show that such a policy *with* the traditional salary schedule—which includes the long, lockstep time period to move up to a higher salary—has little positive, and sometimes a negative, effect on recruiting new, quality teachers. A policy of raising all teachers' salaries simply encourages current teachers—good or not—to remain in education, thus reducing the number of entry positions. This policy, combined with the long time it takes to reach the top salary, results in an overall decline in teacher quality.

Ballou and Podgursky argue that for an overall teacher salary hike to improve teacher quality, it must be combined with some type of pay-for-performance plan that (a) provides salary increases only to those teachers who have more expertise; (b) allows new teachers to move up the salary schedule more quickly, based on their professional knowledge and skills; and (c) provides increases to teachers (we would say as a faculty) who produce higher levels of student learning. In sum, they argue that higher overall salaries will work to recruit and retain quality teachers only if such a policy is combined with a major overhaul of the current salary structure.

Although the new Cincinnati pay plan (described in Chapter 5) does what Ballou and Podgursky recommend, only research will tell if the program will have those predicted long-term effects. In the meantime, formative research suggests that the plan is having some positive impacts. In a Consortium for Policy Research in Education (CPRE) study of the 1999-2000, 10-school pilot of Cincinnati's new evaluation system, 75% of teachers said the new teaching standards were valid descriptions of good teaching, with younger teachers supporting them at higher percentages than more senior teachers. But school principals varied widely in their implementation of the evaluation system across the 10-school pilot, which raised questions about the system's fairness. When principals did a good job, however, teachers liked the system, and vice versa. That's why Cincinnati is taking 2 years to "perfect" the evaluation system, with intensive training for principals and peer assessors, before using the results to trigger pay levels.

At the Vaughn New Century Learning Center in Los Angeles, a CPRE survey of teachers showed that most teachers were motivated by the knowledge-and-skills pay amounts and that 75% of them wanted the program to continue. As testimony to these beliefs, nearly all teachers are participating in efforts to improve their skills in the areas that the school rewards. Furthermore, the survey found that 81% of Vaughn teachers thought it was fair to give bonuses to teachers when student learning rose; 84% said they were motivated by the bonus; and 79% said the bonus program should be continued. Perhaps most important, nearly all teachers have now opted into the new system, which is voluntary. Finally, Vaughn has anecdotal evidence that their pay program is attracting quality, younger teachers because of its pay-for-performance orientation and the ability it provides to earn a higher salary faster (Milanowski & Kellor, 2000b).

As described in Chapter 6, research also shows the viability of school-based bonus programs. Research on the programs in Kentucky, Maryland, Charlotte-Mecklenburg, and Dallas has found that school-based award programs can help to boost student performance (Clotfelter & Ladd, 1996; Kelley, Heneman, & Milanowski, 2000). Such programs seem to encourage teachers to focus their work efforts on the areas of student performance that are being measured—primarily the core academic areas of mathematics, science, social studies, and reading. In these programs, teachers valued monetary bonuses, but bonuses of $1,000 were generally viewed as too small. Research in the private sector has found that to affect a worker's motivation, annual bonuses need to be at least 5% to 8% of salary—about $2,000 for a typical teacher. This is generally consistent with the reactions of teachers to the Kentucky and Charlotte-Mecklenburg programs.

There is little research yet on educational policies to provide salary increments for shortage areas and hard-to-staff, low-performing, or high-poverty schools. But private-sector research shows that without such similar kinds of salary adjustments, organizations lose their ability to recruit and retain quality workers. Many policymakers have recognized the importance of market considerations as districts struggle to attract math, science, and technology-related teachers away from more lucrative, private-sector opportunities. Even the American Federation of Teachers has recognized the critical nature of teacher shortages in certain subject areas and is encouraging local districts to consider contract language that allows for salary incentives to address teacher shortages (Archer, 2001).

Finally, there is some evidence that the size of salary adjustments affect the numbers of teachers who seek National Board certification. The states that provide the largest salary supplements also have the most Board-certified teachers. Although additional research is needed, early evidence suggests that Board-certified teachers outperform noncertified teachers on a variety of performance measures, including student performance (Bond, Richard, Smith, & Hattie, 2000). Furthermore, evidence from states that provide incentives for Board certification suggests that a salary increase can positively encourage teachers to seek what is now considered a desirable but hard-to-attain goal—National Board certification.

Although knowledge- and skills-based pay and group performance pay are the two basic structural changes that are occurring, many other compensation initiatives are developing across the country. Several states (e.g., Arizona, Iowa, Nebraska, and South Carolina) and numerous districts (e.g., New York City, Philadelphia) want somehow to raise teacher salary levels to compete for teacher talent in the labor market. Other districts are providing higher pay for teachers in shortage areas (mathematics, science, and technology), and still others are providing pay incentives for individuals who take jobs in hard-to-staff, high-poverty, or low-performance schools to increase the level of teacher quality in those difficult schools. District and state teacher compensation task forces are also using or proposing signing bonuses, moving expenses, and housing allowances in high-cost communities (big cities and Silicon Valley). In short, there are numerous, varied, and rapidly emerging innovations in teacher compensation, all of which suggest the time is ripe for change and all of which will provide a rich natural laboratory for research and analysis.

Resource A: Generic Models of Knowledge- and Skills-Based Pay

This section describes more generic examples of knowledge- and skills-based pay structures, beginning with a model that adds some key knowledge and skills to a traditional single-salary schedule and including a model that completely restructures that schedule. All four models also appear in the first edition of this book.

Adding Knowledge- and Skills-Based Pay to the Current Single-Salary Schedule

Figure A.1 is a model that retains the current single-salary schedule and adds some important knowledge and skills pay elements to it. All elements in the model should be viewed as suggestive; it is the general framework for the model that should be emphasized. The model suggests two categories of knowledge and skills: those common across a district and those specific to a school. The common or professional knowledge and skills include greater knowledge of the subject matter taught, licensure in a second area, licensure in a shortage area (shortage to be defined by the district), and National Board certification. The locally assessed knowledge and skills would be determined by school-specific needs.

The major rationales for this model are threefold: (a) It signals that deep knowledge of subject matter content is important; (b) it supports advanced recognition—certification—by the National Board for Professional Standards; and (c) the infrastructure is in place to implement it fairly quickly. Since scholars and teacher leaders suggest teachers need to

Figure A.1. Model 1: Current Step and Column Salary Schedule With Knowledge- and Skills-Based Pay Additions (Professionally and Locally Assessed)

Experience	Column 1 BA	Column 2 BA+	Column 3 MA	Column 4 MA+	Skill-Based Pay Increments (professionally assessed)	Skill-Based Pay Increments (examples) (locally assessed)
Step 1					Passing a content test in area of license	Nongraded primary school
Step 2					Licensure in a second area	Cooperative learning
Step 3					Licensure in a shortage area	Reading recovery
Step 4					Certification from National Board for Professional Teaching Standards	Computer skills
Step 5						
Step 6						
Step 7						
Step 8						
Step n						

NOTE: Model 1 maintains the current single-salary schedule structure with annual increments for years of experience (steps) and additional educational units (columns). To this structure salary it adds increments for skills demonstrated through professional assessment procedures and for skills identified and assessed locally by the school or district. Local districts could determine the degree to which educational units (columns) would need to be related to areas of licensure and local educational needs. Currently, some local districts and states make these requirements; others do not. Specific dollar amounts would be identified for each cell in this model.

learn subject matter content more deeply, particularly for the emerging curriculum content standards, this model would provide a salary increase if a teacher passed an advanced subject matter examination. All a state or district would need to implement this competency element is an appropriate subject matter test. The model also provides a salary increase for licensure in a second subject or in a shortage area. The former reinforces the increasing number of curriculum programs that are multidisciplinary or thematic in nature and also helps to ensure that teachers assigned outside of their primary licensure area have at least the beginning set of knowledge and skills in the second subject (Gardner & Boix-Mansilla, 1994). By providing a salary increment for a shortage area, the schedule also provides an incentive for teachers to learn the beginning set of skills in areas that currently are short of qualified teachers; definitions of shortage areas would be set either by districts or states. Finally, the schedule formally provides salary increments for developing an advanced set of professional knowledge and skills as demonstrated by earning certification from the National Board for Professional Teaching Standards.

The local skills are suggestive; they are included to reinforce the notion that each school site may need a particular set of knowledge and skills depending on the vision of high performance the school decides to implement. The local skills identified also include specific second-language skills because schools increasingly are populated by students for whom English is not the primary language.

Another attractive feature of this model is that the knowledge and skills areas could be a rationale for additional education funding from either a local district or a state. A new educational enhancement fund could be created to provide salary incentives for teachers to develop the needed knowledge and skills. But the financial rewards would be given only to teachers who had developed new knowledge and skills deemed needed and important by the state, district, or site. This could start a process of linking pay directly to needed expertise.

Requiring Competence to Earn
Annual Salary Increments

Figure A.2 is also an example of a knowledge- and skills-based salary model that could be implemented quite quickly and actually is being tried in a variety of states and districts around the world. This model has several important features. First, it replaces the automatic annual increments for years of experience with annual increments that are contingent upon a

Figure A.2. Model 2: Performance Reviews for Annual Increments Combined With Skills-Based Pay Elements

Annual Performance Reviews	Additional Local Skills/Knowledge and Skills	
Performance Review 1	Skill Area A	
Performance Review 2	Skill Area B	*Certification from National Board for Professional Teaching Standards:* 5% to 10% salary addition over base salary from both columns 1 and 2 but only after performance review at some step, e.g., step 4.
Performance Review 3	Skill Area C	
Performance Review 4	Skill Area D	
Performance Review 5	Skill Area E	
Performance Review 6	Skill Area F	
Performance Review 7		
Performance Review 8		
Performance Review 9		
Performance Review 10		

NOTE: Model 2 modifies the current single-salary schedule by providing annual salary increments (steps) only for those teachers who have successfully passed a performance review, ideally, conducted through a professional, peer review process. Teachers would also receive pay increments for the demonstration of skills and knowledge identified by the local school or district as skills needed to achieve student achievement goals. These specified skills could be learned in a variety of ways (such as through course work, staff development, individual research, or professional networking opportunities) and would replace the educational units in the traditional single-salary schedule. In addition, teachers who achieved certification from the National Board for Professional Teaching Standards would receive a 5% to 10% pay increase. Specific dollar amounts would need to be identified for each cell in this model.

successful performance review, either annually or every 2 or 3 years. This stipulation makes pay increases not just automatic but a reward for some type of accomplishment, such as developing teaching practice to a set of increasingly rigorous professional standards.

A key element in making this stipulation function as intended is the nature of the performance review. Too often, districts or states implementing this plan assign the review function to principals but neither provide adequate training for a substantive review nor adequately describe the standards of teaching knowledge and skills that teachers would need to meet. This was a shortcoming of the first career teaching program implemented beginning in 1992 in Victoria, Australia, and of a similar program in Douglas County, Colorado. In Douglas County, however, it encouraged teachers and administrators to take teacher evaluation more seriously and to make concerted efforts to develop and set teaching standards and train principals in effective assessment techniques. Principal review of teaching practice to standards is also part of a revised, 1996 teacher career structure in Victoria, Australia, but, again, good implementation was impeded by lack of rich descriptions of teaching practice to standards and of principal training to conduct such a complex review.

The career teaching programs in Cincinnati, Ohio, and Rochester, New York, however, have avoided both of these shortcomings and are examples of how local performance reviews to solid professional standards can be a contribution to high-quality instruction. The ideal approach would be to take the written teaching standards that have been developed by both the Interstate New Teacher Assessment and Support Consortium (INTASC) and the National Board, write a set of local standards that form a series of steps from beginning to more advanced practice, and link performance reviews and skill assessments to these increasingly challenging standards. This would help provide specificity to the local performance review and link it to broader expectations for practice that have been created by the profession. By making any type of annual salary increment contingent on successfully completing such a performance review, the system in Figure A.2 connotes that monetary rewards should appropriately be connected to the level of individual practice vis-à-vis professionwide standards.

The second important feature of Figure A.2 is the addition of knowledge and skills required either by a local district or by a particular site, as described in Figure A.1. Third, this model eliminates the education units and degrees portion of the current single-salary schedule and replaces it with lanes for knowledge and skills; essentially, the model replaces the indirect measures that education credits now provide with more direct measures of professionally and locally defined knowledge and skills. However, education courses still could help teachers acquire new knowledge and skills. Finally, this model also includes salary recognition for

teachers who earn National Board certification. The model provides a significant salary increase, as a percentage of base salary, to any teacher earning Board certification. Although some districts now provide some type
of salary reward for Board certification, many do so as a fixed dollar
amount and often as a one-time bonus. The idea in Figure A.2 is that
Board certification represents advanced, accomplished, professional practice that should be rewarded each year after it is earned by a 5% to 10%
increase in base salary.

Taking Advanced Professional Practice Seriously

Figure A.3 begins moving to a more dramatic version of knowledge-
and skills-based pay. This model *replaces* the current salary schedule with
a knowledge- and skills-based salary structure; it also includes, although
conditionally, increments for years of experience.

The major thrust of this model is the structure of lane one. Teachers
would first begin as probationary teachers or interns with a salary below
the professional beginning salary, until they earned their full professional
license. Then they would enter at the beginning salary. They would earn
either annual or biennial salary increases, however, only by advancing
their professional expertise toward Board certification. They would receive no salary increase for years of experience until *after* they had earned
Board certification. The concept behind this structure is that it is only
teachers with advanced, accomplished expertise that the education system—district or state—would want to retain and reward with an automatic annual salary increment. Rather than assuming that additional
years of experience produce a more accomplished teacher, this schedule
requires demonstration of advanced competence both through early
competency assessments and by passing the National Board's rigorous
assessment to high professional standards.

Figure A.3 also provides salary increments for teachers who earn a
license in a second area as well as for enhancing their knowledge and skills
in that second area to some degree beyond initial licensure. Districts using
this model also could link tenure with an assessment of some level of practice beyond that required for initial licensure, level 2 in the proposed
model. Thus tenure would become something more than conferral of job
security: an indication of enhanced knowledge and competence. This
type of model takes very seriously the need for today's teachers to have a
much stronger repertoire of core subject matter knowledge and related

Figure A.3. Model 3: A Skills-Based Teacher Compensation Schedule for Board Certification and Retention

Primary Content Specialty	Second Content Specialty
Entry level with a full teacher license	Extra amount for a full second license
Advanced 1	Advanced 1
Advanced 2 (Tenure?)	Advanced 2
Advanced 3	
Advanced 4	
Advanced 5	
National Board certification—years of experience after Board certification	
Step 1	
Step 2	
Step 3	
Step 4	
Step 5	
Step n = ???	

NOTE: Model 3 completely replaces the current single-salary schedule with a knowledge- and skills-based compensation schedule. Under this plan, teachers would receive pay increments for the demonstration of knowledge and skills identified by the teaching profession as reflective of what excellent teachers should know and be able to do at various stages in their careers. Only after being certified by the National Board for Professional Teaching Standards would teachers begin to receive annual increments for years of experience beyond Board certification. This would provide an incentive for outstanding teachers to remain in the teaching profession. Teachers could also receive additional pay for the demonstration of skills in a second content area. Specific dollar amounts would need to be identified for each cell in this model.

instructional skills, and it signals that professional competence is the key variable on which to base salary.

A Complete Knowledge- and Skills-Based
Teacher Salary Schedule

Figure A.4 moves another step and represents a structure for a full-fledged, knowledge- and skills-based teacher salary structure. The model does not include any salary increments for either years of experience or education units or degrees; it replaces them with salary increments for knowledge and skills only.

The first lane represents knowledge and skills for the primary area of licensure. Salary increments would be earned for deepening and broadening professional expertise in that primary area. Again, tenure could be linked to an assessment of advanced professional expertise. Districts could vary the number of different levels between initial licensure and Board certification, but one to five levels appear to be feasible.

The model also includes salary increments for licensure in a second area as well as additional salary increments for advanced expertise in the second teaching area—but not all the way to Board certification. The concept behind this second lane is that an individual fully prepared to teach in two different subject areas is more valuable to a school than a teacher licensed in only one subject. Schools always seem to be short of teachers in various subjects; by providing a salary increment for teachers who earned licensure in a second area, a school would be improving the probability that it could always assign teachers to classes in which they are fully prepared and thus could reduce, minimize, and, it is hoped, even eliminate having faculty teach a class in a subject for which they are not fully prepared.

Figure A.4 also provides for specific site expertise. The knowledge and skills listed are expertise in a second language and expertise in a tutoring model for reading. These are just examples. Districts and schools would identify the specific, additional knowledge and skills they needed beyond the core knowledge and skills represented by lanes one and two.

The last two lanes specifically list various knowledge and skills teachers need in restructured and site-based managed schools—counseling, professional development, curriculum development, leading teams, community outreach, program evaluation, budgeting, and so forth. Again, this list is suggestive but identifies several of the functional and managerial areas of knowledge and skills that teachers in such schools could be reasonably expected to develop to engage professionally in these tasks.

Clearly, other models of competency pay could be developed either to add to the current salary structure or to replace it. But the models pre-

Figure A.4. Model 4: A Comprehensive Competency-Based Teacher Compensation Schedule: High School Version

First Content Specialty	Second Content Specialty	School Site Expertise (examples)	Breadth Skills	Management Skills
Entry		Spanish fluency	Counseling	Decision-making team leader
Provisional license	Provisional license	Hmong fluency	Professional development	School operations
Professional license	Professional license	Korean fluency	Curriculum development	Budgeting
Advanced 1	Advanced 1	Reading recovery	School-to-work transition	Accounting and financial mgt.
Advanced 2 tenure	Advanced 2 tenure		Computers and technology	Marketing
Advanced 3 recertification			Community outreach	Program evaluation
Advanced 4			Family liaison	
Advanced 5				
National Board certification				

NOTE: Model 4 builds on Model 3 but adds opportunities for pay increments for the demonstration of skills and knowledge identified by the school or district as important to achieve local educational goals. This model provides for tailoring of teacher skill development to needs of the local school context, including specific depth and breadth skills, geared to the local student population, and management skills that may be required for local management of school operations. Specific dollar amounts would need to be identified for each cell in this model.

sented here provide several ideas of both what paying for knowledge and skills means and how such new ideas could be used to reshape the teacher salary structure.

Choosing Among Models

There are no clear rationales for choosing among the above models, and, as stated, additional models or variations of the above models could be created. The first two models can more quickly be adopted; they are more closely linked to the current single-salary structure and add elements of knowledge- and skills-based pay to them. Models A.3 and A.4 are much more aligned with the high-standards, high-performance school discussed in Chapter 2 and would be more appropriate for a school system or state moving aggressively to create these kinds of schools, places with a standards-based education reform, including substantial, site-based school management.

Resource B: Principles for Implementing Change in Teacher Compensation

Generally, notions of knowledge- and skills-based pay and group-based performance awards are still relatively new to schools and education systems. However, many other organizations have been using these forms of pay for several years. This experience provides information on the design and development of these compensation approaches, which addresses both technical and process issues. Interestingly, studies show that although the technical issues are obviously important, the process issues are more important (Jenkins, Douglas, Ledford, Gupta, & Doty, 1992). Thus we first discuss the process and then the technical issues.

Process Principles

There are 10 key process principles, each contributing to the successful development, design, and implementation of a new compensation system that includes either knowledge- and skills-based pay or school-based performance awards or both:

❖ *Involvement of all key parties,* especially those whose compensation is being changed, is the preeminent principle for successfully changing compensation structures. Teachers and their unions, administrators, school boards, and the public all should be centrally involved in the process of development, design, and implementation.

❖ *Broad agreement on the most valued educational results.* Compensation incentives help focus attention on important organizational goals. Thus all parties—teachers, administrators, board members, parents, and the public—need to agree on the results that are most valued.

❖ *Comprehensive evaluation systems.* Sound mechanisms need to be in place to assess teacher knowledge-and-skill development in a skill-based pay system as well as organizational products and processes to be rewarded through group-based performance awards. Such assessment mechanisms might include measures of student achievement, parent satisfaction, and teacher and administrator skills, knowledge, and performance.

❖ *Adequate funding.* A lack of funding and a lack of a long-term funding commitment have been key aspects of the downfall of many efforts to reform compensation in education. Transition funds often are needed to move from the old to the new structure, and performance bonuses need a stable funding pool. Funds integrated in the school finance and budgeting structures are less likely to be vulnerable to cuts than a separate funding pool.

❖ *Investments in ongoing professional development* are key to knowledge- and skills-based pay systems. Such investments should be in the range of 2% to 4% of the operating budget.

❖ *No quotas.* Quotas are the bane of many compensation changes. Although not all individuals will want or need to master all knowledge and skills areas, quotas should not be imposed. All schools— not just a fixed percentage of schools—that meet performance improvement targets should be rewarded. Organizational excellence is dependent on consistent rewards for improvements in performance.

❖ *General conditions of work.* The better the conditions of work in a school (teacher involvement in decision making, sound facilities, availability of materials, safety, good principal leadership, central office support for schools, etc.), the more likely a new form of compensation can be implemented successfully. A corollary to this principle is that the compensation system should be designed with the general conditions of work in mind. For example, skills assessment in a high-involvement school should incorporate teachers fully in the assessment process.

❖ *Management maturity.* Administrators and the school board should have good working relations, and the administration should develop a history of working cooperatively with teachers and their unions to further system goals and objectives. Restructuring the salary schedule should occur in an environment characterized by interest-based bargaining in which each party recognizes the interests and concerns of the other parties and all work together to design solutions that meet the needs of all parties in the local context.

❖ *Labor maturity.* Teacher unions, associations, and their members need to have positive commitment to the academic goals of the school, good working relations among themselves, and a tradition of working with management toward education system key goals.

❖ *Persistence* until the plan is "perfected." Most plans have initial bugs and are viewed with skepticism by some employees. Thus persistence is needed to continue implementation, to revise the plan when problems are identified, and to encourage full participation to see how the plan works when fully implemented.

General Technical-Design Principles

Although there are numerous technical-design issues, the following key principles should guide the design of any new compensation system:

❖ *Fairness.* Everyone from teachers to school board members should perceive the system as fair.

❖ *Comprehensibility.* If it is to provide an incentive for high performance or for knowledge and skills development, the system will need to be understood by all who are affected. Although this does not mean that it must be simplistic, it does mean that the elements of any new compensation plan, and how salary increments or bonuses are earned, will need to be readily comprehended.

❖ *Incentive-behavior compatibility.* The new compensation system must provide incentives that lead to the appropriate types of teacher behaviors, for example, collegial work within schools, active learning of new skills, knowledge and professional expertise, and deployment of energies to produce desired results for all students.

Knowledge- and Skills-Based Pay Principles

The following applies specifically to competency-based pay components of compensation plans:

❖ *Clear, specific, and measurable skills.* The skills should be directly related to the needs of a particular school system—state, district, or site—and described in written form with clear standards. Such teacher knowledge and skills and rubrics for the evaluation system could be designed locally and could utilize the development of standards of the Interstate New Teacher Assessment and Support Consortium (INTASC), PRAXIS III, Danielson's (1996) Framework for Teaching, and the National Board for Professional Teaching Standards (NBPTS). Each has written documents about 25 pages long that describe the knowledge and skills needed for licensure, performance, or certification in several teaching areas.

❖ *An objective, sound, and credible assessment system* to determine skill attainment. Teachers and administrators should be involved in skill assessment that is done locally. In the long term, core curriculum and instruction skill blocks should probably be assessed by a state or national teaching-standards board, as is done in many other professions (Kelley & Taylor, 1995). These assessments should be set according to an external professional standard. Teachers whose performance will be judged by it should view the assessment system as fair, and different assessors should provide consistent assessments for different teachers.

Performance Awards

The following principles should guide development of performance awards:

❖ *Provide awards only on a group, probably a whole-school, and not an individual basis.* This is important because it reflects the collaborative nature of teaching and schools. Usually, this means everyone in a school—professional and classified staff members—is eligible.

❖ *Be very clear about what performance is most valued*—student achievement, student and teacher attendance, parent satisfaction, and so forth. The system will get more of what is in the performance measure and less of other system outcomes. Thus if the system focuses on achievement, it should incorporate a full range of achievement measures over a range of subject areas.

❖ *Base the performance standard for each school on improvements* over some historic base. Although the specific standard should reflect local context, the improvement targets should be revisited each year and could be based on multiple years of data. The core goal for all schools should be improving student performance to specific levels by a specific target date. The performance assessment should recognize changes in the student population, such as student mobility, which may impede accurate measures of progress.

❖ *Provide an integrated and protected funding pool* that will make all schools that meet or exceed performance targets eligible for the performance award. When performance award funds are integrated into the entire fund structure, these awards are a less convenient target for budget cuts. Stability in performance award funding is essential for the awards to serve as an incentive for future performance improvements.

❖ *Provide awards that are valued by teachers.* Such awards could be salary enhancements or dollars to be used, for example, for school improvement activities, expanding technology, additional opportunities for additional professional development, or a venture capital pool for developing innovative practices. We think average bonuses in the $2,000 to $3,000 range should be the goal.

❖ *If offering a salary award, provide it as a bonus, not as an addition to base pay.* The award could be a percentage of each individual's salary or a specific dollar amount; the percentage or dollar amount could vary by staffing category—classified, professional, principal. The amount should be sufficient to be a relevant incentive and should be paid as a bonus to provide a continuing incentive for high performance each year. The amounts also should be part of retirement pay.

❖ *Provide teachers with professional control over the work environment.* If teachers are to be held responsible for student results, they need to have the capacity to improve organizational effectiveness. Knowledge, power, and information should be devolved to teachers to give them the capacity to make the changes needed to create performance improvements (Mohrman, Wohlstetter, & Associates, 1994; Wohlstetter, Mohrman, & Robertson, 1997; Wohlstetter, Van Kirk, Robertson, & Mohrman, 1997).

References

Adams, J. (1993). School finance reform and systemic school change: Reconstituting Kentucky's public schools. *Journal of Education Finance, 18,* 318-345.

Adams, J. (2000). *Taking charge of curriculum: Teacher networks and curriculum implementation.* New York: Teachers College Press.

Allen, M. (2000). Focusing policy on hard-to-staff schools. *State Education Leader, 18*(2), 1-4.

American Federation of Teachers. (2000). *Survey and analysis of teacher salary trends 1999.* Washington, DC: Author. Retrieved April 19, 2001, from the American Federation of Teachers from the World Wide Web: www.aft.org/research/survey99/index.html

American Federation of Teachers. (2001). *Professional compensation for teachers.* Retrieved April 24, 2001, from the American Federation of Teachers from the World Wide Web: www.aft.org/edissues/teacherquality/profcomp4tchrs.htm

Archer, J. (2001, February 21). AFT to urge locals to consider new pay strategies. *Education Week, 20*(23), 3.

Bacharach, S. B., & Conley, S. C. (1986). Educational reform: A managerial agenda. *Phi Delta Kappan, 67*(9), 641-648.

Bacharach, S. B., Conley, S. C., & Shedd, J. B. (1990). Evaluating teachers for career awards and merit pay. In J. Millman & L. Darling-Hammond (Eds.), *The new handbook of teacher evaluation: Assessing elementary and secondary school teachers* (pp. 133-146). Newbury Park, CA: Sage.

Bacharach, S. B., Lipsky, D. B., & Shedd, J. B. (1984). *Paying for better teaching: Merit pay and its alternatives.* Ithica, NY: Organizational Analysis and Practice.

Ball, D. L., Cohen, D. K., Peterson, P. L., & Wilson, S. M. (1994, April). *Understanding state efforts to reform teaching and learning: Learning from teachers about learning to teach.* Paper presented at the annual meeting of the American Educational Research Association, New Orleans, Louisiana.

Ballou, D., & Podgursky, M. (1997). *Teacher pay and teacher quality.* Kalamazoo, MI: W. E. Upjohn Institute for Employment Research.

Bandura, A. (1997). *Self-efficacy: The exercise of control.* New York: W. H. Freeman.

Baugh, W. H., & Stone, J. A. (1982). *Mobility of wage equilibrium in the educator labor market.* Eugene, OR: Center for Educational Policy and Management.

Bellon, E. C., Bellon, J. J., Blank, M. A., Brian, D. J. G., & Kershaw, C. A. (1989, March). *Alternative incentive programs for school-based reform.* Paper presented at the annual meeting of the American Educational Research Association, San Francisco, California.

Blair, J. (2001, February 21). Lawmakers plunge into teacher pay: Shortages spur action in many states. *Education Week, 20*(23), 1, 16.

Blinder, A. S. (Ed.). (1990). *Paying for productivity: A look at the evidence.* Washington, DC: Brookings Institution.

Bond, L. (1998). Disparate impact and teacher certification. *Journal of Personnel Evaluation in Education, 12*(2), 211-220.

Bond, L., Richard, J., Smith, T., & Hattie, J. (2000). *Accomplished teaching: A validation of National Board certification, executive summary.* Retrieved December 14, 2000, from the National Board for Professional Teaching Standards from the World Wide Web: www.nbpts.org/Press/exec_summary.pdf

Bradley, A. (1994, April 20). Pioneers in professionalism. *Education Week, 13*(30), 18-27.

Bransford, J., Brown, A., & Cocking, R. (1999). *How people learn.* Washington, DC: National Academy Press.

Bransford, J., Goldman, S., & Vye, N. (1991). Making a difference in people's abilities to think: Reflections on a decade of work and some hopes for the future. In L. Okagaki & R. J. Sternberg (Eds.), *Directions of development: Influence on children's thinking* (pp. 147-180). Hillsdale, NJ: Lawrence Erlbaum.

Brophy, J., & Good, T. (1986). Teacher behaviors and student achievement. In M. Wittrock (Ed.), *Handbook of research on teaching* (3rd ed., pp. 328-375). New York: Macmillan.

Bruer, J. T. (1993). *Schools for thought: A science of learning in the classroom.* Cambridge: MIT Press.

Carnegie Forum on Education and the Economy. (1986). *A nation prepared: Teachers for the 21st century.* New York: Carnegie Corporation.

Carter, P. (1992). Becoming the "new women": The equal rights campaigns of New York City schoolteachers, 1900-1920. In R. J. Altenbaugh (Ed.), *The teacher's voice: A social history of teaching in twentieth-century America* (pp. 40-58). London: Falmer.

Chan, Y., Galarza, G., Llamas, S., Kellor, E., & Odden, A. (1999). *A case study of the Vaughn Next Century Learning Center's school-based performance award program.* Madison: University of Wisconsin–Madison, Wisconsin Center for Education Research, Consortium for Policy Research in Education. Retrieved April 24, 2001, from the World Wide Web: www.wcer.wisc.edu/cpre/tcomp/

Clardy, A. (1988). *Compensation systems and school effectiveness: Merit pay as an incentive for school improvement.* College Park: University of Maryland. (ERIC Document Reproduction Service No. ED 335 789)

Clotfelter, C., & Ladd, H. (1996). Recognizing and rewarding success in public schools. In H. Ladd (Ed.), *Holding schools accountable* (pp. 23-64). Washington, DC: Brookings Institution.

Cohen, D., & Ball, D. L. (Eds.). (1990). *Educational Evaluation and Policy Analysis, 12*(3), entire issue.

Cohen, D. K. (1990). A revolution in one classroom: The case of Mrs. Oublier. *Educational Evaluation and Policy Analysis, 12,* 327-345.

Cohen, D. K. (1996). Rewarding teachers for student performance. In S. H. Fuhrman & J. A. O'Day (Eds.), *Rewards and reform: Creating educational incentives that work* (pp. 60-112). San Francisco: Jossey-Bass.

Cohen, D. K., McLaughlin, M., & Talbert, J. (Eds.). (1993). *Teaching for understanding: Challenges for policy and practice.* San Francisco: Jossey-Bass.

Cohen, M. (1983). Instructional, management and social conditions in effective schools. In A. Odden & L. D. Webb (Eds.), *School finance and school improvement: Linkages for the 1980s* (pp. 17-50). Cambridge, MA: Ballinger.

Conley, S. C. (1991). Review of research on teacher participation in school decision making. In G. Grant (Ed.), *Review of Research in Education* (Vol. 17, pp. 225-266). Washington, DC: American Educational Research Association.

Conley, S. C. (1994). Teacher compensation: From merit pay and career ladders to knowledge-based pay. In L. Ingvarson & R. Chadbourne (Eds.), *Valuing teachers' work: New directions in performance appraisal* (pp. 46-69). Victoria, Australia: Australian Council for Educational Research.

Conley, S. C., & Bacharach, S. B. (1990). From school-site management to participatory school-site management. *Phi Delta Kappan, 71,* 539-544.

Conley, S. C., & Odden, A. (1995). Linking teacher compensation to teacher career development: A strategic examination. *Educational Evaluation and Policy Analysis, 17,* 253-269.

Conley, S. C., Schmidle, T., & Shedd, J. B. (1988). Teacher participation in the management of school systems. *Teachers College Record, 90,* 259-280.

Conti, E. (2000). *Turning experience into expertise: A multiple case study analysis of school districts aligning teacher compensation with high performance.* Unpublished doctoral dissertation, University of Wisconsin–Madison.

Corcoran, T. B. (1995, June). *Helping teachers teach well: Transforming professional development* (RB-16). New Brunswick, NJ: Consortium for Policy Research in Education, Rutgers University.

Cornett, L. M. (1994, April). Ups and downs of incentive programs. *Southern Regional Education Board Career Ladder Clearinghouse,* 1-2. Atlanta, GA: Southern Regional Education Board.

Crandall, N. F., & Wallace, M. J., Jr. (1998). *Work and rewards in the virtual workplace.* New York: American Management Association-Amacom.

Cumming, C. M. (1994). Incentives that really do motivate. *Compensation and Benefits Review, 26*(3), 38-40.

Cunningham, D. H. (2000, June). *The link between New York state student performance standards and teaching.* Paper presented to the Education Finance Research Consortium, Albany, New York.

Danielson, C. (1996). *Enhancing professional practice: A framework for teaching.* Alexandria, VA: Association for Supervision and Curriculum Development.

Danielson, C., & McGreal, T. (2000). *Teacher evaluation to enhance professional practice.* Alexandria, VA: Association for Supervision and Curriculum Development.

Darling-Hammond, L. (1994, November). *National Commission on Teaching and America's Future: Briefing paper.* New York: Teachers College, Columbia University.

Darling-Hammond, L. (1996). Restructuring schools for high performance. In S. H. Fuhrman & J. A. O'Day (Eds.), *Rewards and reform: Creating educational incentives that work* (pp. 144-192). San Francisco: Jossey-Bass.

Darling-Hammond, L., & McLaughlin, M. W. (1995). Policies that support professional development in an era of reform. *Phi Delta Kappan, 76,* 597-604.

Darling-Hammond, L., Wise, A. E., & Klein, S. P. (1995). *A license to teach: Building a profession for 21st century schools.* Boulder, CO: Westview.

David, J. (1994). School-based decision making: Kentucky's test of decentralization. *Phi Delta Kappan, 75,* 706-712.

Dwyer, C. A. (1994). *Development of the knowledge base for the Praxis III: Classroom performance assessment criteria.* Princeton, NJ: Educational Testing Service.

Dwyer, C. A. (1998). Psychometrics of Praxis III: Classroom Performance assessments certification. *Journal for Personnel Evaluation in Education, 12*(2), 163-187.

Educational Research Service Report. (1978). *Methods of scheduling salaries for teachers.* Arlington, VA: Educational Research Service.

Elmore, R. F. (1996). Getting to scale with good educational practice. *Harvard Educational Review, 66,* 1-26.

Elmore, R. F. (with Burney, D.) (1997). *Investing in teacher learning: Staff development and instructional improvement in community school district #2, New York City.* New York: National Commission on Teaching and America's Future, and the Consortium for Policy Research in Education.

English, F. (1992). History and critical issues of educational compensation systems. In L. Frase (Ed.), *Teacher compensation and motivation* (pp. 3-25). Lancaster, PA: Technomic.

Farkas, S., Johnson, J., & Foleno, T. (2000). *A sense of calling: Who teaches and why.* New York: Public Agenda.

Federico, R. F., & Goldsmith, H. B. (1998, July/August). Linking work/life benefits to performance. *Compensation and Benefits Review,* 66-70.

Ferris, J., & Winkler, D. (1986). Teacher compensation and the supply of teachers. *Elementary School Journal, 86,* 389-404.

Firestone, W. (1994). Redesigning teacher salary systems for education reform. *American Educational Research Journal, 31,* 549-574.

Firestone, W. A., & Pennell, J. R. (1993). Teacher commitment, working conditions, and differential incentive policies. *Review of Educational Research, 63,* 489-525.

Freiberg, H. J., & Knight, S. L. (1991). Career ladder programs as incentives for teachers. In S. C. Conley & B. S. Cooper (Eds.), *The school as a work environment: Implications for reform* (pp. 204-235). Boston: Allyn & Bacon.

Fuhrman, S. (Ed.). (1993). *Designing coherent education policy*. San Francisco: Jossey-Bass.

Fuller, W. E. (1982). *The old country school: A story of rural education in the Middle West*. Chicago: University of Chicago Press.

Galbraith, J. R., & Lawler, E. E., III. (1993). *Organizing for the future: The new logic for managing complex organizations*. San Francisco: Jossey-Bass.

Gardner, H., & Boix-Mansilla, V. (1994). Teaching for understanding in the disciplines—and beyond. *Teachers College Record, 96,* 198-218.

Geber, B. (1992, June). Saturn's grand experiment. *Training,* 27-35.

Goertz, M., Floden, R., & O'Day, J. (1995). *Evaluating education reform: Systemic reform, Vol. 1: Findings and conclusions*. New Brunswick, NJ: Consortium for Policy Research in Education, Rutgers University.

Gold, R. (2001, February 22). Teacher bonuses get mixed grades: States give higher marks to merit based awards than hiring incentives. *Wall Street Journal,* p. B17.

Goodlad, J. I. (1984). *A place called school*. New York: McGraw-Hill.

Gupta, N., & Mitra, A. (1998). The value of financial incentives: Myths and empirical realities. *ACA Journal, 7*(3), 58-66.

Hall, G. E., & Caffarella, E. P. (1996). *First-year implementation of the Douglas County, Colorado, school district performance pay plan for teachers*. Greeley: University of Northern Colorado, School of Education.

Hall, G. E., & Caffarella, E. P. (1997). *Third-year implementation assessment of the Douglas County, Colorado, school district performance pay plan for teachers*. Castle Rock, CO: Douglas County School District.

Hall, G. E., & Caffarella, E. (1998). *Third-year implementation assessment of the Douglas County, Colorado, school district performance pay plan for teachers (1996-97)*. Greeley: University of Northern Colorado, School of Education.

Hammer, M., & Champy, J. (1993). *Reengineering the corporation*. New York: Harper Business.

Hanushek, E. A. (1994). *Making schools work: Improving performance and controlling costs*. Washington, DC: Brookings Institution.

Hanushek, E. A. (1997). Assessing the effects of school resources on student performance: An update. *Educational Evaluation and Policy Analysis, 19*(2), 141-164.

Harp, L. (1995, April 26). Ky. schools put on the line in bonus budgeting. *Education Week, 14*(31), 1, 9.

Harris, L., & Associates. (1995). *The Metropolitan Life survey of the American teacher, 1984-1995: Old problems, new challenges.* New York: Metropolitan Life Insurance.

Hart, A. W. (1994). Work feature values of today's and tomorrow's teachers: Work redesign as an incentive and school improvement policy. *Educational Evaluation and Policy Analysis, 16*, 458-473.

Hart, A. W. (1995). Reconceiving school leadership: Emergent views. *Elementary School Journal, 96*, 9-28.

Hart, A. W., & Murphy, M. J. (1990). New teachers react to redesigned teacher work. *American Journal of Education, 98*, 224-250.

Hatry, H. P., Greiner, J. M., & Ashford, B. G. (1994). *Issues and case studies in teacher incentive plans* (2d ed.). Washington, DC: Urban Institute Press.

Haycock, K. (2000). No more settling for less. *Thinking K-16, 4*(1), 3-12.

Heneman, H. G., III. (1998). Assessment of motivational reactions to teachers of a school-based performance award program. *Journal of Personnel Evaluation in Education, 2*(2), 43-59.

Heneman, H. G., III, & Milanowski, A. (1999). Teachers' attitudes about teacher bonuses under school-based performance award programs. *Journal of Personnel Evaluation in Education, 12*(4), 327-342.

Heneman, H. G., III, & Schwab, D. P. (1972). An evaluation of research on expectancy theory predictions of employee performance. *Psychological Bulletin, 78*, 1-9.

Heneman, H. G., III, & Schwab, D. P. (1979). Work and rewards theory. In D. Yoder & H. G. Heneman, Jr. (Eds.), *ASPA handbook of personnel and industrial relations.* Washington, DC: Bureau of National Affairs.

Heneman, H. G., III, & Young, I. P. (1991). Assessment of a merit pay program for school district administrators. *Public Personnel Management, 21*(1), 35-47.

Heneman, H. G., III, Schwab, D. P., Fossum, J. A., & Dyer, L. (1989). *Personnel/human resource management* (4th ed.). Homewood, IL: Richard D. Irwin.

Heneman, R. L. (1992). *Merit pay: Linking pay increases to performance ratings.* Reading, MA: Addison-Wesley.

Heneman, R. L., & Ledford, G. E., Jr. (1998, June). Competency pay for professionals and managers in business: A review and implications for teachers certification. *Journal of Personnel Evaluation in Education, 12*(2), 103-121.

Heneman, R. L., Ledford, G. E., Jr., & Gresham, M. T. (2000). The changing nature of work and its effects on compensation design and delivery (pp. 195-240). In S. L. Rynes & B. Gerhart (Eds.), *Compensation in organizations: Current research and practice.* San Francisco: Jossey-Bass.

Heneman, R. L., & Von Hippel, C. (1995). Balancing group and individual rewards: Rewarding individual contributions to the team. *Compensation and Benefits Review, 27*(4), 63-68.

Herzberg, F. (1968). One more time: How do we motivate employees? *Harvard Business Review, 46*(1), 53-62.

Herzberg, F., Mausner, B., & Snyderman, B. B. (1959). *The motivation to work.* New York: Wiley.

Huberman, M. (1995). Professional careers and professional development: Some intersections. In T. R. Guskey & M. Huberman (Eds.), *Professional development in education: New paradigms and practices* (pp. 193-224). New York: Teachers College Press.

Imazeki, J. Y. (2000). *School finance reform and the market for teachers.* Unpublished doctoral dissertation, Department of Economics, University of Wisconsin-Madison.

Interstate New Teacher Assessment and Support Consortium. (1995a). *Model standards for beginning teacher licensing and development: A resource for state dialogue.* Washington, DC: Council of Chief State School Officers.

Interstate New Teacher Assessment and Support Consortium. (1995b). *Model standards in mathematics for beginning teacher licensing and development: A resource for state dialogue.* Washington, DC: Council of Chief State School Officers.

Iowa State Department of Education. (2000). *A proposal for a new teacher compensation system based on teacher performance, career development and the national labor market.* Des Moines, IA: Author.

Jacobson, S. L. (1987). Merit pay and teaching as a career. In K. Alexander & D. H. Monk (Eds.), *Attracting and compensating America's teachers* (pp. 161-177). Eighth annual yearbook of the American Educational Finance Association. Cambridge, MA: Ballinger.

Jaeger, R. M. (1998). Evaluating the psychometric qualities of the National Board for Professional Teaching Standards Assessments:

A methodological accounting. *Journal of Personnel Evaluation in Education, 12*(2), 189-210.

Jenkins, G. D., Jr., Ledford, G. E., Jr., Gupta, N., & Doty, D. H. (1992). *Skill-based pay: Practices, payoffs, pitfalls and prescriptions.* Scottsdale, AZ: American Compensation Association.

Jenkins, G. D., Jr., Mitra, A., Gupta, N., & Shaw, J. D. (1998). Are financial incentives related to performance? A meta-analytic review of empirical research. *Journal of Applied Psychology, 83*(5), 777-787.

Johnson, H., Leak, E., Williamson, G., Kellor, E., Milanowski, T., & Odden, A. (1999). *A case study of the state of North Carolina's school-based performance award program.* Madison: University of Wisconsin–Madison, Wisconsin Center for Education Research, Consortium for Policy Research in Education.

Johnson, S. M. (1986). Incentives for teachers: What motivates, what matters? *Educational Administration Quarterly, 22*(3), 54-79.

Jordan, H., Mendro, R., & Weerasinghe, D. (1997). *Teacher Effects on Longitudinal Student Achievement.* Paper presented at the annual meeting of the Consortium for Research on Educational Accountability and Teacher Evaluation, Indianapolis, Indiana.

Kannapel, P. J., Coe, P., Aagaard, L., Moore, B. D., & Reeves, C. A. (2000). Teacher responses to rewards and sanctions: Effects of and reactions to Kentucky's high-stakes accountability program. In B. L. Whitford & K. Jones (Eds.), *Accountability, assessment, and teacher commitment: Lessons from Kentucky's reform efforts.* New York: SUNY Press.

Katz, M. B. (1987). *Reconstructing American education.* Cambridge, MA: Harvard University Press.

Katzenbach, J. R., & Smith, D. K. (1993). *The wisdom of teams: Creating the high-performance organization.* Boston: Harvard Business School Press.

Kelley, C. (1996). Implementing teacher compensation reform in public schools: Lessons from the field. *Journal of School Business Management, 8*(1), 37-54.

Kelley, C. (1997). Teacher compensation and organization. *Educational Evaluation and Policy Analysis, 19*(1), 15-28.

Kelley, C. (1998). The Kentucky school-based performance award program: School-level effects. *Educational Policy, 12*(3), 305-324.

Kelley, C., Conley, S., & Kimball, S. (2000). Payment for results: The effects of the Kentucky and Maryland group-based performance award programs. *Peabody Journal of Education, 75*(4), 159-199.

Kelley, C., Heneman, H., III, & Milanowski, A. (2000). *School-based performance award programs, teacher motivation, and school performance: Findings from a study of three programs* (CPRE Research Report Series RR-44). Philadelphia: University of Pennsylvania, Graduate School of Education, Consortium for Policy Research in Education.

Kelley, C., & Kimball, S. (in press). Financial Incentives for National Board Certification. *Educational Policy.*

Kelley, C., & Odden, A. (1995). *New ideas for reinventing teacher compensation.* Madison: University of Wisconsin–Madison, Wisconsin Center for Education Research, Consortium for Policy Research in Education.

Kelley, C., & Protsik, J. (1997). Risk and reward: Perspectives on the implementation of Kentucky's school-based performance award program. *Educational Administration Quarterly, 33*(4), 474-505.

Kelley, C., & Taylor, C. H. (1995). *Compensation and skill development in four professions and implications for the teaching profession.* Madison: University of Wisconsin–Madison, Wisconsin Center for Education Research, Consortium for Policy Research in Education.

Kellor, E., & Odden, A. (2000). *Cincinnati: A case study of the design of a school-based performance award program.* Madison: University of Wisconsin–Madison, Wisconsin Center for Education Research, Consortium for Policy Research in Education.

Kellor, E., Milanowski, A., & Odden, A. (2000). *How Vaughn Next Century Learning Center developed a knowledge- and skills-based pay program.* Madison: University of Wisconsin–Madison, Wisconsin Center for Education Research, Consortium for Policy Research in Education.

Kennedy, C. W., Fossum, J. A., & White, B. J. (1983). An empirical comparison of within-subjects and between-subjects expectancy theory models. *Organizational Behavior and Human Performance, 32,* 124-143.

Kentucky Department of Education. (1995, February). *Kentucky teacher.* Frankfort, KY: Author.

Kentucky Institute for Education Research. (1995, January). *An independent evaluation of the Kentucky Instructional Results Information System conducted by the Evaluation Center, Western Michigan University.* Frankfort, KY: Author.

Kerchner, C. T., Koppich, J. E., & Weeres, J. G. (1997). *United mind workers: Unions and teaching in the knowledge society.* San Francisco: Jossey-Bass.

King, R. A., & Mathers, J. K. (1997, Fall). Improving schools through performance-based accountability and financial rewards. *Journal of Education Finance, 23,* 147-176.

Klein, S., & Hamilton, L. (1999). *Large scale testing: Current practices and new directions.* Santa Monica, CA: RAND.

Klein, S. P. (1998). Standards for teacher tests. *Journal of Personnel Evaluation in Education, 12*(2), 123-138.

Klein, S. P., Hamilton, L., McCaffrey, D., & Stecher, B. M. (2000). *What do test scores in Texas tell us?* Santa Monica, CA: RAND.

Knapp, M. S., Shields, P. M., & Turnbull, B. J. (1995). Academic challenge in high poverty classrooms. *Phi Delta Kappan, 76,* 770-776.

Kohn, A. (1993). *Punished by rewards: The trouble with gold stars, incentive plans, A's, praise, and other bribes.* Boston: Houghton Mifflin.

Koretz, D. M., Barron, S., Mitchell, K. J., & Stecher, B. M. (1996). *Perceived effects of the Kentucky Instructional Results Information System.* Institute on Education and Training. Santa Monica, CA: RAND.

Ladsen-Billings, G. (1997). *Dream keepers: Successful teachers of African American children.* San Francisco: Jossey-Bass.

Lawler, E. E., III. (1971). *Pay and organizational effectiveness: A psychological view.* New York: McGraw-Hill.

Lawler, E. E., III. (1973). *Motivation in work organizations.* Monterey, CA: Brooks/Cole.

Lawler, E. E., III. (1981). *Pay and organizational development.* Reading, MA: Addison-Wesley.

Lawler, E. E., III. (1986). *High-involvement management.* San Francisco: Jossey-Bass.

Lawler, E. E., III. (1990). *Strategic pay: Aligning organizational strategies and pay systems.* San Francisco: Jossey-Bass.

Lawler, E. E., III. (1992). *The ultimate advantage.* San Francisco: Jossey-Bass.

Lawler, E. E., III. (1995). The new pay: A strategic approach. *Compensation and Benefits Review, 27*(4), 14-22.

Lawler, E. E., III. (1996). *From the ground up: Six principles for building the new logic organization.* San Francisco: Jossey-Bass.

Lawler, E. E., III. (2000a). *Rewarding excellence: Pay strategies for the new economy.* San Francisco: Jossey-Bass.

Lawler, E. E., III. (2000b). Pay strategy: New thinking for the new millennium. *Compensation and Benefits Review,* Jan./Feb., 7-12.

Lawler, E. E., III, Mohrman, S. A., & Ledford, G. E., Jr. (1995). *Creating high performance organizations.* San Francisco: Jossey-Bass.

Ledford, G. E., Jr. (1991). The design of skill-based pay plans. In M. Rock & L. Berger (Eds.), *Handbook of compensation* (pp. 199-217). New York: McGraw-Hill.

Ledford, G. E., Jr. (1995a). Designing nimble reward systems. *Compensation and Benefits Review, 27*(4), 46-54.

Ledford, G. E., Jr. (1995b). Paying for the skills, knowledge, and competencies of knowledge workers. *Compensation and Benefits Review, 27*(4), 55-62.

Ledford, G. E., Jr., Lawler, E. E., III, & Mohrman, S. A. (1995). Reward innovations in Fortune 1000 companies. *Compensation and Benefits Review, 27*(4), 76-80.

Lieberman, A., & Miller, L. (Eds.). (1991). *Staff development for education in the '90s* (2d ed.). New York: Teachers College Press.

Leithwood, K. (2000, November). *School leadership in an era of external accountability initiatives.* Paper presented at the University Council for Educational Administration Research Conference, Albuquerque, New Mexico.

Lipsky, D. B., & Bacharach, S. B. (1983). The single salary schedule vs. merit pay: An examination of the debate. *Collective Bargaining Quarterly, 11*(4), 1-11.

Little, J. W. (1982). Norms of collegiality and experimentation: Workplace conditions of school success. *American Educational Research Journal, 19,* 325-40.

Little, J. W. (1993). Teachers' professional development in a climate of educational reform. *Educational Analysis and Policy Analysis, 15,* 129-152.

Little, J. W., & McLaughlin, M. W. (Eds.). (1993). *Teachers' work: Individuals, colleagues and contexts.* New York: Teachers College Press.

Locke, E. A. (1968). Towards a theory of task motivation and incentives. *Organizational Behavior and Human Performance, 3,* 157-189.

Lortie, D. C. (1975). *Schoolteacher: A sociological study.* Chicago: University of Chicago Press.

Louis, K. S., Marks, H. M., & Kruse, S. (1995). *Teachers' professional community in restructuring schools.* Madison: University of Wisconsin–Madison, Wisconsin Center for Education Research, Center on Organization and Restructuring Schools.

Malen, B., Murphy, M. J., & Hart, A. W. (1987). Restructuring teacher compensation systems: An analysis of three incentive strategies. In K. Alexander & D. H. Monk (Eds.), *Attracting and compensating America's teachers: Eighth annual yearbook of the American Educational Finance Association* (pp. 91-142). Cambridge, MA: Ballinger.

Manski, C. F. (1987). Academic ability, earnings, and the decision to become a teacher: Evidence from the National Longitudinal Study of the High School Class of 1972. In D. A. Wise (Ed.), *Public sector payrolls* (pp. 291-316). Chicago: University of Chicago Press.

Marks, H. M., & Louis, K. S. (1995). *Does teacher empowerment affect the classroom? The implications of teacher empowerment for teachers' instructional practice and student academic performance.* Madison: University of Wisconsin–Madison, Wisconsin Center for Education Research, Center on Organization and Restructuring Schools.

Maryland State Department of Education. (1997). *Maryland school performance report, 1997: State and school systems.* Annapolis, MD: Author.

McAdams, J. L. (1995). Design, implementation and results: Employee involvement and performance reward plans. *Compensation and Benefits Review, 27*(2), 45-55.

McGregor, D. M. (1992). The human side of the enterprise. In J. M. Shafritz & J. S. Ott (Eds.), *Classics of organization theory* (3d ed., pp. 174-180). Pacific Grove, CA: Brooks/Cole. (Original work published 1957)

McLaughlin, M. W., & Yee, S. M.-L. (1988). School as a place to have a career. In A. Lieberman (Ed.), *Building a professional culture in schools* (pp. 23-44). New York: Teachers College Press.

Mento, A. J., Steel, Robert P., & Karren, R. J. (1987). A meta-analytic study of the effects of goal setting on task performance: 1966-1984. *Organizational Behavior and Human Decision Processes, 39,* 52-83.

Milanowski, A. (1999). Measurement error or meaningful change? The consistency of school achievement in two school-based performance award programs. *Journal of Personnel Evaluation in Education, 12*(4), 343-363.

Milanowski, A. (2000). School-based performance award programs and teacher motivation. *Journal of Education Finance, 25*(4), 517-544.

Milanowski, A. (2001). *The varieties of knowledge- and skill-based pay design: A comparison of seven new pay systems for K-12 teachers.* Madison: University of Wisconsin–Madison, Wisconsin Center for Education Research, Consortium for Policy Research in Education.

Milanowski, A., & Kellor, E. (2000a). Preliminary Report on the Performance Pay Survey. Madison: University of Wisconsin, Wisconsin Center for Education Research, Consortium for Policy Research in Education.

Milanowski, A., & Kellor, E. (with assistance from H. Heneman III and A. Odden). (2000b). *Teacher and evaluator reactions to standards-based teacher evaluation in the Cincinnati public schools: An evaluation of the 1999-2000 field test of the new evaluation system.* Report prepared for the Cincinnati Public School District. Madison: University of Wisconsin–Madison, Wisconsin Center for Education Research, Consortium for Policy Research in Education.

Milanowski, A., Odden, A., & Youngs, P. (1998). Teacher knowledge and skill assessments and teacher compensation: An overview of measurement and linkage issues. *Journal of Personnel Evaluation in Education, 12*(2), 83-101.

Miles, K. H. (1996). *Rethinking school resources in high performing schools.* Madison: University of Wisconsin–Madison, Wisconsin Center for Education Research, Consortium for Policy Research in Education.

Miskel, C. (1982). Motivation in educational organizations. *Educational Administration Quarterly, 18*(3), 65-88.

Miskel, C., DeFrain, J., & Wilcox, K. (1980). A test of expectancy work motivation theory in educational organizations. *Educational Administration Quarterly, 16*(1), 70-92.

Miskel, C., McDonald, D., & Bloom, S. (1983). Structural and expectancy linkages within schools and organizational effectiveness. *Educational Administration Quarterly, 19*(1), 49-82.

Mitchell, T. R. (1974). Expectancy models of job satisfaction, occupational preference, and effort: A theoretical, methodological, and empirical appraisal. *Psychological Bulletin, 81,* 1053-1077.

Mohrman, A., Mohrman, S. A., & Odden, A. (1996). Aligning teacher compensation with systemic school reform: Skill-based pay and group-based performance awards. *Educational Evaluation and Policy Analysis, 18,* 51-71.

Mohrman, A. M. (1989). *Deming versus performance appraisal: Is there a resolution?* Los Angeles: Center for Effective Organizations, School of Business Administration, University of Southern California.

Mohrman, S. A., Cohen, S. G., & Mohrman, A. M., Jr. (1995). *Designing team-based organizations: New forms for knowledge work.* San Francisco: Jossey-Bass.

Mohrman, S. A., & Lawler, E. E., III. (1996). Motivation for school reform. In S. H. Fuhrman & J. A. O'Day (Eds.), *Rewards and reform: Creating educational incentives that work* (pp. 115-143). San Francisco: Jossey-Bass.

Mohrman, S. A., Lawler, E. E., III, & Mohrman, A. M., Jr. (1992). Applying employee involvement in schools. *Education Evaluation and Policy Analysis, 14,* 347-360.

Mohrman, S. A., Wohlstetter, P., & Associates (Eds.). (1994). *School-based management: Organizing for high performance.* San Francisco: Jossey-Bass.

Moss, P. A., Schutz, A. M., & Collins, K. (1998). An integrative approach to portfolio evaluation for teacher licensure certification. *Journal of Personnel Evaluation in Education, 12*(2), 139-161.

Murnane, R. J. (1983). Quantitative studies of effective schools: What have we learned? In A. Odden & L. D. Webb (Eds.), *School finance and school improvement: Linkages for the 1980s* (pp. 193-209). Cambridge, MA: Ballinger.

Murnane, R. J., & Cohen, D. K. (1986). Merit pay and the evaluation problem: Why most merit pay plans fail and a few survive. *Harvard Educational Review, 56,* 1-17.

Murnane, R. J., Singer, J. D., Willett, J. B., Kemple, J. J., & Olsen, R. J. (1991). *Who will teach? Policies that matter.* Cambridge, MA: Harvard University Press.

Murphy, J., & Beck, L. G. (1995). *School-based management as school reform: Taking stock.* Thousand Oaks, CA: Corwin.

National Board for Professional Teaching Standards. (1994a). *Adolescence and young adulthood/mathematics standards for National Board Certification.* Detroit, MI: Author.

National Board for Professional Teaching Standards. (1994b). *Early adolescence/English language arts standards for National Board Certification.* Detroit, MI: Author.

National Board for Professional Teaching Standards. (1994c). *Early adolescence/generalist standards for National Board Certification.* Detroit, MI: Author.

National Board for Professional Teaching Standards. (1994d). *Early childhood/generalist standards for National Board Certification.* Detroit, MI: Author.

National Board for Professional Teaching Standards. (1995). Press release. Detroit, MI: Author.

National Board for Professional Teaching Standards (Ed.). (1999). National Board certification. *Teaching and Change [Special issue], 6*(4).

National Center for Education Statistics. (1995). *Third International Science and Mathematics Study* [Video]. Washington, DC: Author. Retrieved April 24, 2001, from the Internet: /nces.ed.gov/TIMSS/timss95/video.asp

National Center for Education Statistics. (2000). *Projections of Educational Statistics to 2010.* Washington, DC: U.S. Department of Education.

National Commission on Excellence in Education. (1983). *A nation at risk: The imperative for educational reform.* Washington, DC: U.S. Department of Education.

National Commission on Teaching and America's Future. (1996). *What matters most: Teaching in America.* New York: Teachers College Press.

National Council of Teachers of Mathematics. (1989). *Curriculum and evaluation standards for school mathematics.* Reston, VA: Author.

National Council of Teachers of Mathematics. (1991). *Professional standards for the teaching of mathematics.* Reston, VA: Author.

Newmann, F., & Associates. (1996). *School restructuring and student learning.* San Francisco: Jossey-Bass.

Newmann, F., & Wehlage, G. (1993). Standards for authentic instruction. *Educational Leadership, 50*(7), 8-12.

Newmann, F., & Wehlage, G. (1995). *Successful school restructuring.* Madison: University of Wisconsin–Madison, Wisconsin Center for Education Research, Center on Organization and Restructuring of Schools.

Newmann, F., Bryk, A., & Nagaoka, J. (2001). *Authentic intellectual work and standardized tests: Conflict or coexistence?* Chicago: Consortium on Chicago School Reform.

Newmann, F. M., Marks, H. M., & Gamoran, A. (1995). *Authentic pedagogy and student performance.* Madison: University of Wisconsin–Madison, Wisconsin Center for Education Research, Center on Organization and Restructuring Schools.

O'Dell, C. (1987). *People, performance and pay.* Houston, TX: American Productivity Center.

Odden, A. (1996). Incentives, school organization and teacher compensation. In S. H. Fuhrman & J. A. O'Day (Eds.), *Rewards and reform: Creating educational incentives that work* (pp. 226-256). San Francisco: Jossey-Bass.

Odden, A. (2001). Rewarding Expertise. *Education Matters, 1*(1), 16-24.

Odden, A., & Archibald, S. (2000). *Reallocating resources: How to boost student achievement without spending more.* Thousand Oaks, CA: Corwin.

Odden, A., & Archibald, S. (2001). *The elements and costs of effective professional development.* Madison: University of Wisconsin-Madison, Wisconsin Center for Educational Research, Center on Organization and Restructuring of Schools.

Odden, A., & Clune, W. (1995). Improving educational productivity and school finance. *Educational Researcher, 24*(9), 6-10, 22.

Odden, A., & Clune, W. (1998). School finance systems: Aging structures in need of renovation. *Educational Evaluation and Policy Analysis, 20*(3), 157-177.

Odden, A., & Conley, S. (1992). Restructuring teacher compensation systems. In A. Odden (Ed.), *Rethinking school finance: An agenda for the 1990s* (pp. 41-96). San Francisco: Jossey-Bass.

Odden, A., & Kelley, C. (1997). *Paying teachers for what they know and do: New and smarter compensation strategies to improve schools.* Thousand Oaks, CA: Corwin.

Odden, A., & Kelley, C. (in press) *Assessing teacher quality and supply through compensation policy.* Albany, NY: State Department of Education.

Odden, A., & Kellor, E. (2000). *How Cincinnati developed a knowledge and skills-based salary schedule.* Madison: University of Wisconsin–Madison, Wisconsin Center for Education Research, Consortium for Policy Research in Education.

Odden, A., Kellor, E., Heneman, H., & Milanowski, A. (1999). School-based performance award programs: Design and administration issues synthesized from eight programs. Madison: University of Wisconsin–Madison, Wisconsin Center for Education Research, Consortium for Policy Research in Education. Retrieved April 24, 2001, from the World Wide Web: www.wcer.wisc.edu/cpre/tcomp

Odden, A., Monk, D., Nakib, Y., & Picus, L. (1995). The story of the educational dollar: No academy awards and no fiscal smoking guns. *Phi Delta Kappan, 77,* 161-168.

Odden, A., & Odden, E. (1994, April). *Applying the high involvement framework to local management of schools in Victoria, Australia.* Paper presented at the annual meeting of the American Educational Research Association, New Orleans, Louisiana.

Odden, A., & Odden, E. (1995). *Educational leadership for America's schools*. New York: McGraw-Hill.

Odden, A., & Picus, L. O. (2000). *School finance: A policy perspective* (2nd ed.). New York: McGraw-Hill.

Odden, A., Wohlstetter, P., & Odden, E. (1995). Key issues in effective school-based management. *School Business Affairs, 61*(5), 4-16.

Odden, A. R., & Busch, C. (1998). *Financing schools for high performance: Strategies for improving the use of educational resources*. San Francisco: Jossey-Bass.

Odden, E., & Wohlstetter, P. (1995). Strategies for making school based management work. *Educational Leadership, 52*(5), 32-36.

Pankratz, R. S., & Petrosko, J. M. (Eds.). (2000). *All children can learn: Lessons from the Kentucky reform experience*. San Francisco: Jossey-Bass.

Pearlman, M. (2001). *Implementing standards-based performance appraisal systems for teachers*. Princeton, NJ: Educational Testing Service.

Pechman, E. M., & LaGuarda, K. G. (1993). *Status of new curriculum framework standards, assessment, and monitoring systems*. Washington, DC: Policy Studies Associates.

Pfeffer, J. (1994, September). *Managing human resources for competitive advantage: Barriers to change*. Paper presented at a conference, sponsored by the Industrial Relations Centre, Queen's University, Ontario, Canada.

Poggio, J. P. (2000). Statewide performance assessment and school accountability. In R. S. Pankratz & J. M. Petrosko (Eds.), *All children can learn: Lessons from the Kentucky reform experience* (pp. 75-97). San Francisco: Jossey-Bass.

Protsik, J. (1996). History of teacher pay and incentive reforms. *Journal of School Leadership, 6*(2), 265-289.

Purkey, S. C., & Smith, M. S. (1983). Effective schools: A review. *Elementary School Journal, 83*, 427-452.

Resnick, L. B. (1994). Performance puzzles. *American Journal of Education, 102*, 511-526.

Resnick, L. B., & Klopfer, L. E. (Eds.). (1989). *Toward the thinking curriculum: Current cognitive research*. Washington, DC: Association for Supervision and Curriculum Development.

Richards, C. E., Fishbein, D., & Melville, P. (1993). Cooperative performance incentives in education. In S. Jacobson & R. Berne (Eds.), *Reforming education: The emerging systemic approach* (pp. 28-42). Thousand Oaks, CA: Corwin.

Richards, C. E., & Sheu, T. M. (1992). The South Carolina school incentive reward program: A policy analysis. *Economics of Education Review, 11,* 71-86.

Richardson, J. (1994, May 25). Va. district to give bonuses to top-rated teachers. *Education Week, 13,* 13.

Richardson, J. G., & Hatcher, B. W. (1983). The feminization of public school teaching, 1870-1920. *Work and Occupations, 10,* 81-99.

Robertson, P. J., Wohlstetter, P., & Mohrman, S. A. (1995). Generating curriculum and instructional innovations through school-based management. *Educational Administration Quarterly, 31,* 375-404.

Rosen, S., & Flyer, F. (1994). *The new economics of teachers and education.* Chicago: University of Chicago Department of Economics.

Rosenholtz, S. J. (1989). *Teachers' workplace: The social organization of schools.* New York: Longman.

Rosenshine, B., & Stevens, R. (1986). Teaching functions. In M. Wittrock (Ed.), *Handbook of research on teaching* (pp. 376-391). New York: Macmillan.

Rothman, R. (1995). *Measuring up.* San Francisco: Jossey-Bass.

Rothman, S. M. (1978). *Woman's proper place: A history of changing ideals and practices, 1870 to the present.* New York: Basic Books.

Rothstein, R., & Miles, K. H. (1995). *Where's the money gone?* Washington, DC: Economic Policy Institute.

Rowan, B. (1996). Standards as incentives for instructional reform. In S. H. Fuhrman & J. A. O'Day (Eds.), *Rewards and reform: Creating educational incentives that work* (pp. 195-225). San Francisco: Jossey-Bass.

Runge, C. F. (1984). Institutions and the free ride: The assurance problem in collective action. *Journal of Politics, 46*(1), 154-181.

Sanders, W. L., & Horn, S. P. (1994). The Tennessee Value-Added Assessment System: Mixed-model methodology in educational assessment. *Journal of Personnel Evaluation in Education, 8,* 299-313.

Sanders, W. L., Saxton, A. M., & Horn, S. P. (1997). The Tennessee Value-Added Accountability System: A quantitative, outcomes-based approach to educational assessment. In J. Millman (Ed.), *Grading teachers, grading schools: Is student achievement a valid evaluation measure?* (pp. 137-162). Thousand Oaks, CA: Corwin Press.

Sandham, J. L. (2001, January 24). Calif. test-based bonus plan gets off to rocky start. *Education Week, 20*(19), 1, 20.

Schlechty, P. C. (1989). Career ladders: A good idea going awry. In T. J. Sergiovanni & J. H. Moore (Eds.), *Schooling for tomorrow: Directing reforms to issues that count* (pp. 356-376). Boston: Allyn & Bacon.

Schlechty, P. C., & Vance, V. S. (1983). Recruitment, selection, and retention: The shape of the teaching force. *Elementary School Journal, 83,* 469-487.

Scholtes, P. R. (1994a). *Alternatives to performance appraisal: Twelve guidelines for creating "debundled" policies.* Madison, WI: Scholtes Seminars and Consulting.

Scholtes, P. R. (1994b). *Performance without appraisal.* Madison, WI: Scholtes Seminars and Consulting.

Scholtes, P. R. (1995). *Dr. Deming's vision of the organization.* Madison, WI: Scholtes Seminars and Consulting.

Schuster, J. R., & Zingheim, P. (1992). *The new pay: Linking employee and organizational performance.* New York: Lexington Books.

Senge, P. M. (1990). *The fifth discipline: The art & practice of the learning organization.* New York: Doubleday Currency.

Sharpes, D. K. (1987). Incentive pay and the promotion of teaching proficiencies. *The Clearing House, 60,* 406-408.

Shedd, J. B. (1988). Teacher unions: Participation through bargaining. In S. B. Bacharach (Ed.), *Educational reform: Making sense of it all* (pp. 92-102). Boston: Allyn & Bacon.

Shedd, J. B., & Bacharach, S. B. (1991). *Tangled hierarchies: Teachers as professionals and the management of schools.* San Francisco: Jossey-Bass.

Shephard, L. A., & Smith, M. L. (1989). *Flunking grades: Research and policies on retention.* Philadelphia: Falmer.

Shulman, L. (1986). Those who understand: Knowledge growth in teaching. *Educational Researcher, 15,* 4-14.

Shulman, L. (1987). Knowledge and teaching: Foundations of the new reform. *Harvard Educational Review, 57,* 1-22.

Sizer, T. (1992). *Horace's school: Redesigning the American high school.* Boston: Houghton Mifflin.

Sizer, T. (1996). *Horace's hope: What works for the American high school.* Boston: Houghton Mifflin.

Smith, M. S., & O'Day, J. (1991). Systemic school reform. In S. H. Fuhrman & B. Malen (Eds.), *The politics of curriculum and testing* (pp. 233-267). Bristol, PA: Falmer.

Smith, C., Rothackerand, J. W., & Griffin, A. (1999, August 6). ABCs show schools' progress: Area educators cheer improved year-end results.

Charlotte Observer. Retrieved April 20, 2001, from the Internet: charlotte.com/schools/abcs99/0806abc.htm

Smylie, M. (1991). Organizational cultures of schools: Concept, content and change. In S. C. Conley & B. S. Cooper (Eds.), *The school as a work environment: Implications for reform* (pp. 20-41). Boston: Allyn & Bacon.

Smylie, M. (1994). Redesigning teachers' work: Connections to the classroom. In L. Darling-Hammond (Ed.), *Review of research in education* (Vol. 20, pp. 129-177). Washington, DC: American Educational Research Association.

Smylie, M., & Smart, J. C. (1990). Teacher support for career enhancement initiatives: Program characteristics and effects on work. *Educational Evaluation and Policy Analysis, 12*(2), 139-155.

Southern Regional Education Board. (1994). *Reflecting on ten years of incentive programs: The 1993 SREB career ladder clearinghouse survey.* Atlanta, GA: Author.

Spring, J. (1994). *The American school 1642-1993* (3d ed.). New York: Longman.

Spuck, D. W. (1974). Reward structures in the public high school. *Educational Administration Quarterly, 10,* 22-42.

Stecher, B. M., & Barron, S. (1999, April). *Test-based accountability: The perverse consequences of milepost testing.* Paper presented at the annual meeting of the American Educational Research Association, Montreal, Canada.

Steffy, B. E. (1993). *The Kentucky education reform: Lessons for America.* Lancaster, PA: Technomic.

Steffy, B. E., Wolfe, M. P., Pasch, S. H., & Enz, B. J. (2000). *Life cycle of the career teacher.* Thousand Oaks, CA: Corwin.

Stringfield, S., Ross, S., & Smith, L. (1996). *Bold plans for school restructuring: The new American schools designs.* Mahwah, NJ: Lawrence Erlbaum.

Stronge, J. H., & Tucker, P. (2000). *Teacher evaluation and student achievement.* Washington DC: National Education Association.

Talbert, J., & McLaughlin, M. W. (1994). Teacher professionalism in local school contexts. *American Journal of Education, 102*(2), 123-153.

Timar, T. (1992). Incentive pay for teachers and school reform. In L. Frase (Ed.), *Teacher compensation and motivation* (pp. 27-60). Lancaster, PA: Technomic.

Tyack, D. B. (1974). *The one best system: A history of American urban education.* Cambridge, MA: Harvard University Press.

Tyack, D. B., & Strober, M. H. (1981). Jobs and gender: A history of the structuring of educational employment by sex. In P. A. Schmuck, W. W. Charters Jr., & R. O. Carlson (Eds.), *Educational policy and management: Sex differentials* (pp. 131-152). New York: Academic Press.

Urbanski, A., & Erskine, R. (2000). School reform, TURN, and teacher compensation. *Phi Delta Kappan, 81*(5), 367-370.

Viadero, D. (2001, February 21). Researcher: Teacher signing bonuses miss mark in Mass. *Education Week, 20*(23), 13.

Vroom, V. H. (1964). *Work and motivation.* New York: Wiley.

Walker, S. (Ed.). (2000). Teaching quality: Hard-to-staff schools. *State Education Leader [Special issue], 18*(2). Retrieved April 19, 2001, from the World Wide Web: www.ecs.org/clearinghouse/11/87/1187.htm

Wanous, J. P., Keon, T. L., & Latack, J. C. (1983). Expectancy theory and occupational/organizational choices: A review and test. *Organizational Behavior and Human Performance, 32,* 66-86.

Wiersma, U. J. (1992). The effects of extrinsic rewards on intrinsic motivation: A meta-analysis. *Journal of Occupational and Organizational Psychology, 65,* 101-114.

Welbourne, T. M., & Mejia, L. R. G. (1995). Gainsharing: A critical review and a future research agenda. *Journal of Management, 21,* 559-609.

White, K. A. (1998). *Kentucky bids KIRIS farewell, ushers in new test.* Retrieved April 24, 2001, from Education Week from the Internet: edweek.com/ew/ewstory.cfm?slug=32ky.h17

Wise, A. E. (1995). The new professional teacher project. *Quality teaching: The newsletter of the National Council for Accreditation of Teacher Education, 4*(2), 2-3.

Wise, A., & Leibbrand, J. (1993). Accreditation and the creation of a profession of teaching. *Phi Delta Kappan, 75,* 133-136.

Wohlstetter, P. (1995). Getting school-based management right: What works and what doesn't. *Phi Delta Kappan, 77*(1), 22-26.

Wohlstetter, P., & Odden, A. (1992). Rethinking school-based management policy and research. *Educational Administration Quarterly, 28,* 529-549.

Wohlstetter, P., Mohrman, S., & Robertson, P. (1997). Successful school-based management: Lessons for restructuring urban schools. In D. Ravitch & J. Viteritti (Eds.), *New schools for a new century: The redesign of urban education.* New Haven, CT: Yale University Press.

Wohlstetter, P., Smyer, R., & Mohrman, S. A. (1994). New boundaries for school-based management: The high involvement model. *Educational Evaluation and Policy Analysis, 16,* 268-286.

Wohlstetter, P., Van Kirk, A., Robertson, P., & Mohrman, S. (1997). *Organizing for successful school-based management.* Alexandria, VA: Association for Supervision and Curriculum Development.

Wright, P. M. (1989). Testing the mediating role of goals in the incentive-performance relationship. *Journal of Applied Psychology, 74,* 699-705.

Wright, P. S., Horn, S. P., & Sanders, W. L. (1997). Teacher and classroom context effects on student achievement: Implications for teacher evaluation. *Journal of Personnel Evaluation in Education, 11,* 57-67.

Yen, W. M., & Ferrara, S. (1997). The Maryland school performance assessment program: Performance assessment with psychometric quality suitable for high stakes usage. *Educational and Psychological Measurement, 57*(1), 60-84.

Youngs, P., Odden, A., & Porter, A. (2000). *State leadership in teacher licensure.* Madison: University of Wisconsin–Madison, Wisconsin Center for Education Research, Consortium for Policy Research in Education.

Zingheim, P., & Schuster, J. R. (Eds.). (1995a). The new pay tools & strategies: How to create and reward high performance in your organization. *Compensation and Benefits Review [Special issue], 27*(4).

Zingheim, P., & Schuster, J. R. (1995b). How are the new pay tools being deployed? *Compensation and Benefits Review, 27*(4), 10-13.

Zingheim, P., & Schuster, J. R. (1995c). Moving one notch north: Executing the transition to new pay. *Compensation and Benefits Review, 27*(4), 33-39.

Zingheim, P., & Schuster, J. R. (1995d). Exploring three pay transition tools: Readiness assessment, benchmarking and piloting. *Compensation and Benefits Review, 27*(4), 40-45.

Zingheim, P. K., & Schuster, J. R. (2000). *Pay people right! Breakthrough reward strategies to create great companies.* San Francisco: Jossey-Bass.

Name Index

235

Subject Index

CORWIN
PRESS

The Corwin Press logo—a raven striding across an open book—represents the happy union of courage and learning. We are a professional-level publisher of books and journals for K–12 educators, and we are committed to creating and providing resources that embody these qualities. Corwin's motto is "Success for All Learners."

Made in the USA
Middletown, DE
13 March 2018